Care & Feeding of the Aging Human Male Species: A Sassy Primer

By Irene Shere

with
**Helen Weels, Ph.D.* in Manthropology
& Rae Jean Beech, B.S.* in Mengineering**

*Ph.D. = Piled higher and Deeper
*B.S. = Bad Sassyass

Published by Blue Wildfire, LLC
Sarasota, Florida
©2021 Irene Shere

All rights reserved. No part of this book may be used or reproduced in any manner whatsoever without written permission except in the case of brief quotations embodied in critical articles and reviews.

Blue Wildfire, LLC, and Irene Shere have no responsibility for the persistence or accuracy of URLs for external or third party internet websites referred to in this publication and do not guarantee that any content on such websites is, or will remain, accurate or appropriate.

Designations used by companies to distinguish their products are often claimed as trademarks. All brand names and product names used in this book and on its cover are trade names, service marks, trademarks and registered trademarks of their respective owners. The publishers and the book are not associated with any product or vendor mentioned in this book. None of the companies referenced within the book have endorsed the book.

The anecdotes described within are written to the best of the author's recollection. The names have been changed to protect the innocent and the guilty.

First Edition
Paperback ISBN: 978-1-734494-2-6
Ebook ISBN: 978-1-7344494-0-2
Library of Congress Control Number: 2020904359

Edited by Rachel Abileah
Cover Design by Mary Ann Smith
Illustrations by Andy "Doodles" Baker
Interior Design/Typography/Production by Asya Blue

sassyprimer.com

This Sassy Primer is dedicated to

My mother, **Rebecca**, who, with much patience and compassion—and selective deafness—survived sixty-five challenging years with my stubborn father. —*Irene Shere*

My funny brother **Ron**, who taught me from day one how to love a wackadoodle male, and my sweet Bill, my amusing muse with silver hair and a golden heart.
—*Helen Weels*

My Precious Old Dames (PODs), my best Boomer Babes, who not only listen to my life stories, but are right there beside me riding shotgun! Couldn't do it without you! No names—to protect the innocent and the guilty!
—*Rae Jean Beech*

"Listen to everything your man says. Then do what you want."
—Rebecca, *Irene's Mom*

"Humor eases the heart and allows love to flow in."
—Helen Weels

"Be a badass with a good ass."
— Rae Jean Beech

Care and Feeding of the Aging Human Male Species: A Sassy Primer

With a hearty does of piss and vinegar, this **Sassy Primer** offers sage advice and laugh-out-loud stories about surviving and thriving in your Aging Human Partnership—all in 350 pages and four sections of wacky heartfelt truths Grandma never told you.

Buckle up and enjoy the ride as you zip from the sweet and sour snark in **The Field Guy-ed** to the titillating travel tips in **The Roadmap** to the soothing, smoothing suggestions in **The Dame Digest**, all to end with a bang of a vivacious vibe in **The PODs Party Playbook**.

And feel free to go all *Thelma and Louise* rogue and hop, skip, and jump around—with or without compression stockings—to any chapter in any order. After all, what do women want? Choices!

Intros 1

The Field Guy-ed 13
The Field Guy-ed womanplains how to survive your man's quirks and burps, and answers the question: Does everything with an Aging Human Male begin and end with sex?

The Roadmap to Traveling Route 66+ Together 91
The Roadmap offers travel tips for oiling your relationship, fighting fair when the wheels fall off your car, and continuing to love your vintage jalopy.

The Dame Digest 197
The Dame Digest supports your bra-very as your nurture your feelings and passions while balancing your life—all on arthritic knees?

The Precious Old Dames' Party Playbook 277
The POD Party Playbook is a mega-bonus of games and gab guides for schmoozing with your gal pals.

Epilogue: The Reveal 310
What's a **Sassy Primer** without something a little revealing?

A to Z for the Glossary-Eyed 317
The Women's Truth Foundation (WTF) collection of new, fun, and scandalous aging-relationship words and concepts in this book.

Table of Contents

The Aging Human Male Species: A Treat-Us by Helen 1

The Aging Human Male Species: A Complain-Us from Rae Jean 4

The Skinny on this Fat and Sassy Primer: FAQs with Irene 6

The Field Guy-ed 13

Intro. Is He an Aging Human Male?
Are You an Aging Human Female? Checklist It Out 14

Chapter 1. Sex 16

    Lesson 1. The Little Blue…Isn't He a Pill? 17

    Lesson 2. The Geezer Triangle: **Sex▲Sustenance▲Sports** 19

    Lesson 3. Two Beds or not Two Beds:
        That is the Question that Shakes Peers Up 22

    Lesson 4. How Do I Love Thee? Let Me Count the (Had-Sex) Days . 24

    Lesson 5. Two Heads are Better than One: His and Hers Lust Lists . . 27

Chapter 2. Competence: Questions? 31

    Lesson 1. Bueller? Bueller? Questions, Anyone? 32

    Lesson 2. Don't Be a Repeat Ask-fender 37

Chapter 3. Control + Alt + Delete the Power Struggle 39

    Lesson 1. Don't Ask, Don't Tell: Unsolicited Advice (UA) 40

    Lesson 2. Don't Ask, But Be Told Anyway: Mansplaining 42

    Lesson 3. I (Com)Promise to Love, Honor and Cherish:
        Over-giving and Under-appreciating 44

Lesson 4. Right Brain, Left Brain:
  The I-Am-Always Right Brain 47

Lesson 5. Hard-Boiled Eggs or Chicken and Waffles?
  You Choose! 49

Lesson 6. To Coddle or not to Coddle:
  What's the Eggspectation? Or Does it All Get Scrambled? . . 51

Chapter 4. It Takes a Worried Man. 52

Lesson 1. Anxiety and Control: Dance to Whose Tune? 53

Lesson 2. Enough Already, Einstein 57

Chapter 5. Aging: "Who Me? What Mirror?" 59

Lesson 1. Butt Ugly: Homeostayinplacis 61

Lesson 2. It's My Body and I'll Cry If I Want To:
  H.E.R.S. versus H.I.S. 64

Lesson 3. Home is Where the Fart Is 67

Lesson 4. Can You Hear Me Now? The Deaf Leading the Deaf 68

Lesson 5. 50 Shades of Grey… Hair, That Is 69

Lesson 6. The Truth about ADHD and Sports 70

Lesson 7. Memories, Light the Cobwebs of My Mind. 72

Chapter 6. Lifestyle Issues: Fashions and Passions. 74

Lesson 1. Fashions that Cause Foes to Pause: Fashion Mis-Takes 75

Lesson 2. Maynard G. Krebs and "Werk?!" 78

Lesson 3. I'll Have the Meat and Potatoes,
  With a Side of Boredom:
  Does Only Heinz Ketchup have 57 Varieties? 80

TABLE OF CONTENTS

Lesson 4. Game? Who's Got Game?
    The Only Game in Town is on TV 82

Lesson 5. Male Friendships: A Carton of Codgers 84

Chapter 7. Sex... Not Again!. 86

The Roadmap to Traveling Route 66+ Together 91

Intro. Sharing the Road. 92

Chapter 8. Traveling Route 66+ Together, Pitstops and Potholes. 93

  Lesson 1. The AAA Route 66+ Road Trip Checklist. 94

  Lesson 2. Safe Driving Tips 96

  Lesson 3. Retiring: Putting New Tires on an Old Car. 97

Chapter 9. Good Odds to Keep an AHPartnership Even. 101

  Lesson 1. What to Do to Boost the Odds: C.L.O.P or C.L.A.P.?.... 102

  Lesson 2. WTF to Do to Boost the Odds? 104

Chapter 10. Communication: You Just Renewed
    Your-Driving-Me-Crazy License. 107

  Lesson 1. Feelings, Whoa, Whoa, Whoa, Feelings 109

  Lesson 2. No, I Don't Speak French and I Don't Speak Feelings:
    ESL—Emotions as a Second Language. 111

  Lesson 3. Silence of the Lamb Chops 114

Chapter 11. How to Womanhandle an Aging Human Male: The Basics. 117

  Lesson 1. It Takes Two to Tango... and to Tangle: The T & A
    Personality Diagnostic Assessment Instrument. 118

  Lesson 2. Wo-mantras for Tango-ing. 121

Lesson 3. Womanhandling the Mansplaining: **The Rebecca Rule** ... 123

Lesson 4. Womanhandling the Boundaries: *The Erma Edict* 126

Chapter 12. Advanced Womanhandling:
    Competence, Control & Anxiety 127

    Lesson 1. Caring about Competence:
        "Right" Questions are the Wrong Questions 128

    Lesson 2. Controlling Control: Five Tips 130

    Lesson 3. Assuaging Anxiety: Happy 67th Birthday,
        Alfred E. Neuman 132

Chapter 13. Fire Prevention: STOP, DROP, and ROLL 136

Chapter 14. Fight Club: The Rules 138

    Lesson 1. Don'ts 139

    Lesson 2. Do's 141

Chapter 15. Fight #23. Thermostat Wars: Don't Touch that Dial! 144

Chapter 16. Fight #55: Money War$:
    Doe$ Thi$ Make a Li¢k of ¢ent$? 146

    Lesson 1. $pend Time Talking about $pending 147

    Lesson 2. Every Bag Need$ Her Own Money Bag 149

    Lesson 3. Gender and Legal Tender: Who'$ ¢ounting? 150

    Lesson 4. Willing or Not? 152

Chapter 17. Fight #68: Familia—or Too Familiar? 154

Chapter 18. Fight #108: Chores Wars: Garbage In, Garbage Out 161

Chapter 19. Fight #332: Which Restaurant? (aka Who's the Boss?) 164

Chapter 20. Fight #599: 24/7 Togetherness? Lost in Space 166

TABLE OF CONTENTS

Chapter 21. Fight #691: Ohhhh Sayyyy Can You (TL)C?
 In Sickness or in Stealth. 168

Chapter 22. Fight #692: Don't Look a Gift Horse...
 Whoa! Is He a Horse's A__ When It Comes to Gifts? 171

 Lesson 1. Gift-Giving 101: This Time It's Personal 172

 Lesson 2. Gift-Returning 101: Provide a Male Escort 174

 Lesson 3. Retirement Gifts 101: Some Gifts Need to Be Retired. . . . 175

Chapter 23. Fights #1,113-2,045: Sex! 177

Chapter 24. After-the-Fight Heart Hints. 180

Chapter 25. When Good Enough is Not Good Enough:
 Separation and Divorce. 183

Chapter 26. Signing a New Car Lease on an Old Jalopy 186

Chapter 27. The $64,000 Question: I Love You,
 But Do I Like You? 189

Chapter 28. Burma-Shave Road Signs Along Route 66+. 194

The Dame Digest 197

Intro. Yes, Arethra, R-E-S-P-E-C-T!. 198

Chapter 29. Follow Your Heart, Not His Fart 199

Chapter 30. The Dame Diamond:
 Feelings ◊ Revealings ◊ Bods ◊ PODs 200

Chapter 31. The Dame Diamond: Feelings. 202

Chapter 32. The Dame Diamond: Revealings 204

Chapter 33. The Dame Diamond: Bods 207

 Lesson 1. Body Image: Is This a Funhouse Mirror? 208

  Lesson 2. Body Choices: So Many Decisions, So Little Time 214

  Lesson 3. Health TLC: Ten-der Loving Commandments 217

  Lesson 4. Clothes: How's It Hanging? 220

  Lesson 5. Sex: Yet Again?! 221

Chapter 34. The Dame Diamond: PODs (Precious Old Dames) 224

Chapter 35. Wo-mantras to Push-up Your Bra-very 226

Chapter 36. You are "A-OK Boomers!" 228

  Lesson 1. Age-honoring 229

  Lesson 2. Own Your Crone 232

Chapter 37. Gender Benders 236

Chapter 38. Love Your *I Love Lucy* Episodes: Self-Compassion 238

Chapter 39. Be Your Own Best POD:
Self-Kindness and Self-Forgiveness 242

Chapter 40. Your-Self-Healing through Your-Self-Reflection 244

  Lesson 1. I'm Sorry that I Said "I'm Sorry:" Irene's "I wish" 245

  Lesson 2. Gender Discrimination and **The Erma Edict** 249

  Lesson 3. Move Past Your Past 252

  Lesson 4. In Ourselves Do We Trust 254

  Lesson 5. Have a Latte with Your Younger-You 256

  Lesson 6. Have a Heart-to-heart with Yourself 259

Chapter 41. Good Morning, Glory 260

Chapter 42. Yes! 263

Chapter 43. Out Your Outrageous YOU! 265

TABLE OF CONTENTS

    Lesson 1. Who Do YOU Want to BE?........................ 266

    Lesson 2. What Do YOU Want to DO? Your Luna List.......... 268

Chapter 44. What in the World are You Doing?..................... 271

Chapter 45. Baby, It's You, Finally................................ 275

The Precious Old Dames' Party Playbook: Pee POD Poise Parties.... 277

Intro. Like Peas in a POD...................................... 278

Chapter 46. What is a Pee POD Poise Party?..................... 279

    Lesson 1. What is a POD?................................. 279

    Lesson 2. What is a Pee POD?............................. 280

    Lesson 3. The Pee POD Mission Position
        (NOT Missionary Position!)...................... 280

    Lesson 4. What is a Pee POD Poise Party?................... 281

    Lesson 5. Party of One, Anyone?........................... 281

Chapter 47. Bring It On: Let's Party!........................... 282

Chapter 48. After Some Laughs: Chick Chat..................... 288

Chapter 49. After Some Tears: Choose to Schmooze.............. 295

Chapter 50. Getting Up Close & Personal: Flow and Tell.......... 302

Chapter 51. Thank You Toasts................................. 308

Chapter 52. The Grand Finale................................. 309

Epilogue: The Reveal................................... 310

A to Z for the Glossary-Eyed......................... 317

xi

The Aging Human Male Species: A Treat-Us

by Helen Weels, Ph.D.* in Manthropology

*Ph.D. = Piled higher and Deeper

In the exhaustive and exhausting study of manthropology — the anthropological study of the Human Male species—it has been observed that the Aging Human Male, **Homo Sappiens** (sic) or **Penus(dic) Erectus**, is characterized by a shining hairless head, hairy ears, hairy nostrils, an extended belly, brightly-plumaged tropical shirts, saggy shorts, knobby knees, and flat odiferous feet.

The call of the Aging Human Male is a shriek-like cry, often heard in the wilds of a leather recliner: "Where's my beer? Where's my beer? Where's my beer?"

The cry of the Aging Human Male can also be heard in the darkness of the bedroom: "Where's my Viagra? Where's my Viagra? Where's my Viagra?" This cry is often followed shortly by: "Yes! Yes! Yes!" whereupon a puff of cigarette smoke ensues.

Brain research in the Aging Human Male (AHMale) indicates that, with aging, there is a self-perceived shrinking in the **Competence Area** of the brain as well as an accompanying increase in the **Need-for-Control** area of the brain. These brain changes manifest themselves in complaining, crankiness, and bossiness, as well as diminishing skills, such as the ability to make oneself a sandwich. These brain changes are best managed by an Aging Human Female (AHFemale) with skill, expertise, finesse, and an occasional sharp tongue-lashing.

The care and feeding of the Aging Human Male is complex and requires tact, patience, and an amazing partner, otherwise known as a Precious Old Dame. (**Please note:** "old" is used affectionately, as in a sweet and comfortable "old" friend!)

CARE & FEEDING OF THE AGING HUMAN MALE SPECIES: A SASSY PRIMER

This manthropological **Sassy Primer** is designed to help an AHFemale navigate her happy golden years with her AHMale with finesse… and a few strong drinks. (Stay tuned for the forthcoming companion recipe book, *Stiff Drinks for Boomer Babes Living with a Stiff!*)

To be honest, this book was plagiarized: it was copied directly from the lives of Aging Human Females. This **Sassy Primer** is a collection of literary selfies of real aging women as they talk, eat, sleep (with and without sex), and share their bathroom sink with their real aging men, all while doing their best to cope with the accompanying awe, frustration, disbelief, confusion and love. All names have been changed to protect the innocent… and the guilty.

Rae Jean and I have been more than connected at the hip for years, so when she and I retired years ago with our own partners, we all descended together into the same hot Florida jungle of aging males and females, all delightfully eager to form friendships. And in these emerging friendships, patterns began to emerge. During every conversation with our girlfriends, common themes of living with an aging man caught us by surprise. It was almost as if we were all married to or partnered with the same man and struggling with the same challenges. There seemed to be a universal "Aging Human Male Species."

Our men (were they new aging men or newly aging men) were acting out their anxieties and fears about aging in similar ways, ways that had us shaking our well-coifed heads. And, as we women often do, sharing our concerns helped us cope, bond, laugh, cry and sigh. And we learned a little bit, too.

According to Statista.com, in 2019 there were over 117 million people in the U.S over age 50. That means that there are millions and millions of aging women in this country dealing with millions and millions of aging men of all shapes and sizes and colors in all forms of relationships. It is the hope of this book to help those millions of us Aging Human Females become better manthropologists, mengineers, friends, partners, and lovers.

First we decided to put these experiences into chapters in a lengthy Word document, but then the book basically began writing itself. It was uncanny. After a conversation with an AHFemale—one of our Precious Old Dames (PODs)—or after a conflict with one of our AHMales, a chapter emerged. Just as real life happened naturally, a chapter happened naturally. And, luckily, the humor flowed naturally, too, to take the sting out of our frustrations, bewilderment and wounds when dealing with our aging men. Laughter is often the best medicine—and in laughing, we didn't have to deal with the high cost of a Laugh-and-Feel-Better Pill with or without Medicare Part D!

Rae Jean's intro follows, but watch out, she tends to shoot from the hip and with a lot of lip!

— *Helen, in a sunny Florida state of mind*

The Aging Human Male Species: A Complain-Us

by Rae Jean Beech, B.S.* in Mengineering

*B.S.=Bad Sassyass

So you just heard from the softy. **Helen** has an open heart and empathy, compassion and patience—all that shit that aging is supposed to bring to you. For some of us, old age just means that our ass gets tougher, like aged leather, and our mouth gets sassier, like we're sucking sour lemons. But we can handle it! Old age, bring it on! In the words and spirit of Bill Cullen on *The Price is Right*: "Old guys, come on down!" But in a good, sexy way!

So **Helen** did the "treat-us" intro; everyone needs a Pollyanna sometimes. And I will do the "complain-us" intro, as everyone needs a Sassyass sometimes. And let it be known that I am a credentialled Bad Sassyass as I have a B.S. in mengineering. Mengineering is the Aging Human Female study of relationship principles in order to design a model wherein an Aging Human Male (AHMale), despite being occasionally well-oiled and equipped with some obsolete parts, can function optimally in building an Aging Human Partnership (AHPartnership).

I am also a certified Complainer Trainer, an Aging Human Female who is an expert in helping Boomer Babes learn to complain, although many of us don't need any training—it comes with the aging territory. I was born a complainer; right after my trip down Vagina Lane, I looked up at my mom from between her knees and said, "Quit your bellyachin'! What took you so long?" And boy, or should I say, old man, can we professional complainers have a field day with the Aging Human Male Species.

So it's hard to know where to start complaining about an Aging Human Male, and it's hard to know how and when to finish! The setting is important. Ideally complaining is said and done with a collection of your favorite Precious Old Dames (PODs) over a delicious meal, which whets the appetite for juicy talk. But in a pinch, a phone call, text, FaceTime, or Zoom will do.

And it helps to have the details fresh, as well as a fresh collection of tissues for laughing or crying.

Complaining about one of the Aging Human Male Species has no rules. There are no taboo topics. Everything from sexual positions and performance, to madras shorts with crocs and socks, to his intense stubbornness, to his need to alphabetize the spice shelf, to his inability to use a vacuum, to his attempts to learn "feelings as a second language" are on the table (and also sex on the table, folding laundry on the table, and leaving crumbs on the table)! Let's release those collective sighs of: "OH NO!" and "You're kidding!" and "I know! I know!" And then, after we Boomer Babes have sliced and diced and pared and pureed our Boomer Buddies, we can breathe a sigh of relief that we are not alone. And then we Boomer Babes can start feeling some of our appreciation and sweetness for these Boomer Boobs... oops, Boomer Buddies.

Once the complaining is over and we have come to some appreciation of the Aging Human Male that is in our life, whatsagirltodo about his stubbornness, need for control, anxiety and ever-present mansplaining? Have no fear! The **Sassy Primer** for frustrated Aging Human Females is here!

'Tis Time To...

Unwrinkle your heart
Unetch the character lines in your face
Untangle your frustrated hair knots
Unwedgie your panties
And
Unsnit your fit.
Call up your bellbottom spirit
Sweeten up your tongue

Jazz up your smile
Shake up your booty
Rev up your engine
Juice up your vag
And confetti up your life's parade
All at once!
You go-go girl!

—*Rae Jean, in a sassyass state of mind*

The Skinny on this Fat and Sassy Primer: FAQS

by Irene Shere

For Boomer Babes, asking questions is like breathing. We always need to know more, especially about our Boomer Buddies, who have been puzzling since time immemorial. And since Aging Human Males seem to be allergic to Q & A (preferring T & A), here are some answers from a trusted Precious Old Dame.

How will this Sassy Primer help me?

With a hearty dose of piss and vinegar, this primer answers all your questions with sage advice and laugh-out-loud stories about surviving your Aging Human Partnership—all with wacky, heartfelt truths Grandma never told you.

The Field Guy-ed womansplains how to survive your man's quirks and burps, and answers the question: Does everything with an Aging Human Male begin and end with sex?

The Roadmap offers travel tips for oiling your relationship, fighting fair when the wheels fall off your car, and continuing to love your vintage jalopy.

The Dame Digest supports your bra-very as you nurture your feelings and passions, while balancing your life—all on arthritic knees!

The Precious Old Dames' Party Playbook is a mega-bonus of games and gab guides for schmoozing with your gal pals.

And every woman likes to be a little revealing, so be sure to check out **Epilogue: The Reveal**.

Need a chuckle? Be sure to check out the **A to Z for the Glossary-Eyed**, The Women's Truth Foundation (WTF) collection of new, fun, scandalous, aging-relationship words and concepts. It is chock full of all kinds of sexy junk. (Junk. *Noun*. What comes in the male.)

What is a primer?

According to *Wikipedia*, "primer" refers to "any book that presents the most basic elements of any subject." And what could be more basic than your average Aging Human Male?

In the spirit of over 400 years of textbook primers beginning with Benjamin Harris's *The New-England Primer* (1688), this **Primer** continues Harris's high standards of tradition by being "affordable, portable, and compatible with the predominant worldview." More specifically, this **Primer** represents the "worldview" of many Precious Old Dames, predominantly asking "Who is this Aging Human Male and what did he do with my sweet, attentive, loving partner?!"

Note on pronunciation: Primer can be pronounced with a short "i," which then sounds like "primmer" and this **Primer** is definitely not prim or even primmer; or primer can be pronounced with a long "i," which then sounds like pr-eye-mer, as in a "primer for preparing to paint," and this **Primer** definitely prepares you to paint a _____ (fill-in-the-blankety-blank) picture of your AHMale.

Why should I read this Sassy Primer?

Inside this **Sassy Primer** you will find the wacky, challenging, and heartfelt truths about aging that Grandma never told you.

Every AHFemale wants to be heard. This **Primer** hears you without a hearing aid.

Every AHFemale wants to be understood. This **Primer** understands you on the daily-chore-list level and on the deep love-and-appreciate-me-better level.

Every AHFemale needs a good laugh sometimes. Ahem, lots of times.

Every AHFemale needs a good cry sometimes. Not just once a month before the red tide that no longer arrives.

Every AHFemale is tired of mansplaining! (According to *The Merriam-Webster Dictionary*, mansplaining is explaining "something to a woman in a condescending way that assumes she has no knowledge about the topic.") In other words, mansplaining is a simple explanation from a simple man simply looking for trouble. What the world needs now is more womansplaining, a simple explanation from a simply marvelous woman simply telling it like it is.

Every AHFemale needs positive support for her aging concerns. Ok, so that crow's foot wasn't there yesterday and today an entire flock of crow's feet has alit on your face. Cry! Then cope! This is the youngest you will ever look for the rest of your life.

Every AHFemale needs this burning question answered: "Is this 'normal' AHMale behavior?" Or is "NORMAL" just a setting on the washing machine?

Every AHFemale requires female oxygen—life support in the form of her Precious Old Dames (PODs). Every woman has the inalienable right to have a POD to cry with over the stupid thing her AHMale said or her disastrous conversation with her daughter, or her anguish over her growing-old pains. A gaggle of women in the Pee POD Poise Parties described in this **Sassy Primer** is essential for every aging woman's health.

Every AHFemale with an AHMale needs advice, tips, and unlimited access to appletinis. Call **Sassy Primer** 9-1-1.

Every Aging Human Female knows that over the past decades, aging female roles, expectations and possibilities have changed at lightning speed. This **Primer** provides a blueprint for changing aging blues into rapturous rainbows and imprinting your new-you with a joyous stamp of your own. This **Primer** shines a light on an aging woman's path to re-dreaming her dreams and outing her outrageous self.

How should I read this Sassy Primer?

What do women want? Choices! Read this **Primer** any way you want, in any order you want. Each lesson can serve as a stand-alone as you navigate ways to stand-with your Aging Human Male.

Where should I read this Sassy Primer?

You can read it on a train. You can read it on a plane. You can read it in the rain. You can read it to complain. You can read it here and there. You can read it anywhere! (with special thanks to Dr. Seuss!)

Read it locked in the bathroom while sitting on the throne as the newly crowned Latrine Queen of Quarantine, as you cry with anger and frustration over way too much 24/7 time with your super aggravating, obnoxious Aging Human Male on the umpteenth day of dealing with social isolation.

Read it in the new-tire waiting room at COSTCO™ as you moan with exasperation since you were dragged there to keep your partner company during the one-hour tire rotation that is turning into three hours.

Read the mansplaining lesson to your AHMale to explain that mansplaining doesn't help. Good luck with this womansplaining!

Read it in the morning in bed for a wake-up chuckle.

Read it in Denny's™ as you eat your Early-Bird Special with your silent Aging Human Partner who is busy enjoying his food and ignoring your attempts at scintillating conversation.

Read it with your PODs at a Pee POD Poise Party, with a glass of bubbly in your hand, while you Depend™ on your Poise™ to hold you in good stead as you all laugh and cry with joy and frustration.

How often should I read this Sassy Primer?

Ten out of ten female psychiatrists recommend one to four daily doses of this **Primer** to ease the effects of an AHFemale suffering from *Acute Neurological Geriatric Enraged Response (ANGER)* or from a serious case of *Aging So Sucks (ASS) Rash*. These doses will help an aging woman relieve pain and help her grow some big balls—oops, grow some big ovaries!

So what's the deal on the research cited in this Sassy Primer? Truth or dare?

Some of the research and sources cited in this **Primer** are authentic and true. In these instances, the sources and research cited will be followed by "(TRUTH)."

If the sources and information cited in this **Primer** are not followed by "(TRUTH)," it is important to know that the research may have been concocted and conducted either at a Pee POD Poise Party after four drinks by AHFemales who were obviously at the height of their game (just don't ask, "What game?") or behind closed doors by The (fictional) Women's Truth Foundation (WTF).

Does this Sassy Primer walk the straight and narrow?

We are all aging, no matter what our sexual orientation. We live in a world of ever lengthening acronyms; LGBTQIA (Lesbian-Gay-Bisexual-Trans-Queer-Intersex-Asexual) is an important one for aging humans of all genders to wrap our older brains around and embrace. If your relationship is not cookie-cutter heterosexual, please accept our apologies for the phrase "Aging Human Male" and change the "l" to a "t" in your head to make it "Aging Human Mate." Please accept our apologies that some discussions of body parts such as nose and ear hair and balls, may not apply. But enjoy the relationship similarities, no matter what sexual body parts and sexual mindsets are present in your Aging Human Partnership.

How is this Sassy Primer age-honoring?

Amidst all the teasing, whining, and tongue-lashing in this book about Aging Human Males—and sometimes about AHFemales—our intention is to honor the aging of the Aging Human Species.

Popularly, a geezer is a cranky old man. This **Primer** uses "geezer" with affection.

This **Primer** invented the term "geezess" (pronounced with a "hard g," as in the first "g" in "gorgeous") to describe a cranky old woman because we have to admit that 1-2% of the time we Aging Human Females can be cranky! This **Primer** uses "geezess" affectionately and with a sweet smile.

In this **Primer**, a "crone" is not an old wrinkly biddy, but a "<u>c</u>reative <u>r</u>aunchy <u>o</u>ldster with <u>n</u>ever-ending <u>e</u>xpertise." A crone is a "WOW," a Woman Of Wisdom.

THE SKINNY ON THIS FAT AND SASSY PRIMER: FAQS

If we can't joke about ourselves—and our partners and our PODs— then who can we joke about?! And, as in all of life, including aging, laughter is the best medicine. Even though laughter is not covered by Medicare and doesn't come in a child-proof container, laughter can heal the heart —and it can be found over the counter, over the kitchen counter, that is, having coffee with a Precious Old Dame!

Should I read this Sassy Primer if I'm not in an Aging Human Relationship?

The Field Guy-ed and The Roadmap lessons in this Primer are primarily proposed for Aging Human Females in their Aging Human Partnerships. The Dame Digest and The Precious Old Dames' Party Playbook lessons in this Primer are written to include all Precious Old Dames, whether flying solo or with a co-pilot, dames who are positively pumped to polish and perfect their own precious lives!

Will I have to take a test after reading this Sassy Primer?

There are plenty of fun tests in this Primer! The Field Guy-ed starts with two tough quizzes: "Is He an Aging Human Male?" and "Are You an Aging Human Female?" In The Roadmap, the "T and A Personality Diagnostic Assessment" scores who starts your fights (duh!) and then takes a steep incline down the road to the "Name that Tune" pop quiz, which tries to put the brakes on how controlling your man is. The Dame Digest provides fill-in-the-blank questions about your life, and there are, thankfully, no wrong answers! There are also wacky charades and pong games in The Precious Old Dames' Party Playbook that will definitely challenge your ability to think while you drink!

But, no, there will not be a test at the end of this Primer. The test of life is quizzical enough!

So, you Precious Old Dame you, why not keep this Sassy Primer by your side—in your purse or on your nightstand—helping you further perfect the art and craft of aging well with your Aging Human Partner.

—Irene, in a smartypants,
Dear Abby state of mind

The Field Guy-ed

"When God made man, she was practicing."
—Rita Mae Brown, writer, activist

The Field Guy-ed* is every Boomer Chick's guide to the prickles and pratfalls of living with and loving an Aging Human Male. And, yes, these broad basics literally begin and end with chapters on SEX.

The Field Guy-ed relies on the new branch of science called "psuedo-science" (science based on whatever psued's your fancy). And if your fancy doesn't include snarky Latin names about brain parts and you are wanting a lighter experience—and what Aging Human Female doesn't want to be lighter?—please feel free to move your tush around to any chapter in any order in this **Sassy Primer**.

***Guy-ed.** Noun. 1. A guy guide. 2. A guide with balls—oops, a guide with big ovaries!

Intro.
Is He an Aging Human Male? Are You an Aging Human Female? Checklist It Out

> *"Being a woman is a terribly difficult task, since it consists principally in dealing with men."*
> —Joseph Conrad, British writer

Should an Aging Human Female have questions on whether her man is an Aging Human Male, the following scientific checklist is provided.

The Aging Human Male: Dirty Dozen Checklist

Which of the following dozen questions would be answered, "Damn straight!" by your man? Check it off… the questions, not the man!

_____ Real men don't take baths.

_____ Love is blind. So is lust.

_____ Feelings matter. Somewhat… sometimes… maybe.

_____ You can never have too many beers… or too much ESPN.

_____ *Sex and the City*—NO! Sex anywhere in the city—YES!

_____ I am always right.

_____ A man's man cave is his castle.

INTRO. IS HE AN AGING HUMAN MALE? ARE YOU AN AGING HUMAN FEMALE?

_____ I still have my mojo.

_____ *Rocky I/II/III/ad nauseum*—YES to dick flicks!

_____ I am never stubborn, especially about being stubborn.

_____ My woman is stubborn.

_____ I BBQ, therefore I am.

_____ (Baker's dozen to sweeten the quiz) I am not a curmudgeon. Ever.

Scoring:

0-1 checkmarks: Is he a member of the human male species?

2-4 checkmarks: He is definitely aging.

4-6 checkmarks: His curmudgeon barometer is rising rapidly.

7+ checkmarks: Honey, buckle-up your seatbelt! It's going to be a wild ride. You've got a live one: should you fish or cut bait? (sorry to mix metaphors... you can mix a drink later). He is definitely a member of the Aging Human Male Species and he is getting crankier by the minute!

The Aging Human Female: A Checklist of One

And just in case you are wondering if you are an Aging Human Female, an AHFemale is defined as any woman over the age of eighteen who is with an AHMale, as being with an Aging Human Male can age any Human Female, often astonishingly rapidly!

Chapter 1.
Sex

"Good sex is like good bridge. If you don't have a good partner, you'd better have a good hand." — Mae West

The Field Guy-ed Sighting #1.

Observation: Manthropologist *Helen Weels* and Mengineer *Rae Jean Beech* take notes on the Aging Human Male in his native habitat as, throughout the day, he moves from the bedroom ("scratching balls") to the kitchen ("scratching around fridge for food") to the golf course ("dreaming of being a scratch golfer") to his Man Cave ("scratching his head as his team loses") and back to the bedroom ("hoping his Aging Human Partner will scratch his itch.")

Hypothesis: Leave it to Mae West to put her finger on a handy, handsy solution to an age-old problem, one that gets harder with age… or does it? For older dames and dudes, dancing in the sheets can look more like a slow dance than a foxy-trot.

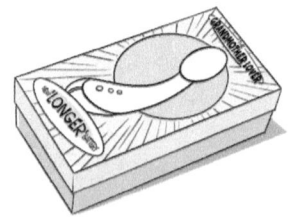

Question (for the ages) requiring further study: Do all members of Aging Human Male Species spend their days pursuing sex, food and drink, and sports?

CHAPTER 1. SEX

Lesson 1.
The Little Blue...
Isn't He a Pill?

"Sex at age 90 is like trying to shoot pool with a rope."
—George Burns

Brain Research has shown that the Aging Human Male (AHMale) brain is comprised of two sections: the **Sexus Maximus** area and the **Sexus Maximus** area. And, yes, these two areas do overlap, to the maximus.

'Nuff said.

Or not "'nuff said." From MRI research of aging men conducted by The Women's Truth Foundation (WTF), there are brain developments in Aging Human Males that result in their brain evolving into one of two sexual brain types: **Sexual Campus Type 1**, and **Sexual Campus Type 2**, or, more simply, there are two "sexual camps." An aging man whose brain has evolved into **Sexual Campus Type 1** has a raging campfire burning 24/7, with smoldering rarely occurring, and then only when dampened by rain (or alcohol). An aging man whose brain has evolved into **Sexual Campus Type 2** has wood (for the campfire, of course), but there is no way to light this fire, not a match or tinderbox to be found within fifty miles, come rain or come shine (or come alcohol), actually, come nothing. Nothing comes.

And, according to an AHFemale survey, aging women tend to complain

CARE & FEEDING OF THE AGING HUMAN MALE SPECIES: A SASSY PRIMER

about their Aging Human Boy Scouts no matter which sexual camp their aging man has joined. Apparently there is a natural brain evolution in the aging man wherein being with a cool aging woman fosters evolution of an aging male brain into *Sexual Campus Type 1* andnd being with a hot aging woman fosters the brain evolution of an aging man into *Sexual Campus Type 2*.

And so this mismatch often results in a condition known as *Incompatibility Erectus*, as in, this incompatibility e-wrecks the sex life of the AHMale and the AHFemale.

AHMale Boy Scout Motto: Be Prepared, or Not.

AHFemale Motto: Be Prepared, or Not, to Be Disappointed.

Now, 'nuff said."

Or not "nuff said" again. Don't cue the violins! Male researchers to the rescue! Ta-da! There is always The Little Blue Pill, appearing magically at your doorstep via Canada, appearing magically by your aging man's bedside table at night, appearing magically at your aging man's pecker and call. That Little Blue Pill is the only medication on earth whose reported negative side effect is its best advertisement: "For erections lasting more than 4 hours…" strikes either joy or terror in the heart (and gonads) of the taker or the takee. Instant erection—wow! Thanks to modern medical science, an AHMale in *Sexual Campus Type 2* can be initiated into *Sexual Campus Type 1* in just thirty minutes—if the bottle is not topped with a child-safety twist-off! Magic—the unscrewing of a medicine cap can lead to a screwing in a snap! There's a Viagra slogan for ya!

But wait! There is an additional warning side effect from Rodney Dangerfield: "I'm taking Viagra and drinking prune juice—I don't know if I'm coming or going."

CHAPTER 1. SEX

Lesson 2.
The Geezer Triangle:
Sex ▲ Sustenance ▲ Sports

"I'm at the age where food has taken the place of sex in my life. In fact, I've just had a mirror put over my kitchen table."
—Rodney Dangerfield

Geometry can describe various situations. The ancient Greeks appreciated the beauty of The Golden Rectangle, the natural proportions that are pleasing to the eye. There are legends about The Bermuda Triangle, into which boats and planes appear to disappear. In some cultures, there is The Devil's Triangle, a way to pleasure three bodies. And, since time immemorial, the Aging Human Male Species has worshipped **The Geezer Triangle: Sex ▲ Sustenance ▲ Sports**.

The Geezer Triangle is an equilateral triangle, all sides being equal in a day in the life of an aging man.

Sex: Whatever turns you on and gets you off.
Desired Frequency: Once a day minimum, either in real life or fantasy life or virtual life, that is, while watching any electronic device.

Sustenance: Any food that is found in the fridge or pantry, preferably food that has "Chili," "Nachos," or "BBQ" on the label, and/or any drink that has sat in an old wooden container to ripen with age in order to help the aged ripen.
Desired Frequency: Three meals a day, plus snacks, especially snacks while indulging in the other two sides of **The Geezer Triangle:** sweet gooey snacks like whipped cream and chocolate sauce during gymnastic sex or spicy crunchy snacks while watching TV sports with booby cheerleaders.

Sports: Anyone moving any object toward anything with anything, often with one person trying to best another person doing that thing. This is a catch-all definition that encompasses every sport from baseball to foosball, and even bridge and hot-dog-eating contests!
Expanded definition of sports: Any consuming passion that brings pleasure within its own activity, such as cars, video games, coin collecting, knitting, reading history books, astronomy, hiking, gardening, painting, cooking, daydreaming about winning the lottery... whatever floats an aging boat.
Desired Frequency: It's always sports time somewhere in the world, either the live game itself or the endless TV recaps or then the rating of the recaps, ad infinitum!

Pleasures are simple for an AHMale. Just three sides to **The Geezer Triangle** to make for a complete and satisfying day, a dream day, or a daydream of a day!

CHAPTER 1. SEX

In contrast, the geometry of basic needs of a Geezess—an Aging Human Female that is, with "Geezess" pronounced with a "hard g," such as the first "g" in "gorgeous"—can be described as a diamond, of course. As Carol Channing sang in the 1949 movie *Gentlemen Prefer Blondes*, "A diamond is a girl's best friend," and every glittering, glowing *Dame Diamond* draws attention and generates energy. The multi-facets of an Aging Human Female's *Dame Diamond* are **Feelings ♦ Revealings ♦ Bods ♦ PODs!** See *The Dame Digest* (Chapters 30-34) to learn more about the complex beauties of *The Dame Diamond*.

Thus, 'tis the simple **Geezer Triangle** of **Sex ▲ Sustenance ▲ Sports** versus the complex *Geezess Dame Diamond* of **Feelings ♦ Revealings ♦ Bods ♦ PODs** that can create "issues." When **The Geezer Triangle** meets the many facets of *The Geezess Dame Diamond*, sparks will fly… and glow!

> **Diane and David and The Geezer Triangle**
>
> Diane and David met and married in their late 50s while they were both working at stressful jobs for the federal government. They retired and moved to Albuquerque for a quieter lifestyle. After six months of retirement, David was driving Diane crazy!
>
> "All you do is sit around and watch sports on TV," was Diane's constant refrain as David sat in a nacho-infested stupor in front of ESPN 24/7. "Don't you want to do some sight-seeing? Meet new friends? Play tennis?"
>
> David just sat with a happy smile, a smudge of cheesy chip and a speck of beer foam on his lips, and said, "I am sooo fine." David was satisfying his **Geezer Triangle** of needs—**Sex ▲ Sustenance ▲ Sports**—to the max.
>
> Diane started meeting their neighbors, joined a book club, began gardening and volunteered at the local elementary school. Diane started tending to her own *Dame Diamond* needs. Diane stopped nagging David to be more like her. They both realized that their needs and joys were very different and that this had been accentuated in retirement without their office jobs. Retirement smoothed out as Diane learned to respect David's **Geezer Triangle** of needs and David learned to respect Diane's *Geezess Dame Diamond* of needs. *Vive le différence!*

Lesson 3.
Two Beds or not Two Beds: That is the Question that Shakes Peers Up

"Laugh and the world laughs with you, snore and you sleep alone."
—*Anthony Burgess, British writer and composer*

To be or not to be… in the same bed? That is the question. Whether an Aging Human Female is nobler in the mind to suffer the slings and arrows of an Aging Human Male's tongue while he talks in his sleep or to try to sleep and, perchance, to dream amidst the snores and snores and more snores. Out, damn snores!

Ay, there's the rub. 'Tis nobler—but is it more fun and is it practical?—to share the same bed or to shuffle off the shared mattress coils? It gives an AHFemale pause, especially if sexual consummation is a wish for the morning. To leave for a separate bedroom mid-night, perchance to dream one's dreams alone. What is it worth to an aging woman for a quiet night's snoreless, not-being-kicked, not-being-scratched-in-the-leg-by-toenails sleep? And what is it worth to a woman not to be sharing a bed with her AHMale and his sleep apnea? Any AHFemale who, even in her wildest fantasies thought of a *menage a troi*, never imagined it would be with her aging man and his CPAP device! Romeo, Romeo, wherefore art thou, Romeo? Underneath the Darth Vader CPAP mask! Oh, a kingdom for quiet, deep, peaceful sleep.

And when a houseguest passes the second bedroom on the way to the bathroom and sees that the bed is unmade and has been slept in—does that guest get down and dirty in your business and think, "Aha, they are not sleeping together and not having sex?" What does that do to an aging woman's reputation as

CHAPTER 1. SEX

"a hot patootie?" Is this thought a *Shaming of the True-th*? (as opposed to a *Taming of the Shrew*!) Did the woman get herself to the nunnery of the guest room? Or did the aging woman get herself to the guest room to lure her man to have some hot sex and exclaim to him at the height of passion, "GOOD NIGHT, SWEET PRINCE!"

Lesson 4.
How Do I Love Thee? Let Me Count the (Had-Sex) Days

From the movie Annie Hall (split screen scene):
His therapist: "Do you have sex often?"
Alvy Singer: "Hardly ever. Maybe three times a week."
Her therapist: "Do you have sex often?"
Annie Hall: "Constantly. I'd say three times a week."

CHAPTER 1. SEX

The latest research by sexologists Heethemaster and Hegottajohnson has identified a part of the brain in every AHMale that they call the **Cometab**. This **Cometab** is in the right hemisphere of the male brain—an AHMale is always right—and the **Cometab** has been proven to unconsciously keep a running number of how many times a week a man has had an ejaculation with his woman. During MRIs of AHMales, it is observed that the **Cometab** seems to contain an unconscious digital counter, which Heethemaster and Hegottjohnson have called the *"nookie number,"* a number that runs from from 0 to 1 for pessimists as diagnosed on the MMPI (Macho Male Penis Index) and that runs from 1 to 100 in every AHMale who scores as an optimist on the MMPI. (***Please note:*** The *nookie number* resets to 0 every week and the previous week's *nookie number* is permanently erased from **Cometab** memory, as every AHFemale knows).

Research has shown that when the **Cometab nookie number** of an AHMale is in the 0 to1 range, that AHMale scores very high on the AMIBLU (Assessment of Mental Illness Because of Large Undersexment), a test of low self-esteem and depression.

Research has also shown that when the **Cometab nookie number** of an AHMale brain averages scores (ahem!) of 7 or more each week, then oxycontin, the body's "happiness drug," runs rampant in the bloodstream of an aging man and he can be seen hopping, skipping, and jumping throughout his day, regardless of his arthritis.

In addition, every woman knows that when her man's **Cometab nookie number** reaches 7 or more each week, there is a special window of opportunity available. When the **Cometab nookie number** is 7 or greater, that is called Family Jewel Time: when the aging man's "family jewels" are happy, then it is time for an aging woman to cash in on her own need for jewels!

Furthermore, the latest research by sexologist Heethemaster and Hegottajohnson has identified a similar part of the aging female brain that is a digital counter. In the left hemisphere of the aging female brain (many AHFemales are concerned with being left) is the *TickTockOrgasmaclock*. This automatic brain counter keeps a second-by-second timer of how long it takes from first kiss to the "end," the "end" being AHMale satisfaction. This *TickTockOrgasmaclock* is ONLY activated when an older woman is not feeling particularly sexy but wants to help her older man with his **Cometab**

nookie number, since every aging woman knows that life in general and LIFE IN EVERY WAY is easier when her aging man has a high ***Cometab nookie number.***

A loving aging woman respects the importance of her aging man's ***Cometab nookie number***, even while mentally counting the seconds or counting sheep or calculating the discounts available with her Macy's coupon as her ***TickTockOrgasmaclock*** counts on. And so the question becomes: is there an upper limit to the ***TickTockOrgasmaclock***? How much can it tock before someone gets ticked? Is the ***TickTockOrgasmaclock*** an alarm clock—just turn it off when it gets to a certain tock and go on about your own womanly business? Or is the ***TickTockOrgasmaclock*** an endless counter that goes on and on and on and on until he goes off? This is a tough question, to be decided with your private parts and with your man's private parts within the private parts of your own home.

CHAPTER 1. SEX

Lesson 5.
Two Heads are Better than One: His and Hers Lust Lists

"Sex is emotion in motion." — Mae West

"Sex is crotch motion for an Aging Human Male."
— Rae Jean Beech

Just like two monogrammed towels on a towel rack that are marked His and Hers, so can sex in the bedroom be labelled His and Hers. His "shlong head" is where foreplay happens, whereas her "head head" is where foreplay happens. One penile noodle becoming hard begets an Aging Human Male's desire, whereas one fantasy in the noodle of her head begets an Aging Human Female's desire. How does a couple coordinate the two different sexual triggers, physical and emotional, so that they both shoot off at the same time? (Excuse the mixed metaphors of noodles and guns!)

For most aging men, their gun sits in the holster ready to fire at the touch of a finger(s), and perhaps with the help of a friend. But for some aging women, after menopause, their libido has gone libid-lo and it is even hard to find the holster that used to sit somewhat comfortably on their hips. In the words of Erma Bombeck: "I haven't trusted polls since I read that 62% of women had affairs during their lunch hour. I've never met a woman in my life who would give up lunch for sex."

So the questions are: How can an AHFemale turn her libid-lo to libid-go and then libid-O? And, how can he and she use his physical head and her fantasy head for mutual fireworks?

For most AHFemales, the key is in their fantasmagoric orgasmic imagination.

What movie scenes are a turn-on? The action in *Gone with the Wind* when Rhett Butler picks up Scarlett and carries her to the bedroom? The romance in *Ghost* where Patrick Swayze seduces Demi Moore as he embraces her from behind as she is working clay on the potter's wheel? The fun talk, talk, talk, talk, talk in *When Harry Met Sally* when they realize their friendship has turned to love? The sexual heat with Tom Cruise in *Eyes Wide Shut*? What reads are a turn-on? *Fifty Shades of Grey? The Joy of Sex? Penthouse Letters?* Or is it gifts that turn on an AHFemale: Flowers? Chocolate? Sweet words? Appreciation? What turns low libido to go-go: slow dancing to "Your Song," playful teasing, hot movies or steamy books, fantasy play, sex toys, romantic gestures, sweet words?

Every woman needs a **Lust List**, a list of personal turn-ons, very personal turn-ons. This **Lust List** can be in her personal diary or it can be shared with her man to increase the likelihood of sexual man-ifestation, ahem, woman-ifestivities. And the **Lust List** can even be numbered to be called out, as in, *"Let's set a date for **Lust List #5** this evening."* This provides lots of time to put that special book on the nightstand, get that steamy movie set up from On Demand, or stop at the store for her favorite flowers. Foreplay in the mind provides the warm and exciting anticipation for foreplay in the body as the time draws closer.

And why not share and compare each partner's **Lust List**? Odds are, His **Lust List** is shorter than Her **Lust List**, but then, size doesn't really matter!

> **Bob and Karen and their Lust Lists**
> Bob and Karen both enjoy making love, but have different need-schedules and different turn-ons that get them to that, "OH, YES!" place. Bob would love to have sex every day—his favorite color is "blue pill"—and Karen would like to relax in the evenings before bed with her TV shows and make love once a week. (Two-times-a-week sex can seem "constantly" to her!) Their **Lust Lists** look like this:

Karen's Lust List:
This is a Warming-My-Heart-Warms-My-Hoo-Ha Guide for You, Bob…

1. You giving me back rubs and cuddles at unexpected moments

2. You calling me "Beautiful," "Cutie," "Sweet Lips," "Brilliant"

3. You bringing me flowers, chocolate,or making plans for a surprise dinner out

4. You planting deep, deep, deep, sizzling, tongue-filled kisses on me as we do a deep dip

5. You suggesting we make love that day and giving me a choice of when, so I have about 30 minutes beforehand to switch gears and get tuned in to my own fantasies

6. Us dancing to our song, "Unchained Melody" by The Righteous Brothers

7. You turning off the game, asking about my day and REALLY, REALLY listening

8. You thanking me for making fantastic coffee/muffins/children

9. You talking sexy and telling me how much you crave my body

10. You being patient with me as my aging body is slower to respond to touch

11. You loving me and telling me often

12. You vacuuming the living room rug without being asked—yes, this is sexy!

> **Bob's Lust List:**
> **I am Always Hot for You, Karen...**
>
> 1. You touching my private parts
>
> 2. Us watching sexy movies or reading soft-core porn to each other
>
> 3. You touching my privates
>
> 4. You in that red teddy
>
> 5. You choosing the sex toys
>
> 6. You touching my whatever

So how do these two reconcile the mutual joining of his physical noodle (penile sensitivity) and her feeling noodle (heartwarming romantic gestures) so that they make a delicious lo mein noodle dish that leads to low moans of mutual satisfaction? Over the years—yes, good things are worth waiting for—Bob and Karen have found their noodle rhythm.

On any given day Bob recalls Karen's **Lust List** and puts at least one of Karen's list requests into sexy motion. Here is the important part: **What do women want? Choices!!!**

After deep, deep kissing, Bob suggests they think about their **Lust Lists** and he asks Karen if and how and when and where she would like the kiss to go. He provides her with time to get in touch with her **Lust List**. When Karen has a choice, she can decide to go with the flow and be spontaneous or not. If "not," she can focus on their future plan for fun and can fantasize about that time and all the juicy details about what she wants to wear, what sexy movies she wants to use as foreplay, what sex toys may be exciting.

Bob loves to have some hot action planned and Karen loves to regulate the temperature.

Bob and Karen's **Lust Lists** honor their sexual differences. Sharing **Lust Lists** can turn take-for-ever play into torrid fore-play. **Lust Lists** can turn fizzling libid-los into sizzling libid-gos and screaming libid-Os!

Chapter 2.
Competence: Questions?

"An aging man's sense of his competence is as crucial to him as an aging woman's sense of her lovability is to her—without question."
—Helen Weels

The Field Guy-ed Sighting #2.

Observation: Manthropologist *Helen Weels* and Mengineer *Rae Jean Beech* take photos of the Aging Human Male in his native habitat as he responds to unwanted questions from his Aging Human Female. The photos include him with his mouth spewing colorful language, his body all bent out of shape, and his eyes aglow with anger.

Hypothesis: There are many things that a Boomer Chick can call her Boomer Buddy, but calling him out on his competence is a definite *EGO* no-no. An AHFemale's innocent question can ignite an AHMale's internal question of competence and spark a slew of fireworks!

Questions requiring further study: Do all members of The Aging Human Male Species snap, crackle, and pop when questioned by their Aging Human Partner?

Lesson 1. Bueller? Bueller? Questions, Anyone?

"A man's ego is just as fragile as a woman's heart."
—*Lana Del Rey, singer, songwriter, poet, model*

If an Aging Human Female has a question, the best way to pose this question to an Aging Human Male is... DON'T!

If an Aging Human Female has a question, the one thing that she never, ever wants to do... NOT ASK!

Aging men are into "not connecting" or being disrupted from their one-way brain channel. Questions posed to an aging man are a definite no-no.

CHAPTER 2. COMPETENCE: QUESTIONS?

And aging women are into "connecting" as they multi-process their way through life and share thoughts, info, opinions, politics, grandchildren stories, the weather, clothes, and even aging men issues when they get desperate. Questions are like breathing to AHFemales. **Questions are like breathing polluted air to AHMales.**

In addition, brain research on AHMales has shown that when an AHMale utters the phrase, "I don't know," the *Incompetence Detestus (ID)* area of the brain lights up like a Christmas Tree (or a Hannukah Menorah, or Kwanzaa Kinara) and all sorts of bells and whistles cause a chain reaction in the *Everlasting God Omnipotence (EGO)* area of his brain, causing the *EGO* to crash and burn. The consequences are not pretty. This is evidenced by brain research taken during an AHMale's utterance of the phrase, "I don't know." During this brain study, MRIs taken during "I don't know" showed clear evidence of mass brain confusion and a complete shutting down of both the *ID* and the *EGO*. The resulting "I don't know" MRIs appeared to resemble the scarecrow's brain in *The Wizard of Oz* and showed mega-activation of the *Rubius Redus Slipperus* portion of the brain, an activation that expresses an unconscious desire to escape the situation and return home to Kansas.

Gwen and George and Questions

Gwen had always wanted to be a writer. During her first year of retirement she began writing a children's book on her laptop. One day her laptop froze and she was very worried that her 100-page rough draft of her book was lost forever.

Gwen: "George, can you come into the office please. You're my IT go-to guy and my computer is frozen and I can't get any keys to do anything."

George (a frustrating hour later): "I can't fix this damn thing."

Gwen: "I'll take it to the Computer Nerds Store to see if they can do anything."

George (in a very snippy voice): "Do that!"

Gwen: "I will! But you don't have to be so snippy about it."

George: "I'm not being snippy. You're being impatient and snippy."

Needless to say, that exchange escalated. It took about two days for Gwen to understand George's snippiness: George's sense of competence had been challenged when he couldn't fix the computer.

Questions—and requests for help—imply there should be an answer. No self-respecting AHMale ever ever ever wants to admit that he doesn't have the answer.

To ask the question or not to ask the question, that is the question—but, oops—we are not supposed to ask questions!

So are any questions safe? Could there possibly be a good question? (Is that question a good question?) The answer is yes. Every aging woman knows that life is smoother when the two most important areas of an aging man are stroked regularly. Every female knows about the first stroking area; this lesson deals with the stroking of the second area, the *EGO* area in the brain.

The *EGO* area in the male brain becomes automatically activated and massaged when the chest area of an AHMale becomes puffed up, thus softening the utterings that come from his mouth. Thus life runs more smoothly for the female questioner. Chest-puffing questions affect the *EGO* area instantaneously, bypassing all other sections of the brain. These chest-puffing questions, **ChestPuffers,** as they are sometimes called, are also known as "no-brainers."

ChestPuffers Category 1: Competence *EGO* Stroking Questions

1. How did you ever learn how to do that?
2. Have you always been so smart?
3. How could one guy know so much?
4. Were you always so competent?
5. That is so cool! Can you teach me to do that?
6. Aren't you amazing?!

If saying any of these six **ChestPuffers,** with or without batting eyelashes, makes an AHFemale nauseous, then she should just deep-six these **ChestPuffers**. Emotional honesty is as emotional honesty does.

CHAPTER 2. COMPETENCE: QUESTIONS?

ChestPuffers Category 2: Hintful *EGO* Stroking Questions

Would that _____ be interesting to try to use on _____?
Examples: hammer…that nail or idea…your friend Harry

Would that _____ you put on the _____ be better in the _____ ?
Examples: butter…table…fridge or sweaty shirt…kitchen counter…laundry bag

Are you also wondering _____?
Examples: if the dog needs to go out or if your mom is being annoying?

Should we _____?
Examples: make love or call AAA to change the flat tire or sell the house?

It's always an AHFemale's prerogative on what, if any, body part or brain part she wants to massage. Questions can be tricky. To use or not use **ChestPuffers**, that is the question. To stoke a spat or to stroke an EGO… there is no easy answer.

CHAPTER 2. COMPETENCE: QUESTIONS?

Lesson 2.
Don't Be a Repeat Ask-fender

"Ask a question once, shame falls on him—if you have activated the ID/EGO section of the AHMale brain. Ask a question twice, shame on you!"—Helen Weels

An AHMale does not change his mind. Do not ask the same question twice! Etch in your AHFemale brain that a decision made by an aging male brain is etched in stone in his brain.

Once an answer is given, the maze of finding an answer has been traversed, never to meander or to be traversed again. A decision made is a decision made, the **Cementus Mentis** section of the aging male brain is activated and the answer is poured in concrete and set instantly. To repeat a question—minutes, hours, or days later—implies that you as an aging female don't understand that the **Manly Trap Door** to the **Cementus Mentis** section of the brain has been locked, never to open again.

To repeat the same question to an AHMale means, "You didn't listen the first time," which is the first offense.

Or, you have committed the second offense: You don't understand that once the **Cementus Mentis** is activated, only a weak AHMale would use the phrase to open the **Manly Trap Door**: "I've changed my mind." That would mean your aging man would lose his membership card in the Aging Human Male Species Club.

Here is an example and while it may be hard to believe, it is taken from real life! Names have been changed to protect the guilty (AHMale).

> **Sherry and Stewart and More Questions?**
>
> **Tuesday**
>
> *Sherry*: "What do you think is the best way to go to that new Pizza Palace tomorrow?"
>
> *Stewart*: "I checked the GPS and found the easiest way to the new Pizza Palace where we are meeting Janet and Joe tomorrow. We can take Vine to 3rd Street."
>
> *Sherry:* "Great!"
>
> **Wednesday**
>
> As Sherry and Stewart prepare to leave for dinner...
>
> *Sherry:* "Why don't we try taking Crabapple Street to 2nd Street? There's parking nearby."
>
> *Stewart:* "I told you yesterday: we are going to take Vine to 3rd."
>
> *Sherry*: "I was just offering a suggestion. You don't listen to me!"
>
> *Stewart:* "No, you never listen to me!"
>
> A fight ensues. Plans are cancelled and neither goes to Pizza Palace.

There is no statute of limitation on decisions made by an AHMale, no expiration date. Once a decision is made by an aging man, it is a decision ad infinitum (or ad nauseum; the wisdom of a decision is in the mind of the beholder).

If an AHFemale breaks the AHMale Ask Code and asks a question, she shouldn't double break the the AHMale Ask Code and be a repeat ask-fender. Exercise to help in this aspect of the care and feeding of the AHMale: Repeat three times: "Only an a__ is a repeat ask-fender, only an a__ is a repeat ask-fender, only an a__ is a repeat ask-fender." Then take two aspirin and go to bed, alone, of course.

Chapter 3.
Control + Alt + Delete the Power Struggle

"Women want a man who is in control, but not a man who is controlling. There's a difference." — JM Storm, author

The Field Guy-ed Sighting #3.

Observation: Manthropologist *Helen Weels* and *Mengineer Rae Jean Beech* record the Aging Human Male in his native habitat as he mansplains with unwanted advice, loudly pounds his chest in a display of superiority, and drones on about how he is in control of every situation. The recordings include faint background sounds of the head-shaking of his Aging Human Female during his mansplaining.

Hypothesis: Hey, Boomer Buddy, the only key to control is on your laptop. Just deal!

Question requiring further study: How can an Aging Human Female interject womanplaining amidst the Aging Human Male's mansplaining?

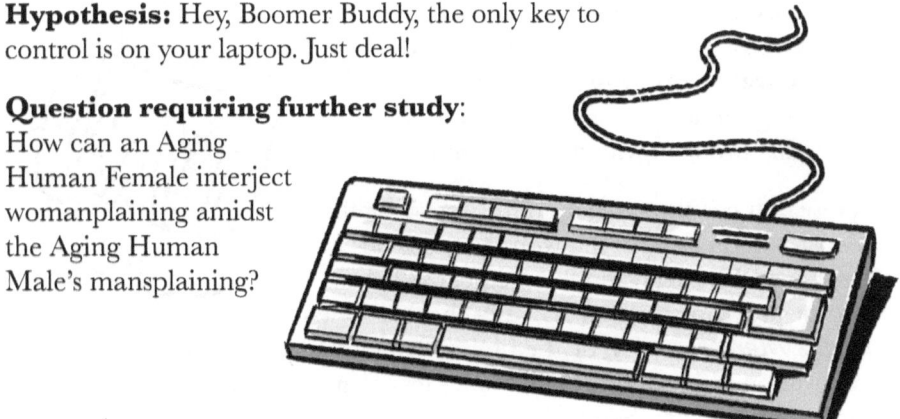

Lesson 1.
Don't Ask, Don't Tell: Unsolicited Advice (UA)

"Take my advice—I'm not using it."
—T-Shirt seen in Fort Lauderdale

We hold these truths to be self-evident:

1. That any AHMale can ALWAYS offer Unsolicited Advice (UA) to any AHFemale at any time, at any place, in any way, on any subject. UA is another term for mansplaining (mansplaining is a simple explanation offered by a simple man simply looking for trouble). In response to UA or mansplaining, a grateful "Thank you!" is all that is expected by an AHFemale in return.

2. That any AHFemale may NEVER offer any Unsolicited Advice (UA) to any AHMale at any time, at any place, in any way, or on any subject—especially regarding traffic or driving directions or a plumbing problem with a kitchen sink or toilet.

Brain research has shown that, in the above conflict situations, as soon as an aging woman opens her mouth to offer UA and words begin to emerge, the UA on the part of the aging woman activates the AHMale's ***Cementus Mentis*** portion of the brain. (See footnote: "written in stone.") This activation results in the aging man's loss of mouth control (snarl), loss of word control ("I can handle it!"), and loss of blood flow to nether parts of the body (resulting in the shutdown of the sexual need of an AHMale for an AHFemale and the accompanying loss of all sweet endearing utterances that may eventually lead to sexual gratification).

CHAPTER 3. CONTROL + ALT + DELETE THE POWER STRUGGLE

This aging male ***Cementus Mentis*** portion of the brain is connected to millions of electrical impulses in the ***Everlasting God Omnipotence (EGO)*** portion of the brain, a connection which is integral to the optimum functioning of the aging male. Any aging female's UA short-circuits this important connection between ***Cementus Mentis*** and ***EGO***, resulting in the dominance of the ***Incompetent Detestus (ID)*** portion of the aging male brain and concomitant verbal releases, such as "F(reeze) U(rself)."

Once the ***Cementus Mentis*** portion of the AHMale's brain is activated, it remains active until the AHMale is able to demonstrate that the AHFemale's UA is incorrect. This deactivation of the ***Cementus Mentis*** can occur with real-time proof or with illogical thinking or with the twisting of reality, whatever it takes for the AHFemale's unsolicited advice to be declared incorrect. Brain research has shown that total de-activation of the AHMale's ***Cementus Mentis*** is only achieved with the AHMale's utterance of the phrase: "See, Honey, I was right."

Harriet and Ralph and Unsolicited Advice

Harriet loved to play golf. Golfing with her girlfriends was fun. Golfing with her husband Ralph often ended up in Unsolicited Advice coming Harriet's way. She started joking with him and saying "UA" whenever he was mansplaining to her about how to improve her golf game.

For the holidays, Harriet gave Ralph a mug from the University of Alabama (even though he hadn't attended college there) because the front of the mug had a big red "UA." Ralph, with a crimson blush appearing on his cheeks, felt fit to be tied. (So, some unsolicited womansplaining for non-Southerners: Alabama is The Crimson Tide.)

Lesson 2.
Don't Ask, But Be Told Anyway: Mansplaining

"Mansplaining. Noun. A simple explanation from a simple man simply looking for trouble."—Rae Jean Beech

According to Rebecca Solnit in her book, *Men Explain Things to Me*, "Mansplaining is not a universal flaw of the (male) gender, just the intersection between overconfidence and cluelessness where some portion of that gender gets stuck… (it is accompanied by) that smug look I know so well in a man holding forth, eyes fixed on the fuzzy far horizon of his own authority." (TRUTH, *Men Explain Things to Me*, Haymarket Books, 2015.)

Mansplaining is a cousin (as a matter of fact, a kissing cousin) to Unsolicited Advice, although it is clear to every AHFemale that mansplaining on his part will not elicit any kissing on her part!

Research studies by The Women's Truth Foundation (WTF) have shown that there appears to be a relationship between sunspots on the sun and mansplaining. For some reason, random sunspot eruptions send brain waves to an AHMale, triggering his *I=Know I'm Naturally Great (I=KING)* brain area. This *I=KING* area then pumps up the AHMale's *Everlasting God Omnipotence (EGO)*. These mega-potent sunspots activate both the *I=KING* and *EGO* so that an aging man begins to believe he is the center of the solar system, which causes him to believe that whatever thoughts he vocalizes are universal truths. Thus, he believes himself to be The King of Knowledge.

How better for an aging man to express his competence and control than to be The King of Knowledge to his adoring Queen. If the aging man were ever to look outward instead of constantly congratulating himself inwardly on his expertise, he might see that his adoring Queen was, in fact, a very bored Queen, shaking her head in disbelief!

CHAPTER 3. CONTROL + ALT + DELETE THE POWER STRUGGLE

Jill and Jack and Mansplaining

Jack and Jill went up a hill
To fetch a pail of water.
Jill fell down and broke her crown
And Jack came mumbling after.

"Oh, Jill," he cried at her side.
"I will get you water,
"You stepped so bad and you are sad
You can't walk as you oughta.

Those shoes you wear are so unfair,
STILETTOS ain't made for WALKING!"
Then Jill did cry, as she gave him the eye,
"And YOUR MOUTH ain't made for TALKING!"

"Jill, you tumbled, such a bumble,
STOP your shrill complaining."
"NO, Jack, I'm fine, just be kind,
And STOP your damn MANSPLAINING!"

For advice on how Jill, and any Aging Human Female, can cope with mansplaining, see Chapter 11. Lesson 3: Womanhandling the Mansplaining: **The Rebecca Rule.**

Lesson 3.
I (Com)Promise to Love, Honor and Cherish: Over-giving and Under-appreciating

"I prefer my pretzels for eating, not as the shape I need to bend myself into to please my man." — Rae Jean Beech

Many Aging Human Females have spent a lifetime learning how to compromise their own needs to satisfy an Aging Human Male. I love, therefore I compromise. I love, therefore I give, and give, and give, and give… until something's gotta give! And when it gives, it's not a pretty picture, more like a full-scale production of *The Taming of the Shrew*, technicolor fireworks included for free!

Brain research has shown that when an aging woman is generous to an aging man, her **Tabbis Humongous** portion of the brain automatically records the deed. It should be noted that if a woman's generosity goes unnoticed or unappreciated, the tally in the aging woman's **Tabbis Humongous** is instantaneously neurologically increased by a factor of 10,000. Yes, she is always keeping an accurate score!

Furthermore, the female's **Tabbis Humongous** section of the brain has a direct connection to her tongue, causing her to automatically verbalize, at any given nanosecond, a description of all unappreciated actions and deeds that have been stored in her brain, forever.

CHAPTER 3. CONTROL + ALT + DELETE THE POWER STRUGGLE

Appreciation for generous acts by AHFemales is often experienced by AHMales in the *Fewandfar Betweenus* portion of the AHMale brain. Activating the *Fewandfar Betweenus* portion of the male brain causes non-verbal vocalizations, such as grunts, more grunts, half smiles, and, should a repetitive tic develop, more grunts.

The interplay between the AHFemale brain and the AHMale brain often takes on a complex and interesting pattern, wherein her *Tabbis Humongous* repeatedly activates her tongue and the AHMale's *Fewandfar Betweenus* repeatedly activates his grunts. So this circular pattern of accusing-grunting-accusing-grunting continues and continues, often at a more highly activated pitch, until additional brain stimulation occurs, often causing either the AHMale or AHFemale's *Dooris Slammo Whammo* to take over.

On the other hand, there is the aging man who feels like he is giving and giving when, in an aging woman's reality, he is hardly inconvenienced. Brain research has shown that the *Tabbis Humongous* portion in an aging male's brain is automatically activated 100 times for only one act, which accounts for the feeling in the aging man that he is doing so much when, in the aging woman's reality, he is doing so little.

Brain scientists explain this disconnect in an AHMale's reality with the *SimpleNeedsSimpleDeeds Supposition.* The *SimpleNeedsSimpleDeeds Supposition* posits that if a person has simple needs, simply little needs doing outside of those simple needs. A geezer has simple needs: **The Geezer Triangle of Sex ▲ Sustenance ▲ Sports**. If a need exists outside that triangular tunnel vision, then the deed requires, in an AHMale's mind and body, a Herculean effort.

In **The Geezer Triangle** world view, there is no need for the living room to be vacuumed, so that the deed of vacuuming the living room rug is a massive feat worthy of an Olympic gold medal and much praise from his Aging Human Partner. In **The Geezer Triangle** mindset, if you don't care about it, you don't have to care for it; if you don't care about, it isn't there. Who needs to apologize for farting? What aging man schedules his own dentist appointments?

And when the aging man's *Tabbis Humongous* automatically ca-chings a mega-tally for one simple deed, the aging man feels he deserves major kudos for his simple deed. And the list of ***SimpleNeedsSimpleDeeds***, that is, simple acts that are deemed simply unnecessary by an AHMale but should be mega-lauded when accomplished, is a never-ending one.

> ### *Judy and Jim and the SimpleNeedsSimpleDeeds Supposition*
>
> ***Judy:*** "I feel like I do all the housework around here. We are both retired and I would like to share the household chores and repairs. When I do all the work, I get grouchy!"
>
> ***Jim:*** "Whadda ya mean?!?! I dusted the living room and dining room furniture!!"
>
> ***Judy:*** "That was four weeks ago!"
>
> ***Jim:*** "But I did a GREAT job!"
>
> ***Judy:*** "I do wayyyyy too much of the work around here!! I do all the laundry."
>
> ***Jim:*** "I put my workout clothes in the washer and dryer!"
>
> ***Judy:*** "That was once and it was two months ago!"
>
> ***Jim:*** "But I did a GREAT job! Alright already, stop your complaining. I even clean the toilets!"
>
> ***Judy:*** "That was once… last year!"
>
> ***Jim:*** "But I did a GREAT job!"
>
> ***Judy:*** "And I even have to remind you to trim your nose hair every week!"
>
> ***Jim:*** "But I do a GREAT job!"
>
> ***Judy:*** (speechless)

It's that dudetude of "you-do-it" on the old fart's part that is not smart. Advice for an AHFemale to share with her AHMale: "Dude, fake that you care about these simple things and do them ungrudgingly—without running up your ***Tabbis Humongous***—and I will love you even more. It's time for you guys to be the ones faking it—but not in bed—out of bed, when changing the bedsheets!"

Lesson 4.
Right Brain, Left Brain: The I-Am-Always Right Brain

"I'm a Man. To save time, let's just assume that I'm never wrong." — T-shirt in Texas

In an Aging Human Male, stubbornness is the layman's term for the more medical diagnosis: *Constipation of the Brain*. *Constipation of the Brain* occurs in an aging male on the I-Am-Always Right side of the brain, and is identified by the following characteristics: it's solid, it's stuck, and it stinks! So what's an older woman to do to cure her older man of *Constipation of the Brain*? There are two solutions for this malady.

Constipation of the Brain Remedy #1. **TLC.** Many AHFemales have found that the best antidote to *Constipation of the Brain* is TLC: Truly Lacy Clothes. TLC can help ensure that the I-Am-Always Right Brain is left behind. TLC (Truly Lacy Clothes) come in many colors and varying dosages and often provide blessed relaxation and overnight relief for *Constipation of the Brain.*

Constipation of the Brain Remedy #2. **The Rebecca Rule** is another solution for *Constipation of the Brain*. Once, when **Irene** was struggling in her Aging Human Partnership, she asked her mother **Rebecca** how she had managed to stay married for sixty-five years to **Irene's** stubborn father. **Rebecca**, who was a very shy and quiet woman said, **"Listen to everything your man says, and then do what you want!"**

And to cure a more advanced case of *Constipation of the Brain*, try a time-release dose of **The Rebecca Rule**. Listen to everything your man says, wait at least 24 hours, and then do what you want. This time-release dose of **The Rebecca Rule** means that, for most issues, within a day any red-blooded aging man can find some exciting sport to capture his attention and he will forget all about the conflict. Then you can skip merrily along and do whatever you want, without the doo-doo. For some, even more advanced cases, it may be better to give **The Rebecca Rule** an even longer time to have an effect on *Constipation of the Brain*, but, luckily, the plus side of being with an aging man is his aging memory.

> *Lashawn and Aiesha and* **The Rebecca Rule**
>
> *Aiesha*: "I want to put hardwood floors in the kitchen when we remodel. They remind me of my grandmother's wood floors in her kitchen in her farmhouse in Georgia."
>
> *Lashawn*: "Hardwood floors are too hard to keep clean. They'll get all wet and warped. We need tile floors in the kitchen."
>
> *Aiesha:* "I hear you."
>
> Six months later, when Aiesha remodelled their kitchen, she quietly installed hardwood floors. Lashawn never noticed and never commented on the kitchen floors.

CHAPTER 3. CONTROL + ALT + DELETE THE POWER STRUGGLE

Lesson 5. Hard-Boiled Eggs or Chicken and Waffles? You Choose!

"My decision making skills are as good as a squirrel that's crossing the street." —T-shirt in a mall in Seattle

A recent survey of Precious Old Dames indicates that in decision-making not all aging men suffer from **Constipation of the Brain.** Some AHMales are not so-hardboiled! Some aging women can be driven to frustration and frazzled hair when it comes to their man not being decisive. Frustration sets in when an aging woman's guy is a "chicken"—not choosy at all, but an old bump-on-a-log chicken (pardon the mixed metaphor). Or how about when her guy is a switchy-choosy "waffler"—switching choices as often as he switches the blades in his razor?!

The Chicken: Here is how one AHMale with a huge heart became a not-gonna-choose "chicken." This geezer wanted to do right by his geezess and so he spent considerable time studying the age-old question: "What do women want?" Then he fortunately—or unfortunately—stumbled across this tale of Sir Gawain from the Middle Ages:

In medieval times, one of Arthur's favorite knights, Sir Gawain, agreed to marry Ragnall, an ugly, wrinkly old hag, in exchange for her telling King Arthur a secret that would save Gawain from death. After the wedding, on their wedding night, Ragnall went to change into something more comfortable as Sir Gawain got into bed.

Then, suddenly, instead of Ragnall, a beautiful, hot young woman appeared. Sir Gawain was shocked. "Where is my wife?" he asked.

"I am your wife," Ragnall replied. She explained that a wicked witch had put a spell on her so that she would change from being beautiful half of the day to being ugly the other half of the day. Ragnall said to her new husband, "You have a choice. You decide if you want me beautiful by night for you to see, and ugly by day, for all the world to see; or beautiful by day for people to see, and ugly by night, for you to see. It is your decision."

Sir Gawain responded, "I want you to be the way you want to be. It is your choice." Unknowingly, with that response, Sir Gawain broke the witch's spell and Ragnall was beautiful all the time. By giving her a choice, Sir Gawain gave Ragnall back her power. (TRUTH, Wikipedia.)

The Sir Gawain-Ragnall story is a beautiful parable about how women can be empowered in a relationship by being given choices. But... can an aging man be too much like Sir Gawain?

Every aging sweetheart has some of Sir Gawain in him, offering his lovely woman choices. But "chickens" take this *wayyy* too far. Some geezers give their geezesses all the choices! Way too many decisions to make! Who wants to always be picking food, movies, friends, hair styles, weekend activities, tattoos, and even when to do an oil change (for the car, not for the guy—or gal!) "HELP! 9-1-1," says an AHFemale with an AHMale chicken. "There is an old man here handing over our lives to ME!"

The Waffler: Waffles start out as mooshy batter, then take shape, and then get crisp. Then comes the maple syrup and, uh-oh, they are mooshy and soggy once more! So an aging man who is a "waffler" is a changer, sometimes taking a stand and making a sharp decision, then changing that decision, and then changing that decision again. It is hard for an aging woman to keep up! What to do with wafflers? Strike while the waffle iron is hot. When the waffle is crisp and ready, and the syrup is still fresh, go for it... before anything—like a mind—can change!

CHAPTER 3. CONTROL + ALT + DELETE THE POWER STRUGGLE

Lesson 6.
To Coddle or not to Coddle: What's the Eggspectation? Or Does it All Get Scrambled?

"I'm more confused than a chameleon in a bag of Skittles."
—*T-shirt in Boulder, CO*

Walking on eggshells, that's what it oftentimes feels like living with a hard-boiled Aging Human Male. The old man sometimes seems like a bantam rooster strutting his stuff in the barnyard of life, an alpha male that doesn't need or want any help from anyone or anything. It's a fine line to walk with the AHMale cock! Does he want help or not want help from an old woman? And it is a fine line for the old woman. Does she offer help or not offer help? How does an aging female live with an aging male's anxiety, fear of incompetence, and need for control without having him feel henpecked? And how does she do all this while remaining a cool chick?

She walks on eggshells with great difficulty and great skill! And she stays strong inside, knowing that she is a generous and nurturing chick who sometimes will be loved and appreciated in return, and sometimes will get ruffled feathers in return. But they are his feathers and he needs to take responsibility for his ruffling. That alpha cock may feel henpecked at times, but that Aging Boomer Bantam Rooster needs to know that his Boomer Chick is loving and nurturing him.

Chapter 4.
It Takes a Worried Man

"There has been much tragedy in my life; at least half of it actually happened." — Mark Twain

The Field Guy-ed Sighting #4.

Observation: Manthropologist *Helen Weels* and *Mengineer Rae Jean Beech* do seismographic recordings of the anxious shaking of the knees of an Aging Human Male as he worries about… well, as he worries about everything. Late-night recordings capture his elevated anxiety as the fridge door slams shut with loud exclamations of, "Who moved my cheese?" The highest seismic readings correspond to his verbalized thoughts: "What is happening to my memory? My belly? My golf swing? My mojo? My libido?"

Hypothesis: When the big world is spinning like a top (which has been happening for millinia) and an AHMale's world is gyrating out of control (which has been slowly happening for a decade or so), many a Boomer Buddy attempts to control the hell out of his outer world ("Where are my car keys?") or retreat into an inner fantasy world ("I do love me some sci-fi movies... 24/7!")

Question requiring further study: How can an Aging Human Female transform her Aging Human Male's anxiety from frantic behavior into romantic behavior? How can she help him dance to a different tune, partnering with him as he calms his (and perhaps her) cha-cha-cha into a slow sexy tango?

Lesson 1. Anxiety and Control: Dance to Whose Tune?

"Some people call me a control freak, but I like to think of myself as a control enthusiast." — paraphrased from Ariana Zakrzewski, "Confessions of a Control Enthusiast," 04/16/2016, theodysseyonline.com

Wondering if your geezer is controlling? Put on your go-go boots and dance to the AHMale Song Quiz to see just how controlling he might be! After all, as Woody Guthrie sings, "It takes a worried man to sing a worried song."

The AHMale Song Quiz: Romantic or Frantic?

Would your AHMale turn these romantic songs into his personal frantic songs to soothe his anxiety and calm his control issues? Count your "YES!" answers.

Note: We've kindly provided singers' names in a key at the bottom, so you don't spend hours Googling: "Who sang ___?" even though you can hear the song in your head and the singer's name is on the tip of your tongue. You are so welcome.

Song 1. **Romantic:** "Try to remember the kind of September when life was slow and oh, so mellow."

Frantic: "Try to remember that the butter goes on the second shelf on the right in the fridge."

Song #2. **Romantic:** "Doolang, doolang, he's so fine, wish he were mine."
Frantic: "We'll get a fine if you park your car too close to that line."

Song #3. **Romantic:** "Dream, dream, dream, all I have to do is dream."
Frantic: "Change? Change is a nightmare!"

Song #4. **Romantic:** Unchained Melody: "Oh, my love, I hunger for your kiss."
Frantic: Fractured melody: "Ewww, don't kiss me with that garlic breath."

Song #5. **Romantic:** "Great balls of fire!"
Frantic: "Don't leave the kitchen with that pot boiling on the stove—it will catch fire."

Song #6. **Romantic:** "Splish, splash, I was taking a bath, long about a Saturday night."
Frantic: "Jeez, woman, you soaked the rug with water when you got out of the shower and now even the floor is wet."

Song #7. **Romantic:** "Blue suede shoes."
Frantic: "Suede stains when it gets wet. I only wear this one style of black Clark's oxfords."

Song #8. **Romantic:** "Mustang Sally, ride, Sally, ride."
Frantic: "Must we do this traffic?! I hate riding in the car with all this traffic and waiting at red lights."

Song. #9. **Romantic:** "He's leader of the pack."
Frantic: "Just don't say anything. I know the directions to Fred and Ethel's house better than you ever have!"

Song #10. **Romantic:** "It's down at the end of Lonely Street at Heartbreak Hotel."

Frantic: "I only stay at Hyatt Houses when we travel. Love their free breakfast."

Song #11. **Romantic:** "Lovely Rita meter maid."

Frantic: "We'll get a ticket if you park in a handicapped space even to run into 7-11 to get a loaf of bread."

Song. #12. **Romantic:** "Like a bridge over troubled water, I will lay me down."

Frantic: "I don't do bridges, I don't do heights, I like my feet solidly on the ground."

Song #13. **Romantic:** "I can't get no satisfaction, as I'm driving in my car with the radio."

Frantic: "My way or the highway."

Song #14. **Romantic:** "To everything there is a season and a time to every purpose under heaven."

Frantic: "The seasoning and herb bottles need to be arranged alphabetically in the spice rack."

Song #15. **Romantic:** "You ain't nothing but a hound dog, cryin' all the time.."

Frantic: "We need to buy a purebred dog with an AKC pedigree, a dog that doesn't shed and doesn't bark and doesn't weigh more than 20 pounds so we can take it on the airplane."

Song #16. **Romantic:** "I heard it through the grapevine."

Frantic: "It is only true when verified by three different independent news sources."

Song #17. **Romantic:** "These boots were made for walking."

Frantic: "Dr. Scholl's Arch Supports and only Dr. Scholl's."

Song #18. **Romantic:** "The answer, my friend, is blowing in the wind."

Frantic #1: "There has to be an answer to this question somewhere! Have you Googled it? This is SOOO frustrating!"

Frantic #2: "Oh, no, what is that smell? Did I fart? Did I forget my deodorant? But I alway put on my deodorant!"

Scoring: If you totalled over three YES! answers, you have objective proof that your Aging Human Male is anxious and controlling—as if you didn't already know!

Singers: **1.** From *The Fantastiks* play **2.** The Chiffons **3.** The Everly Brothers **4.** The Righteous Brothers **5.** Jerry Lee Lewis **6.** Bobby Darrin **7.** Elvis **8.** Wilson Pickett **9.** The Shangri-Las **10.** Elvis **11.** The Beatles **12.** Simon and Garfunkel **13.** The Rolling Stones **14.** *The Old Testament* and The Byrds **15.** Elvis **16.** Gladys Knight and The Pips **17.** Nancy Sinatra **18.** Peter, Paul, and Mary, and Bob Dylan.

CHAPTER 4. IT TAKES A WORRIED MAN

Lesson 2.
Enough Already, Einstein

"If the world were a logical place, men would ride side saddle."
—Rita Mae Brown

The world is not a logical place, and inhabiting the world of the geezer can be beyond logic and reason to a geezess. The Women's Truth Foundation's (WTF) archives reveal that even the Nobel Prize-winning physicist and mathematician Albert Einstein could not come up with a logical equation to help his wife understand his need to shut himself away in his study. Clearly, in his aging, Einstein was trying to try to control his own anxiety and chaos by bringing mathematical order to the chaos of the universe!

Elsa and Albert and The Law of Universal AHMale Control

In a recent discovery amidst Albert Einstein's papers, there appeared a handwritten note that his wife Elsa had scribbled to him.

Elsa's note: "Al, you tell the world your famous equation $E = mc^2$ means that energy and mass are the same thing. I can tell you that as you have gotten older, your increasingly controlling ways and lack of energy are making mass chaos of our lives! You isolate yourself in your office. You neglect me and our family! You spend so much time at your desk staring into space! You make light of all of my complaints! You ignore all our relatives! Enough already! Here is my law of the relative downside of living with an aging male."

Elsa Einstein's Law of Universal AHMale Control

E = mc²

where

E = **E**nough already

m = **m**ale

c² = **c**ontrol x **c**ontrol

As a human male ages and his anxiety increases, his need for control exponentially increases, which creates a flipped equation and a frazzled frau:

mc² = E or **m**ale x **c**ontrol² = **E**xasperated AHFemale!!!!

Chapter 5.
Aging: "Who Me? What Mirror?"

"OMG, I'm rich! Silver in the hair, gold in the teeth, crystals in the kidney, sugar in the blood, lead in the butt, iron in the arteries, and an inexhaustible supply of natural gas. I never thought I would accumulate such wealth!" —Anonymous

The Field Guy-ed Sighting #5.

Observation: Manthropologist *Helen Weels* and *Mengineer Rae Jean Beech* collect data focusing on Bathroom Grooming Habits of an Aging Human Male as he near-sightedly looks in the mirror. They observe that he frequently applies topical hair dye, tries a combover, smooths down his double chin, sucks in his stomach, and furrows his brow as he tries to remember where he put his tweezer to pull out that dang long nose hair.

Hypothesis: For an Aging Human Male during a grooming session, cataracts can be a blessing in disguise.

Hypothesis (Full Disclosure by the Researchers): A similar collection of data focusing on Bathroom Grooming Habits of *Helen* and *Rae Jean* reveals that they each have their own quirky perks relative to facial issues (retina-ing eye cream, masking eye bags, moisturizing lip lines) and body issues (pulling up Spanx, checking out their butts in the mirror, grimacing at their underarm chicken wings… ugh, forget the list).

Question requiring further study: Do Aging Human Males see their twenty-year-old Marlon-Brando-muscle-shirt self when they look in the mirror? Do Aging Human Males develop arthritic hardening of the *EGO (Everlasting God Omnipotence)* section of their brain as they age?

Question (Full Disclosure by the Researchers): Do Aging Human Females channel Bo Derek in *Ten* and smile as they look in the mirror or are they typically found frowning as they rate themselves a very discouraging Six? (See Chapter 33, Lesson 1. Body Image)

CHAPTER 5. AGING: "WHO ME? WHAT MIRROR?"

Lesson 1.
Butt Ugly: Homeostayinplacis

"I promise to still grab your butt—even when you're old and wrinkly."
—Anonymous

Brain research conducted by The Women's Truth Foundation (WTF) has also identified a condition in the Aging Human Male called *Homeostayinplacis*, which is a disease in which the aging male may remain in a petrified body position for 24 hours or more, mesmerized by any TV or electronic screen or device that shows endless sports, rifles, big boobs, cars, video games, or card games. This condition can best be managed just by pulling the plug—on the TV or electronics, not on the life support system!

Homeostayinplacis has symptoms similar to tetanus, commonly known as "lockjaw." Unlike tetanus, *homestayinplacis* is not transmittable by puncture wounds, but it is known to punch some sizeable holes in an Aging Human Partnership.

Severity of this condition is diagnosed and categorized from an aging AHFemale's anecdotal information of her AHMales's verbal responses, responses often uttered through clenched teeth.

Alice and Fred and Homeostayinplacis Disease

Diagnosis: Homeostayinplacis, Stage 1. Preference Excuse

Alice: "Let's go out to dinner."

Fred: "The game is on in 10 minutes."

Remedy: Negotiation, including trading whatever favors or rewards work, similar to negotiating with a three-year-old.

Diagnosis: Homeostayinplacis, Stage 2. Physical Excuse

Alice: "Let's go out dancing."

Fred: "My knee is acting up."

Remedy: Test for truth: Kick him in the allegedly afflicted body part to either expose a lie or turn the injury into the truth.

Diagnosis: Homeostayinplacis, Stage 3. Anxiety Excuse

Alice: "Let's travel overseas."

Fred: "I haven't had my shots."

Remedy: Drugs work.

Diagnosis: Homeostayinplacis, Stage 4. Non-verbal Response

Alice: "Let's visit my mother."

Fred: Growl

Remedy: Terminal (relationship that is, not the disease)!

Home Remedy for all Diagnostic Categories:

A doozy of a dose of **The Rebecca Rule:** "Listen to everything your man says. Then do what you want."

Lesson 2.
It's My Body and I'll Cry If I Want To: H.E.R.S. versus H.I.S.

"Be careful about reading health books. You may die of a misprint." —Mark Twain

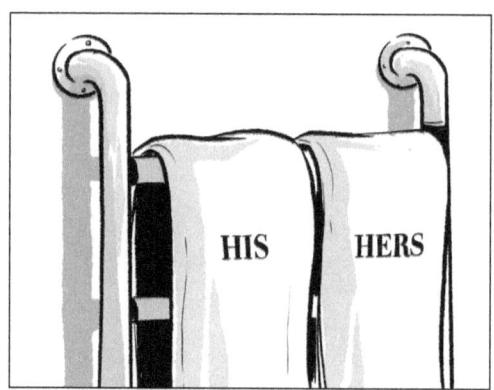

HIS and HERS doesn't just apply to the towels in the honeymoon suite at the Hilton. Men's bodies and women's bodies experience growing pains—and growing gains—in very different universes.

H.E.R.S.: Hormonal Eruptions Running the Show

Throughout the life of an AHFemale, she has had to adjust to many major body changes. Her aging body changes can be characterized as *Hormonal Eruptions Running the Show. (H.E.R.S.)*

Female adolescence: When a female body grows pubic hair and tits, experiences periods with bleeding and cramping, swings with the mood swings, and has the hots for the guys.

Female adulthood: When girls mature, with their women's bodies having lots of protruding parts and intruding parts, and things liquid and bloody coming out of—and sometimes going into—several lower orifices. There are breast exams and hoo-ha exams, IUDs and PAPs, fibroids and pregnancy and periods that sometimes feel like a sentence! Women's bodies also experience an ebb and flow of hormones flying uncontrolled at their own pace and intensity. Thus, women's bodies need lots of maintenance and yearly check-ups, oils, lotions, potions, and meds to keep everything running smoothly and in the groove.

Female menopause: When a female body ceases its bleeding, to be replaced with sweaty nights—not involving sex—and a dry wazoo—involving sex—OUCH! This is a time of non-answerable questions: Is it hot in here or is it me? Am I feeling hot with him or not with him? Am I libid-lo or libid-go today? Can belly fat appear overnight? Am I wearing an invisible cloak when I walk into a restaurant and no guy looks my way? How good does it feel to be "off the rag" forever or do I miss "my friend?!"

Female older age: When a female body experiences drooping of internal organs and external appendages, and an enlarging of the heart with love and gratitude… we hope!

H.I.S.: Hard Into Soft

Throughout the life of an AHMale, he has had to adjust to far fewer major body changes and medical checkups and exams than an AHFemale. His body changes can be characterized as *Hard Into Soft. (H.I.S.)*

Male adolescence: When a male body experiences hair emerging on his balls, face and underarms, as well as a large muscle increase between his legs and between his ears in the *Genitalus Maximus* area in the male brain, thus activating an obsession with sex.

Male adulthood: When the *Genitalus Maximus* becomes enlarged; this enlarged *Genitalus Maximus* is called the *Genitalus Uberallis*, which only increases the teenage obsession with sex… to the max.

Male older age: When the aging male major body parts may become

H.I.S. (Hard into Soft) — abs and pecs, belly, and shlong. Even an AHMale's head becomes *H.I.S.: Hair into Skin!* But the good news for many older men and lucky aging women: his heart may also become *H.I.S... Hard Into Soft.*

So it becomes clear that every aging woman has had to deal with many more body issues that are *H.E.R.S.* throughout her life than every aging man has had to deal with in *H.I.S.* life. An AHFemale may have been poked, prodded, examined, and advised by 5,000+ doctors throughout her life to guide her body through the labyrinth of growing and aging as a female. Brain research has shown that, in this process an AHFemale's brain has developed a very large and sophisticated brain area, called the *Visitme Doctoris,* to help her with her physical issues and to cope with the many bodily metamorphoses that are *H.E.R.S.*

Studies show that an AHMale may have visited doctors only once or twice throughout his adulthood, perhaps for jock itch, or, "What is that bump doing there?" Brain research involving MRIs on AHMales indicate that the *Visitme Doctoris* area of the aging male brain is comparable in size to that of a shriveled pea. (*Note:* 99% of these MRIs were conducted in emergency rooms for conditions that should have triggered the *Visitme Doctoris* portion of the aging male brain months before. Sigh.)

But there is hope. Brain research has shown that the size of an older man's *Visitme Doctoris* may sometimes become somewhat larger (i.e. un-shriveled or re-hydrated) when his partner engages the *Naggus Maximus* portion of her brain in order to activate her older man's *Visitme Doctoris*. Sigh, again. And good luck.

Or, better than luck: Check out the AHFemale's Ten (Loving) Commandments of dealing with an ill/wounded/bleeding/barfing/constipated/whining/concussed AHMale in Chapter 21. Fight #691: Ohhhh Sayyyy Can You (TL)C? In Sickness or in Stealth.

CHAPTER 5. AGING: "WHO ME? WHAT MIRROR?"

Lesson 3.
Home is Where the Fart Is

"I tell you, we are here on Earth to fart around, and don't let anybody tell you different."—Kurt Vonnegut

Research has shown that, as men age, there are two sections of the AHMale brain that become enlarged: the *Wrectus Rectumus* and *Memorees Kaputtus*. These two sections are commonly (and lovingly) referred to as "The Tushy Fart" and "The Brain Fart" sections of an aging male brain.

As a man ages, the increasing sizes of the *Wrectus Rectumus* and *Memorees Kaputtus* are reflected commensurate to increased body output, or, in layman's terms, The Tushy Farts get stinkier—pass the Beano™, please! And The Brain Farts get longer—Google search, anyone?

"Huh?" " What?" " When?" " How?" "Oops, did I do that?" "Did I say that?" So the older man experiences what is referred to in medical terminology as a *Bookend of Farts:* farts that occur from top to bottom.

This *Bookend of Farts* can be managed by an aging woman activating the section of her brain called the *WhatsaGirltodo* area. The *WhatsaGirltodo* area then stimulates an aging woman to either affix a clothespin to her nose, especially at night, or to repeat three times, while shaking her head (and the can of Glade™), "Old farts fart."

Lesson 4.
Can You Hear Me Now?
The Deaf Leading the Deaf

"A good marriage would be between a blind wife and a deaf husband."—Michel de Montaigne, French Renaissance philosopher

Misheard or mislistened? Selective hearing? Faulty hearing aids? Faulty hearing ears? Perhaps more often than not, an AHMale and an AHFemale need to heed the advice of the wise: be in the here and now or, better yet, be in the hear and the know. And please check out those decades of ear wax!

Mary and Michael and a Deafening Roar

Michael: "So I brought you the Chinese carryout pork dish you asked for."

Mary: "I didn't ask for any pork dish!"

Michael: "Yes, you said, 'I want the pork dish.'"

Mary: "No, I said, 'I want more of the dish we had last week!'"

Michael: "That's not what you said!"

Mary: "Yes, it is. You never listen to me!"

Michael: "Yes, I do—I heard you loud and clear!"

Mary: "YOU are the lout!"

Michael: "YOU are the one who needs to get out!"

CHAPTER 5. AGING: "WHO ME? WHAT MIRROR?"

Lesson 5.
50 Shades of Grey...
Hair, That Is

"That's not a gray hair, honey. That's your silver lining."
—Pamela Price, RedWhiteandGrew.com

Grey hair is so distinguished in an AHMale, but only on top of his head. It is not so distinguished when it is fuzzy grey hair curling out of other orifices, such as an ear or a nostril.

But many AHMales insist that all remaining macho grey hair remain unpruned. They resist all offers from an AHFemale to help in the de-fuzzing of ears and nose hairs with tweezers or scissors, almost as if fearing the biblical story of how Samson lost his power when Delilah cut off his hair. As if hair power extends to ear and nose hair! Fifty moans of, "EWWWWW!" arise from an aging woman as she peers at an aging man's Cro-Magnon hairy orifices.

Rae Jean and Her Reluctant Admission

Rae Jean: "And the same goes for an AHFemale. Grey hair in an aging woman seems not so attractive when she looks in the magnifying mirror, finds a grey hair on the bottom of her chin and sees with horror that it is about two feet long! How did she miss that in all her obsessive tweezing?! Out, damn chin hair, out!"

Lesson 6.
The Truth about ADHD and Sports

"If a man watches three football games in a row, he should be declared legally dead."—Erma Bombeck

What if an Aging Human Male's attention is so (mis)directed that he never sees or hears what an Aging Human Female is about? Understanding the truth about ADHD can help an aging woman cope.

It is commonly understood that ADHD refers to Attention Deficit Hyperactivity Disorder, an inability to attend to defined tasks and an overabundance of energy. In other words, an ADHD guy just can't pay attention and sit still.

But, unknown to most of the public, there is a secret *Dramatic Satirical Man-ual* (DSM) published by the Women Psychiatrist's Truth and Acknowledgement (T and A) Association that offers **the true definition of male ADHD:**

DSM #36-24-36. ADHD = Activated Drive to Hunt it or Do It*

*Yes, "Do it" as in "Scroo It!"

From time immemorial, every human male has had intense focus, but only onto prey of type 1 (kill it!), or prey of type 2 (thrill it!). It's in the male DNA: Catch it or snatch it! The remainder of the environment is… well, just is. Situations involving food and sex get a human male's utmost attention, the rest of the environment falls by the wayside.

So perhaps an AHMale does not hear what his AHFemale says. An AHFemale's words, requests, thoughts, and demands may be processed as background noise to the male's hunting and mating focus. And how does the

CHAPTER 5. AGING: "WHO ME? WHAT MIRROR?"

aging process affect the hunting process and the **_Activated Drive to Hunt It or Do It_**? The aging process reinforces this behavior over decades, so that ADHD becomes SADHD, Sad ADHD, that is: sad to an aging woman. Over decades, ADHD petrifies like a rock, or in the eyes of some older women, ADHD putrifies.

And what about ADHD and sports? An AHFemale shouldn't even think about interrupting a sports game on TV. Don't talk; don't ask questions; don't make comments. The hunt for meat/victory in the competitive game, and the hunt for sex in the cheerleaders' big boobs and short skirts equal a double focus, a double whammy. Sports on TV have an ADHD AHMale by both balls!

Lesson 7. Memories, Light the Cobwebs of My Mind

"One of the keys to happiness is a bad memory."
—Rita Mae Brown

To be read very slowly, to increase comprehension… and good luck with that!

Sayonara to the sensible, adios to attention span, ciao to cherished memory, as our beloved thoughts are addled by…

Brain fog… Brain fart… Mist of the mind… Being lost in space… Lazing in la-la land… Word escapement… On-the-tip of my tongue-ness… Numbness in the noggin… Sleepiness in the senses… Out to lunch-ness… What-am-I-doing-in-this-room-ness…

Where's-my-phone-ness… What's-his-name-ness… How-do-I-spell-that-ness…

Where-did-I-park-my-car-ness… What-are-the-keys-doing-in-the-refrigerator-ness… Loss of direction..

Can't-remember-that-song-title-ness… Can't-remember-that-movie-star's-name-ness… Where did I-lose-that-balance… Mistakes in multitasking… Loss-of-password-itis…

What-am-I-supposed-to-get-in-this-grocery-store-aisle-ness… Calamity-of-calendar-confusion…

Weariness-of-what-day-it-is-ness… What-did-I-have-for-breakfast-ness.

All lead to the self-talk "Whatever!" as a follow-up to ease the muddied, muddled mind.

CHAPTER 5. AGING: "WHO ME? WHAT MIRROR?"

And those cobwebs are not gender-biased. Brain farts find the corners of a Boomer Chick brain as well as a Boomer Champ brain. What to do? Memory loss—just fuggettabout it! Easily done!

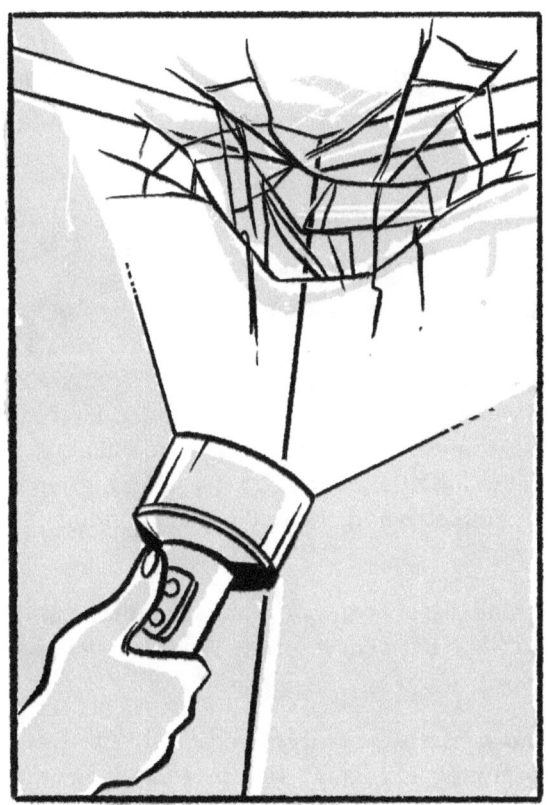

Chapter 6.
Lifestyle Issues: Fashions and Passions

"You're mad, bonkers, off your head. But I'll tell you a secret. All of the best people are." —Alice, in Alice in Wonderland

The Field Guy-ed Sighting #6.

Observation: Manthropologist *Helen Weels* and *Mengineer Rae Jean Beech* roll their eyes so much in disbelief that they can't even take notes as they observe an Aging Human Male's choices of fashion ("You're wearing that faded Hawaiian shirt to the rehearsal dinner?!"), choices of lifestyle ("Sudoku on the couch is a sport?"), choices to limit their food choices ("No, hops in beer does not qualify beer as a vegetable!"), and choices in male bonding ("Sharing grunts is sharing?").

Hypothesis: Nothing like a sweet potpourri of endless complaints about your Aging Human Male to make your day. And why not pour yourself some wine with your whine?!

Question requiring further study: Are we sure Eve was taken from Adam's rib and not from Clark Kent's rib, since Clark Kent (aka Superman) is an alien from another planet who totally has his act together?!

CHAPTER 6. LIFESTYLE ISSUES: FASHIONS AND PASSIONS

Lesson 1.
Fashions that Cause Foes to Pause: Fashion Mis-Takes

"Fashion is like eating, you shouldn't stick to the same menu."
—*Edith Head, fashion designer*

What Aging Human Male doesn't have a leather belt as old as he is? It's hard to part with an old belt, even though the belt is as wrinkled and cracked in places as the man. The belt may be from his high school days and it's as slim as he was then. And how cool was that belt, slung low on the hips and a part of that high school swagger? That old belt just echoes with the total "HEYYY!" of the Fonz!

Does that belt hang even lower today because those gratuitous six-packs of Bud have destroyed the six-pack abs of the teenage bud? Does your aging man look like a geezer Howard Walowitz from *The Big Bang?* Or does his belt rise up to any imaginable occasion like the high-water belt of Urkel in *Family Matters?*

Every aging man has his own individual, cherished fashion faux-pas, as seen through the eyes of his aging woman. Beauty is in the eyes of the beholder, but every older woman is hanging on to the hope that her older partner isn't hanging on to these in his closet, or sporting them on his person, or using them as bodily add-ons— which need to be taken off!

CARE & FEEDING OF THE AGING HUMAN MALE SPECIES: A SASSY PRIMER

Aging Human Male Fashion Freak-outs

Hawaiian Shirt: A shirt only a botanist could love. Looked great at the luau but not smart for the dinner party.

The Comb (It's) Over: That pink skinhead is punk! A combover needs to be looked over.

Muscle Man Undershirt: It only worked for Marlon Brando in *On the Waterfront*, years before the AHMale lost both biceps in The War of the Couch Potato.

Short Short Sport Shorts: These haven't been seen since Michael Jordan hit the court.

Calf Socks with Sneakers: Why?

Any Socks with Sandals: Why and why?

Compression Stockings: Red compressions make for bad impressions!

Fort Knox Necklaces: How many gold chains can one AHMale wear without neck pain?

Patterns Galore: Take it from James Bond, Patterns Galore are not going to get an old man Pussy Galore!

Baggy Clothes: Having baggy clothes matching baggy bodies is wayyy overkill.

Long Tie: Even that tie can't hide a big aging man's gut—way too narrow.

Tight T-shirts: A woman has two nipples of her own—she doesn't need to see more!

Slogan T-shirts: A T-shirt shouldn't do his talking for him!

Hole-y holy T-shirt: A hole in one belongs on a golf course, not a T shirt.

Hole-y holy T-shirts: Yes, the one hidden in the drawer belongs in the Salvation Army pile!

CROCS: Only five-year-olds look cute in these.

Hiphugger Jeans: Not hip!

POP Jeans: The bad answer to "MOM Jeans"—no buts about it, his butt will never look good in those jeans again —and, yes, it is the jeans AND IT IS HIS BUTT!

CHAPTER 6. LIFESTYLE ISSUES: FASHIONS AND PASSIONS

Ear Studs: Only cool on Gen X or Gen Y or Gen Z, not Gen A (A for Aging men).

Tattoos: So cool they are no longer hot, especially when an old man's skin wrinkles, changing his tattoo-ed "Paula" to "Paul."

Fake Tan: Only works for George Hamilton.

Calling AHMales everywhere—please empty out your drawers—clothes drawers, that is —and clear your body of all "enhancements" before your aging woman puts out an APB to the Fashion Police for her man's missing fashion swag!

Lesson 2. Maynard G. Krebs and "Werk?!"

"Hard work never killed anybody, but why take a chance?"
—Edgar Bergen, actor

Human males are hunters. After all, the preservation of the human species needs hunters. But what happens when the Aging Human Male retires? He no longer hunts—that commute and that career is no longer the prey that keeps his instincts keen.

For some aging men, research has shown that at retirement this instinct for hunting activates the male part of the brain known as *Golfismymistress*, and the part of the eyeball known as *Whereiswhiteball*. The more the *Golfismymistress* section of the brain is activated, the larger that section of the brain becomes, until it borders on an addiction that is activated without regard to time, darkness, wind, rain, heat, or hurricane. An addicted aging male golfer subscribes to the belief that "Golf is the most fun you can have without taking your clothes off." (Thank you, pro golfer Chi Chi Rodriguez.)

The *Golfismymistress* section of the brain is also neurologically connected to the muscles of the dominant arm, so that, at times, the *Golfismymistress* section of the brain stimulates the arm to automatically hammer the ground with the golf club a multitude of times after a swing where the

CHAPTER 6. LIFESTYLE ISSUES: FASHIONS AND PASSIONS

Whereiswhiteball section of the eye follows the ball into sand or water.

For some male retirees, the *Golfismymystress* section of the brain never gets activated. These retirees may find themselves activating, or more accurately, de-activating various hunting sections of their brain. Research has shown that for these AHMales, the *Bakedcouchuspotato* brain area is heated up and served daily. And when the *Bakedcouchuspotato* area of the brain becomes hot for hours, it can bake and bake and bake until it gets totally dried and wrinkled. In extreme cases, the *Bakedcouchuspotato* area of the brain may activate the *HalfBakedcouchuspotato* area of the brain, a very small mushy area that results in verbalizations of, "Huh?" every other sentence.

In chronic cases of *Bakedcouchuspotato* and *HalfBakedcouchuspotato*, an AHFemale can try to de-activate these brain areas in one of two ways: (1) with melted sweet butter, such as, "Honey, how about we snuggle for a while?" or (2) with sprinkled sea salt, "Honey, I notice that you haven't moved from that couch and that sports channel for days and the whole room is starting to smell ripe. Get off your tuchus — NOW!"

Solution for an AHMale whose brain is becoming mooshed: Get a job or hobby and get back into the hunt.

Lesson 3.
I'll Have the Meat and Potatoes, With a Side of Boredom: Does Only Heinz Ketchup have 57 Varieties?

"If variety is the spice of life, marriage is the big can of leftover spam."
— Johnny Carson

What happened to "variety is the spice of life?" When did that Young Male Tarzan swinging through the jungle on a vine morph into the Aging Male Archie Bunker vegging in his Lazy Boy Recliner? Does this transformed AHMale have libido or libid-lo? Zest for life or a jest of a life? Same old, same old: Same crispy fried chicken, same TV channels, same on-bottom sex position (okay, it's the arthritic knees), same NFL team, same beer, same leather belt (probably the exact same belt worn at his high school graduation as afore-mentioned), same orthopedic Nike shoes, same wallet style, same Ford/Chevy/Mazda, same facial hair (or not), same head hair (if there), same Wrangler jeans, same hole-y holy ratty T-shirt, same radio station with hits from the 50s/60s/70s/80s, same "guy walked into a bar..." story, same pickup line ("Wanna go_____?"), same guy stories about "that crazy night!"

Since when did Saturday Night Dates with dinner and dancing that ended with a bang melt into a Saturday Night Fate of an Early Bird Special followed by ESPN on the living room couch where the only bang is the "pop" of a beer bottle being opened?

Many AHMales seem to be in a muddy rut, with no desire to oink their way

CHAPTER 6. LIFESTYLE ISSUES: FASHIONS AND PASSIONS

out. Many aging men relish the control, consistency, and safety of peanuts as a dinner appetizer, followed by a hamburger and french fries, often eaten on a TV tray in front of WWF.

One male's rut may be one female's blessed predictability. Sometimes, predictable and steady can be reassuring and wonderful to an Aging Human Female. "Same Aging Human Male" sometimes sounds just fine, and, perhaps, wonderful!

> ### Sally and Jack and Coleslaw and Potato Salad
>
> Sally and Jack were married for 40 years. Jack loved Sally's homemade potato salad and coleslaw, made from his own mother's recipe that she had brought from Russia. Sally made the potato salad and coleslaw fresh every other day and served it for dinner every night at Jack's request. She loved the ease of always knowing what to buy at the grocery store and what sides to serve for dinner.
>
> When guests came for a meal, Sally added some hot vegetables and some biscuits, but there was always potato salad and coleslaw included for Jack. Their family and friends understood, and —along with Jack— they loved the predictability of Sally's delicious side dishes.

Lesson 4.
Game? Who's Got Game? The Only Game in Town is on TV

"There are only three things women need in life: food, water, and compliments." —Chris Rock

Chris Rock got it almost right. It should be "The only four things women need in life: chocolate, wine, a good hair day, and compliments GALORE." Every aging woman thrives on attention, appreciation, and her old man noticing that her butt looks great in those jeans!

So what happened to the young stud who was courting her with sweet words and sweet chocolates and appreciative glances? Did he change or did she change? What happened that his male mojo turned into slo-mo? How did that suaveness turn into bland mauveness? He was so debonair—now it is like he is so nowhere! That male attention and flattery has turned to Attention Deficit Disorder and flatulent conversation.

So every Aging Human in an Aging Human Partnership puts their "best self" onto the shelf at some point—hey, this is real life with an old ratty bathrobe and more grunts than scintillating conversations. And you can say that again—okay, this is real life with an old ratty bathrobe and more grunts than scintillating conversations.

Comfort is good. And chocolate and wine and a good hair day make comfort even better. But doesn't an aging woman deserve something far better than comfort from an aging man? Wouldn't it be lovely if that AHMale sometimes turned off the game on the TV and turned on his AHFemale with

CHAPTER 6. LIFESTYLE ISSUES: FASHIONS AND PASSIONS

his (recently dusted off) sweet words of appreciation, "I love having you in my life. You are the best." Then, and only then, should he go and turn the TV back on.

How can this come to be? Cut this out and scotch-tape it to his TV remote.

Cut here: ------------✂----------------------------------

I love you. I love hearing you say that my butt looks good in my jeans. But best of all, I love hearing you say, "I love you. I love all the blankety-blank things you do for me!"

(and yes you, my loving man, you fill in the blankety-blank!)

Cut here: ---------------------------------✂-----------

Lesson 5.
Male Friendships:
A Carton of Codgers

"A true friend is someone who thinks that you are a good egg even though he knows that you are slightly cracked."
—Bernard Meltzer, radio show host for
"What's Your Problem?"

Many Aging Human Females ask, in the spirit of Jerry Seinfeld, "So what's the deal with Aging Human Males and friends?"

An exhaustive research study conducted by The WTF (Women's Truth Foundation), found that the average older man had 0 to ½ male friends, friends being "people with whom one shares feelings."

But chatter doesn't seem to matter in friendships among aging men. An exhaustive research study conducted by The WATUPS (What? Ask or Tell Ur Personal Story) Foundation found that the average older man had twelve friends, "friends" being "people with whom one shares grunts while engaging

CHAPTER 6. LIFESTYLE ISSUES: FASHIONS AND PASSIONS

in a common activity." In the 1700s, writer Samuel Johnson, said, "Men only become friends by a community of pleasures." In male friendships, men's way together is to play together.

Boomer Chicks have their Precious Old Dames, their PODs. But what to call these Boomer Buddy friendships, which clearly differ from women's friendships? The WTF concluded that AHMale friendships consisted of "a carton of codgers," a "carton" being characterized much like an egg carton—a collection of similar objects compartmentalized into separate sections, never to touch other objects, each good egg to be used for a separate purpose—and a "codger" being an elderly man often eccentric or old-fashioned. So an aging man's friendships are a carton of codgers, each codger with a specific relationship and each codger distinct from the other.

An aging man's carton of codgers might be made up of a dozen of activity-focused friends:

A Beer Codger: Drinking only, no talking, as observing beer foam requires concentration

A Golf Codger: Swinging, but only with clubs, and only discussing their balls

A Car Codger: Car talk is the best, no batteries required

A Football Codger: Talk about scoring, but scoring only on the field

A BBQ Codger: Grilling each other on the best rubs

A Reading Codger: Discussing all the news that's fit to print in papers or books or online

A TV Codger: A series of conversations on the best TV series

A Military Codger: Discussing past and future wars—but not wars at home

A Gadget Codger: Up-to-date on the latest tools and toys for growing boys

A Techie Codger: Speaking in code about the latest IOS and ABC and XYZ

A Good-Old-Days Codger: Glorifying all memories prior to 1999

A Partner-Complainer Codger: Just complaints, no feelings allowed

And the lucky older man has a life filled with a carton of codgers, plus his AHSweetie, his good—no his BEST—egg!

Chapter 7.
Sex... Not Again!

"The basic conflict between men and women, sexually, is that men are like firemen. To men, sex is an emergency, and no matter what we're doing we can be ready in two minutes. Women, on the other hand, are like fire. They're very exciting, but the conditions have to be exactly right for it to occur." — Jerry Seinfeld

The Field Guy-ed Sighting #7.

Observation: Manthropologist *Helen Weels* and Mengineer *Rae Jean Beech* perform an extended 24-hour portable MRI on an Aging Human Male brain to verify that the *Sexus Maximus* in an Aging Human Male dominates his entire living and breathing self from morning 'til night… while rising, showering, dressing, eating, shmoozing with buds, drinking Buds, golfing, goofing around, reading, ESPNing, texting, cooking, cleaning, and dreaming his (wet) dreams.

Hypothesis: For an Aging Human Male, every day should finish with the climax of a happy ending!

Question (for all the ages) requiring further study (cue Henry Higgins and music from *My Fair Lady*): Why can't an aging woman be more like an aging man?

CHAPTER 7. SEX... NOT AGAIN!

Debra and Frank and Libido in a Pill

Debra had a much lower libido than her husband Frank and this caused tension in their relationship, so she spoke to her doctor about this. Her doctor suggested that she try some testosterone for her to get it going between her and Frank. Debra started taking the big T—testosterone pills—and after six days she was in tears of frustration.

"I can't stand it," Debra told her best friend Evelyn. "Every 10 seconds I think about sex. All I think about is sex! It's driving me crazy! I am totally overwhelmed and frustrated! I've been kidnapped by testosterone! Sexual thoughts have overtaken my brain! I have no control over my own thoughts! Sex is my life now. It's horrible!" She was OD-ing on T!

Debra stopped taking the testosterone. Several days later, she was thrilled to have her "normal" thoughts and her "normal" life back and to leave that testosterone-driven life behind (no pun intended).

"I never again want to go through the world being so obsessed with sex and so sexually frustrated all the time!" Debra confided to Evelyn.

So there, once again, is The Aging Human Male Truth, from an Aging Human Female who was the double agent that Boomer Chicks always wanted. Debra was a woman who snuck over to the other (testosterone) side, captured the male libido, and got the full experience (the full monty?) of the male brain. She was captured by sexual obsession, overwhelmed and frustrated, and then escaped and rushed back to the safety of her home turf, the female brain on estrogen.

So what's the deal with the Aging Male Human Species' obsession with sex, "not that there's anything wrong with that," to quote Jerry Seinfeld yet again. Testosterone courses rapidly through the (slightly constricted) veins of every AHMale, seemingly with every beat of his (somewhat calcified) heart. So, how could **Care & Feeding of the Aging Human Male Species: The Field Guy-ed** not begin with "Sex" and end with "Sex… Not Again!"

It is a universal truth to every aging female that her brain is not owned and operated by testosterone, but that her estrogen-laden brain can be nudged or excited to respond to an aging male's testosterone, especially on "any given Sunday," excuse the reference to the NFL slogan, where her AHMale has provided hugs, sweet words, flowers, chocolate, and/or a living room vacuumed by his own hand.

For those who have an appetite for more sex, be sure to read:

The Roadmap. Chapter 23. Fights #1,113-2,045: SEX!

The Dame Digest. Chapter 33 Lesson 4. *The Dame Diamond: Bods* invites AHFemales to get in touch with their bodies, on many levels.

The Precious Old Dames' Party Playbook encourages "talking amongst yourselves" about SEX in groups—that is, talking in groups, not sex in groups— but, to quote Jerry Seinfeld again, "not that there is anything wrong with that!"

A to Z for The Glossary-Eyed womansplains the new and wild sex terms in this **Primer**.

Perhaps the most profound quote on sex was in a conversation overheard by **Helen** at the weight machine area at a YMCA in Florida, as 68-year-old Jimmy lamented:

> *"If only women understood how important sex is to a man."*

CHAPTER 7. SEX... NOT AGAIN!

Male Brain: Frontal view

1. Bakedcouchuspotato
2. Cementis Mentis
3. Cometah
4 Everlasting God Omnipotence
5. Frefrintal Fohe
6. GainpowerthruNO
7. Genitalus Maximus
8. Genitalus Uberallis

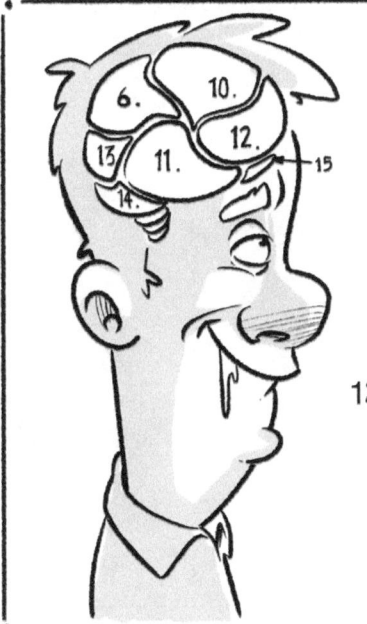

Male Brain: Side view

9. Gluttonusbuttonus
10. Golfismymistress
11. I=king
12. Incompetence Detestus (ID)\ Incompetence Mentis
13. Snippyus Withmylippus
14. Visitme Doctoris
15. WhataPutz

The Roadmap to Traveling Route 66+ Together

"You can't have it all, all at once. Who—man or woman—has it all, all at once? Over my lifespan, I think I have had it all. But in different periods of time, things were rough. And if you have a caring life partner, you help the other person when that person needs it."
—Ruth Bader Ginsburg

The Roadmap offers travel tips, a guide to scenic pullovers, a maintenance schedule for oiling the relationship, directions on how to fight fair when the wheels fall off the car, and how to continue appreciating your aging jalopy. Ladies, this will help you "Start your engines!" as you shift into high gear to zip it up along Route 66+!

Intro.
Sharing the Road

"Marriage has no guarantees. If that's what you're looking for, go live with a car battery." —Erma Bombeck

The good news about older drivers: The American Automobile Association (AAA) reports that, "motorists in their mid to late 80s actually have lower crash rates per mile driven than those in their early 20s." (TRUTH, *Via Magazine*, AAA, Summer 2019.) Perhaps this is because older drivers are more likely to be focusing on the road and less likely to be driving with their right hand holding a bottle of beer, a puff of pot, or their cell phone.

For anything further in this book, AAA refers to the "Aging Automobile Association," which provides a free GPS (Good Partnership Shit!) for Aging Human Females. This GPS is a navigational aid for handling the curves, pitstops and potholes of traveling with an Aging Human Partner on the road trip of their life along Route 66+.

Trip Planning and Packing note: Along Route 66+ and as you read this **Primer**, you will have to supply your own Kleenex to wipe away tears of frustration and to dab your eyes as you cry with laughter. So kick your tires, check your fluids (ahem!), gas up (Beano ™ allowed!), and use this **Primer** to find your fixed point in a spinning world, your True North, your Lodestar—or your Loaded-with-BS-Star!

Chapter 8. Traveling Route 66+ Together, Pitstops and Potholes

"When a man opens a car door for his wife, it's either a new car or a new wife." —Prince Philip

Just as you service your car before any long-distance ride, the Aging Automobile Association GPS includes a Road Trip Checklist and Safe Driving Tips to help you avoid any roadside breakdowns (requiring professional counseling), flat tires (other than the tires around one's middle), or blown gaskets (oh no, not another fight)!

Lesson 1.
The AAA Route 66+ Road Trip Checklist

"Map out your future—but do it in pencil. The trip ahead is as long as you make it. Make it worth the trip."—Jon Bon Jovi

A: *Acknowledge your differences*. He's a Model T and you're a Mustang, or he's a '57 Chevy and you're a Studebaker, or you're an XKE and he's an Edsel. Different styles, different purposes, different tastes, none better or worse than the other—well, except, maybe for the Edsel. Mutual respect is needed for your differing choices of cloth versus leather seats, or automatic versus four-on-the-floor. Choices are not better or worse, just different... as hard as it is not to believe that your way is way better!

CHAPTER 8. TRAVELING ROUTE 66+ TOGETHER. PITSTOPS AND POTHOLES

A: Accept your differences. No one ever solved a disagreement by saying, "My way or the highway." You can't put fins on a '63 Nash. It's difficult, if not impossible, for an AHFemale to change an AHMale; she can only change herself and how she thinks about the AHPartnership differences. Crank up the A/C in the car, stay cool, look out the window, and appreciate the scenery. Okay, your AHMale may be "wrong/cantankerous/stubborn," but "Well, that's how he is!" and, "This is how I am!" can go a long way on the journey. Sometimes the old man drives the car and sometimes the old woman drives the car… and the car still gets where it needs to go. (Even if it takes a very long time because he gets lost and refuses to ask directions… or is it you who is directionally challenged?! Oh well, who cares, blame Siri™!)

A: Appreciate and applaud your differences. This is where the rubber meets the road. You have acknowledged your differences, you have accepted them, and now it's your turn to appreciate and applaud them a few more miles down the road. Now that the new car smell has gone, hope that his pleasant aging male pheromones can get your engine going as you appreciate and celebrate your different AHPartnership models and styles. And if the male pheromones don't make up for the lost new car smell, get some Febreze™ to help with the closeness issues!

95

Lesson 2.
Safe Driving Tips

"At the end of the day, your feet should be dirty, your hair messy and your eyes sparkling." — Shanti, religious leader

The Aging Automobile Association offers these seven driving tips to help you navigate the Nascarness of your Route 66+ life.

1. Stay in your own lane. Swapping lanes can cause (house) wrecks.

2. Beer helps. Decide beforehand who is the designated driver in life, or, better yet, take turns.

3. Use a turn signal (or a hand signal—remember those?) to let your AHPartner know you are changing directions.

4. Going around potholes is easier on the butt than going through potholes.

5. Have a supportive pit crew. Your 911 call automatically connects you with one of your Precious Old Dames!

6. Enjoy the ride as much as your dog does as she puts her head out the window and feels life breeze by.

7. Knowing there is a flag at the finish line can help you round each lap with patience, compassion, and forgiveness, as well as laughter.

CHAPTER 8. TRAVELING ROUTE 66+ TOGETHER, PITSTOPS AND POTHOLES

Lesson 3.
Retiring: Putting New Tires on an Old Car

"A super easy way to check your tire tread: with President Lincoln's head pointed down, insert a penny into the grooves on your tire tread. If any part of Lincoln's head is hidden by the tire tread, your tires are fine. Otherwise your tires are too shallow and it is time to replace your tires."
— Tires Plus, www.tiresplus.com/tires

The Aging Automobile Association offers an adaptation of this Tires Plus tip for an AHFemale as she begins her journey with her AHMale along Route 66+: Turn your AHMale upside down, pointy head pointing to the ground. If any part of his hair is showing, either from his head or his nose or his ears, he is fine. Otherwise, your aging man is too shallow and it is time to re-place him by turning him right-side up and moving to a new retirement place, either geographically or spiritually.

But what happens when your geezer's retirement dream journey is different from your geezess retirement dream journey? Billie and Ted grooved to the travel advice of Yogi Berra (who didn't always know where he wanted to go, except to The World Series), "If you don't know where you're going, you'll end up somewhere else."

You want to boogie on the dance floor and he wants to travel to Bogota. You want to take cooking lessons and he wants to get baked on the beach at Ipanema. He is a glutton for all food that comes from a fryer and your brain fries if you get within 500 feet of gluten. You want to travel to Sweden and he wants to go to the movies and chow down Swedish Fish candy. You want to downsize your *tchotchkes* (random useless clutter) and he wants to down a sizable amount of beer. You want to play pickleball and he wants to pickle cucumbers. You are into Mahjong and he is into more shlong. You are into biking tours and he is into hiking tours. You love sunrises at dawn and he loves the shades drawn. You want to downsize to a new house and he wants to downsize his belly to a smaller size. You want to travel the world in a backpack and he wants to explore the world on the Nat Geo Channel.

How will a geezess and her geezer plan a road trip with all these divergent paths? Luckily, the Aging Automobile Association has drawn up a triptik that helps you navigate the roadmap between his old, crinkly red leather Lazy-Boy recliner at home and your Shangri-la tiki hut in Bali, drawn from the experience of Billie and Ted. Billie and Ted decided to try out different roadmaps to different destinations and see how the maps unfolded… or GPS-ed!

Billie and Ted's Excellent Adventure

Billie and Ted's first act upon their mutual retirement was to host a blast of a champagne party in the Bay Area, their home of forty years. Their second act was a heart-to-heart talk on where to live.

Ted, a retired accountant who liked organizing, created a checklist of "5 Criteria for a Comfortable Conclusion" (Billie didn't like the word "Conclusion," but tolerated Ted's dark sense of humor) to help them focus on where they wanted to live. Ted's "5Cs" were:

Climate: Whether or not weather is important
Congeniality: Is family nearby or are there meet-ups to meet new friends?
Cash: Can we keep enough in our pockets?
Culture: Is there art, theatre, music to keep us happy?
Crime: Will we feel safe?

CHAPTER 8. TRAVELING ROUTE 66+ TOGETHER, PITSTOPS AND POTHOLES

Did they want to downsize in San Fran, "Sittin' on the Dock of the Bay?" Did they want to move near their kiddos in New England or shuffle on down to the shuffleboards in sunny Florida? Or did they want a spicy-hot expat city in Mexico?

And money, of course, was an important retirement issue.

Billie loved yoga, knitting and book clubs with friends. Ted was an outdoorsy guy, smiling on a golf course, sailboat, or tennis court. So, of course, their priorities in the 5Cs were different, but in their wide-open, anything-goes retirement decision, their priority lists helped them focus on the pluses and minuses of each possibility. Billie and Ted both craved newness—new house, new friends, new adventures—so they planned several adventurous routes to test drive on their retirement journey.

Billie and Ted's Excellent Adventure # 1. Travel, Travel, Travel

Billie and Ted did a celebratory two-month-long dream trip to France and Italy, joined by kids and grandkids in Rome. They loved to travel, but it was hard on their feet, hard on their diets—an extra five pounds of French cream sauces and five pounds of Italian pasta—and hard on their wallets. Billie and Ted decided that three or four short travel trips per year was much softer on their backs, their bellies, and their bank account.

Billie and Ted's Excellent Adventure #2. Move near Kids and Grandkids in New England

Billie and Ted spent a summer in New Hampshire with their son Pat and his family. It was great, but Pat's family was very busy, not much time for Gram and Gramps. And Billie and Ted couldn't find many other retirees, especially people who shared their interests. So, Billie and Ted opted for mucho travel time to visit kids and grandkids and to find a retirement community elsewhere with other geezers and geezesses sharing common interests.

> ### Billie and Ted's Excellent Adventure #3. Where is Our H-OM-e?
>
> In search of a peaceful place to call home, Billie and Ted arranged several monthly rentals: a condo in Arizona, a townhouse on the east coast of Texas, a beach apartment on Florida's Gulf Coast, and a villa in Puerto Vallarta. Where did they feel most comfortable in their skin? Their skin was more wrinkled than when they were younger, but it was also more sensitive to what brought smiles to their faces. Ted discovered his fun outdoor sports codgers and Billie her kindred yoga PODs in a retirement community in Arizona.
>
> Billy and Ted were glad that they did an extended test drive of their three possibilities so that they were not taken in by that "new car smell." Billie and Ted's Excellent Adventure had a happy ending, which was actually the happy beginning.

Detours for Alternative Routes: But what if an AHFemale and AHMale have very different retirement wants and needs and are seeking compromise with detours and alternative routes? It may be time to switch from Yogi Berra to Barbara Bush, who said that she, "…[hated] the fact that people think 'compromise' is a dirty word." As we learned in Kindergarten, it is good to share, and it's good to take turns. Some retirees go back and forth between her Boomer Chick favorite place and her Boomer Buddy's favorite place. Some crones and their partner cronies take space and enjoy their own special place and then meet whenever. Retirement is a time to re-tire the old stereotypes about Aging Human Partnerships, including living arrangements. As we old hipsters said way back in the '60s, "If it feels good, do it!"

Chapter 9.
Good Odds to Keep an AHPartnership Even

"Man, they said we better accentuate the positive,
Eliminate the negative,
Latch on to the alternative,
Don't mess with Mr. In-Between."
—Bing Crosby

Most couples' counselors today agree with Der Bingle's advice from 1944: in a successful, melodious Aging Human Partnership, the ratio of positive statements to negative statements should be 10 to 1—good odds for a horse race and for the human race. A Women's Truth Foundation (WTF) study reports that an Aging Human Partnership remains strong when the **Compliment Count** outnumbers the **Criticism Count**, and the blah in-betweens get tossed to the curb. The **Criticism Count** is easily tallied by the number of times that smoke comes out of an aging man's ears.

Lesson 1.
What to Do to Boost the Odds: C.L.O.P or C.L.A.P.?

"You know you're old when someone compliments you on your alligator shoes, and you're barefoot." — Phyllis Diller

Keeping the **Compliment Count** higher than the **Criticism Count** is often challenging on a day-to-day basis on a long road trip. It is easier preached than done. What can an AHFemale do when criticism is about to spew forth from her mouth? How can she perform the mental gymnastics necessary to re-frame the situation in her perfectly-coiffed little head to turn the thought of clopping him over the head into a compliment? How can an aging woman turn a *C.L.O.P. (Criticism Leading to Ostracizing her Partner)* into a *C.L.A.P. (Compliment Leading to Applauding her Partner)*?

Note: A multitude of *C.L.O.P.s* can lead to engine burnout during travels.

Claudia and Jeremy and C.L.O.P.s and C.L.A.P.s

Claudia's C.L.O.P. Thought: "Arg! Jeremy sits in his Lazy Boy lazily watching sports 24/7."

Claudia's C.L.A.P. Thought: "Ahhh… that gives me so much space to do whatever I want!"

Claudia's C.L.A.P. Words: "Jeremy, you so enjoy ESPN. So good that you love all sports. Passions are great! I am leaving now for lunch with Meg and going out to play Mahjong with my PODs. Have fun."

CHAPTER 9. GOOD ODDS TO KEEP AN AHPARTNERSHIP EVEN

> *Claudia's C.L.O.P. Thought*: "That guy sooo wants way more sex than I do. I am just not feeling that sexy."
>
> *Claudia's C.L.A.P. Thought*: "Yes, it does feel nice that Jeremy still desires me so much."
>
> *Claudia's C.L.A.P. Words*: "Sweetie, I am glad that you want me so much. I want you, too, but my libido is so much lower than yours. You are an amazing lover and I would rather make love when I am totally into you since our love-making is so great. How about we check in with each other tomorrow?"
>
> *Claudia's C.L.O.P. Thought*: "Not again! He wants to go to the same restaurant over and over! How boring!"
>
> *Claudia's C.L.A.P. Thought*: "Well, Seaside Grill again. At least it's pretty good there. One thing's for sure: there will be no surprises at dinner."
>
> *Claudia's C.L.A.P. Words*: "Seaside Grill has good food. Jeremy, I am hereby declaring that I am making it my one-year plan to sweep through the menu and try everything once."

And there you have it: Some additional angles to work with **The Geezer Triangle** of **Sex ▲ Sustenance ▲ Sports** with verve and positivity! Much as Dorothy clapped her ruby red slippers together in *The Wizard of Oz*, and said, "There's no place like home," Claudia smacked her ruby red lips together and offered Jeremy the ultimate *C.L.A.P.*, "Sweetie, there's no one like you! You are one of a kind!"

Lesson 2.
WTF to Do to Boost the Odds?

"I think you need to love giving compliments as much as you love receiving them." —Yami Gautam, Indian film actress

What's a Boomer Chick to do when her AHPartnership has hit that low valley where even a "Good Morning" feels too civil, and even shaking hands is too touchy-feely? What to say when the only words that want to flow out of your sweet mouth are unprintable? The WTF (Women's Truth Foundation) suggests that the more verbal partner (odds are 1,000,000,000 to 1 that the "more verbal partner" is the AHFemale) begin turning things around by goosing her **Compliment Count** and squashing her **Criticism Count**. In addition, The WTF publishes a list of positive statements for the desperate times when an AHFemale doesn't even want to be in the same room with her AHPartners, let alone be in the same life together.

WTF Positive Statements for the Desperate: Neutral tone of voice, please! Avoid questions!

1. "Your eyes are so blue." (Make sure to get this one right!)

2. "You are dressed I see."

3. "Did you get a haircut?" (Baldness substitute: "Your head is nicely polished.")

4. "I see you took the dog out."

5. "That shirt is very clean."

6. "You made your own breakfast." (No sarcastic tones allowed!)

7. "How did I ever get hooked up with you?!?!?" (Use this only when numbers 1-6 fail and one partner is ready to activate the **Dooris Slammo Whammo** section of the brain.)

CHAPTER 9. GOOD ODDS TO KEEP AN AHPARTNERSHIP EVEN

If even one of the above elicits a non-growling response, proceed to the next level…

WTF Positive Statements for the Semi-Desperate: Neutral tone of voice, again!

1. "I have always liked your smile." (Hopefully true!)
2. "I was wondering about your plans for the day."
3. "The weather looks like it is going to be _____ today."
4. "I hope you took the dog out and that he pooped." (Omit: "…and that you cleaned it up.")
5. "I am wondering what would be good for dinner."
6. "I plan on going shopping soon."
7. "Can't you ever answer me!?!?!" (Use this only if 1-6 elicit no response, even though they weren't questions.)

Boldly forge ahead to the next suggestions by boldly turning the page.

WTF Positive Statements for the Eternal Optimists: Pollyanna tone of voice, please!

1. "I would love to rewind that tape, forget we even said what we said, and start fresh as if the last ten minutes/hours/months/years (!) never happened."
2. "Let's open a bottle of wine."
3. "Let's pretend we saw each other across a crowded party, our eyes locked, and we moved magnetically towards each other as if in a trance."
4. "Let's order pizza delivery and watch Mission Impossible XII."
5. "I love giving and getting back rubs."
6. "I think we need to get away to our favorite vacation place."
7. "I was just thinking about the day we met. What a great story. Wasn't that something!"

At this point, odds are that you have tried and tried your very best to increase your ***Compliment Count***, and to stay in the same room… the same city… the same continent as your AHMale. If things are still not simpatico between you and your geezer, perhaps it is best to repeat the slogan of the Women's Truth Foundation: ***WTF Says It All!***

Chapter 10.
Communication:
You Just Renewed Your-Driving-Me-Crazy License

"The single biggest problem in communication is the illusion that it has taken place." —George Bernard Shaw, playwright

Remember that 1992 classic best-seller *Men are from Mars, Women are from Venus*? Author Dr. John Gray writes that communication problems arise between the sexes because men generally want to solve problems and women usually want to discuss their feelings about problems. That book was a classic, but perhaps needs updating for an Aging Human Partnership. Many an AHFemale feels that the communication issue is worsened by her AHMale's getting untethered from the space station and totally spacing out when it comes to communicating about feelings.

"Houston, we have a problem."

She feels that her aging man isn't from Mars, but is *way* farther out, lost in space, and their fighting—their Star Wars—start because her old man is from "a galaxy far, far away." After The Big Bang of an eruptive argument, an AHFemale watches in awe as her well-meaning, but unsophisticated, AHMale digs himself into a black hole.

In the words of Yoda, "Listen and understand does he not!"

Some strategic plans on how to reconnect at warp speed and start a trajectory toward the same planet Earth follow.

Scotty, beam us aboard—together!

CHAPTER 10. COMMUNICATION: YOU JUST RENEWED YOUR-DRIVING-ME-CRAZY LICENSE

Lesson 1. Feelings, Whoa, Whoa, Whoa, Feelings

"Men have two feelings—hungry and horny." —Anonymous

Credo of the Aging Human Male:

An Aging Human Male is often more about CONTROL than FEELINGS!

Take Yogi Berra, for instance: "I don't get upset over things I can control, because if I can control them there's no sense in getting upset. And I don't get upset over things I can't control, because if I can't control them there's no sense in getting upset."

Credo of the Aging Human Female:

An Aging Human Female is often more about FEELINGS than CONTROL!

Take writer Gloria Naylor, for instance: "I don't believe that life is supposed to make you feel good, or to make you feel miserable either. Life is just supposed to make you feel."

The latest edition of the *Psychiatric Dramatic Satirical Man-ual* has identified the AHMale malady: fear of feeling feelings, or **feelingafeelingafobia**. **Feelinafeelingafobia** is manifested in the **freefrontal lobe** of the male brain. Further brain research shows that the **feelingafeelingafobia** brain area enlarges as a male reaches puberty and then connects directly to the **Genitallis Uberallis** brain area that governs sexual feelings. As human males age, the **feelingafeelingafobia** merges with the **Genitallis Uberallis**, often elicing the non-medical descriptive phrase "He's a dick!"

So that's the *Psychiatric Dramatic Satirical Man-ual* science behind aging human men having limited feelings thanks to their DNA. But what about nature vs. nurture when it comes to men and feelings? Boys and men have the Goddess-given right to have and share their feelings, no judgments allowed. What's good for the goose, should be good for any gender! In the 1992 movie, *A League of Their Own*, Tom Hanks, as manager of an all-women's baseball team, scolds a woman infielder after her bad ball play and then, after she gets weepy, he yells at her, "THERE'S NO CRYING IN BASEBALL!" Well, for most men in any league in our culture, they hear the message, "There's no crying in life!" From an early age on up until Boomerhood, lots of guys get the message from society that weeping is for wusses: "Man up!" Wouldn't it be so helpful and healthy if all men were given the message to "Woman up!" and let those feelings show and flow?!

> ### *Sofia and Diego and Feelings*
>
> ***Sofia***: "What are you feeling?"
>
> ***Diego:*** "Huh? I dunno."
>
> ***Sofia:*** "How can you not have feelings?"
>
> ***Diego***: "Well, I guess my butt itches."

Lesson 2.
No, I Don't Speak French and I Don't Speak Feelings: ESL—Emotions as a Second Language

"Verbal ability is a highly overrated thing in a guy, and it's our pathetic need for it that gets us into so much trouble."
—Rebecca Gethings, screenwriter, When Harry Met Sally (1989)

Many aging women love to talk; many aging men, when it comes to talk, balk. Verbal sharing for an AHFemale is as easy and necessary as breathing. For many aging men, the language of feelings is like a second language, a language that leaves them tongue-tied and literally at a loss for words!

Neuropsychologist Dr. Gregory Jantz has discovered approximately 100 gender differences in the brain, including gender differences in expressing feelings. Dr. Jantz found that, "females tend to have verbal centers on both sides of the brain, while males tend to have verbal centers on only the left hemisphere… [Males] have less connectivity between their word centers and their memories or feelings… [Males tend] to move onto the next task… rather than analyze their feelings at all." (TRUTH, "Brain Differences between Genders," *Psychology Today,* 02/27/2014.)

Responding to this research finding, the Women's Truth Foundation survey reports that:

33% of AHFemales say, "Vive la difference,"

33% say, "C'est la vie,"

33% say, "Duh," and

100% roll on the floor laughing at such an obvious truth.

Responding to this research finding, the Women's Truth Foundation survey reports that:

100% of AHMales say, "   ." NOTHING, of course!

Mabel and John and Emotions as a Second Language

John: "Honey, I slept in and didn't see you before I left for golf. How has your day been so far?"

Mabel: "Well, I was up a little during the night but finally got back to sleep. Took a hot shower this morning that helped wake me up. Had a good time meeting Betty for breakfast at that new coffee shop around the corner. It's really cozy, decorated all French, and the food was good. The waitress was really cute. Then we went to play tennis. I didn't play well, but it was good seeing Ruth there, and we chatted afterwards. She's all excited about her grandkids coming for a visit. Then I went to volunteer at the homeless shelter. One of the families was new and the little girl was so sweet. Oh! I stopped at the market on the way home, luckily it wasn't too crowded today, although they had a big promo sale going on, and I bought some fresh fruit. Maybe you could cut up some of the melons so we can have them in our fruit salad for dinner later? So that was my day so far. So now I am home for lunch before we head out for that afternoon movie. We'll have to hustle a little so that we get there in time to catch the Tuesday afternoon Senior Discount. How was your golf game this morning?"

CHAPTER 10. COMMUNICATION: YOU JUST RENEWED YOUR-DRIVING-ME-CRAZY LICENSE

John: (Shrug.) "Par for the course. HAHA!"

Mabel: "Doesn't sound good?"

John: (Shrug.)

Mabel: "What did you and your buddies Rick and Bob and John talk about?"

John: (Shrug.)

Mabel: (Tired of grilling John for details, leaving the room—mutter, mutter.)

Later that afternoon, after the movie....

Mabel: "That was an intense movie. It was so scary toward the end. I was afraid of what might happen. Then I cried and cried when Kira's character died, but it was still a good movie, just so sad. Loved the period that they portrayed. The costumes and the manners of the day were so interesting. What a great tearjerker. What did you think of the movie?"

John: "Good action. Good plot."

Mabel: "How did you feel about the movie?"

John: "Well, those seats weren't so comfortable. My back hurts. Now, where should we go for a drink?"

Lesson 3.
Silence of the Lamb Chops

"Silence is so freaking loud!"
—Sarah Desson, author *Just Listen*

"I can't think of anything lonelier than spending the rest of my life with someone I can't talk to, or worse, someone I can't be silent with."
—Mary Ann Shaffer, *The Guernsey Literary and Potato Peel Pie Society*

CHAPTER 10. COMMUNICATION: YOU JUST RENEWED YOUR-DRIVING-ME-CRAZY LICENSE

There sits the Aging Human Male across the table from his Aging Human Female, quietly drinking his wine, picking up his knife and fork, slicing his meat, chewing his cud, looking all around, fiddling with his napkin, looking bleary-eyed. The room is filled with the sound of sips, the crunching of the salad, the burps and sniffles of her aging man. Mega-stuff is going into his mouth, but nothing is coming out of his mouth. No words. No comments. No socializations. No vocalizations. No conversation. The best that comes out of the dining mouth of her aging man is a grunt, a sigh, a rasp, or a clearing of the throat. So where is he? An AHFemale needs words, needs verbal responses, and needs conversation!

Brain research from the The Women's Truth Foundation (WTF) has identified a part of the aging male brain that regulates eating and drinking, scientifically known as the *Gluttonusbuttonus*. Analogously, brain research has identified a part of the aging female brain that regulates eating and drinking, called *Eatdaintily*. Moreover, brain studies have also identified a specialized part present only in the female brain where words and verbal capabilities are processed, known as *Connected Humans Always Talk (CHAT)*.

In studying the brain of an older man dining, scientists have discovered that when the AHMale *Gluttonusbuttonus* is activated during a meal, it short-circuits all other brain functions, so that an aging man single-mindedly focuses on food and drink.

In studying the brain of an older woman, scientists have discovered that when the *Eatdaintily* section of her brain is activated, it hyperactivates the *CHAT* section of her brain, stimulating *CHAT buds* on the tongue of an aging woman, enabling her to eat and converse *at the same time*.

These brain studies clarify why an aging woman sitting at a meal with her aging man might be pondering, "Where is the scintillating conversation of years ago when this very same hot guy was woo-ing me?"

Allison and Allen and Breakfasting Together Alone

Allison: "Allen, what are your plans for the day?"

Allen: (Continues reading the news on his iPad.)

Allison: (Louder) "Allen, what are your plans for the day?"

Allen: (Eyes on iPad.)

Allison: "How are your eggs?"

Allen: (Eyes on iPad) "Mmmhmmm…"

Allison: "What's happening in politics today?"

Allen: (Eyes on iPad) "Nuttin' Honey."

Allison retreats into silence as Allen continues reading his iPad.

Allison: "Allen, I never thought we'd be doing a menage a trois with your iPad!"

Allen: (Eyes on iPad, brain obviously disengaged) "Sounds good to me, Honey."

Chapter 11.
How to Womanhandle an Aging Human Male: The Basics

"The best way to get most husbands to do something is to suggest that perhaps they're too old to do it." —Ann Bancroft

The Merriam-Webster Dictionary defines "to womanhandle" as "to move or manage by female human force." In this **Sassy Primer**, *Helen* womansplains "womanhandling" as "expertly engaging the cooperation of an Aging Human Male, often without his knowing what is happening." This daunting task takes determination, spunk, finesse and, yes, kid gloves—or boxing gloves! The following lessons will help in engaging an AHMale's cooperation, hopefully for the good of the AHPartnership.

Lesson 1.
It Takes Two to Tango... and to Tangle: The T & A Personality Diagnostic Assessment Instrument

"Love is a battlefield." — Pat Benatar

CHAPTER 11. HOW TO WOMANHANDLE AN AGING HUMAN MALE: THE BASICS

Conflict happens. Pick and choose your battles, or make every battle WWIII? To go down swinging or to swing and go down on whoever? What is your high adrenaline, high conflict response? Fight, flight, faint—very Victorian!—or freeze (his balls off)—very Rambo!

So is your AHMale prone to conflict or eager to cooperate? Is he a "Rowdy Pardner" itching for a fight, or a "Howdy, Pardner" wishing to make peace and move on with a minimum of conflict? Which one are you? Are one or both of you conflict-avoidant or ready to "Put up your dukes or your duchesses!" How can you womanhandle these conflict situations to achieve some peace while you have each said your piece?

Are you and your partner prone to tango or to tangle? ***The Tango & Anger Personality Diagnostic Assessment,*** commonly referred to as ***The T & A PDA,*** will help you assess your conflict styles. Bring it on...

The Tango and Anger Personality Diagnostic Assessment

Answer the following questions for yourself; add up your score. Then answer the following questions for your AHPartner and tally up his score.

1. ***How do you calm down when you are upset?***

    a) An hour of yoga followed by a green smoothie: 10 points

    b) A brisk walk with the dog, muttering the whole time (you muttering, not the dog): 0 points

    c) Two hours of kick-boxing at the gym, with a Bud Lite in your hand: -10 points

2. ***After three glasses of wine, you are...***

    a) Ready for a nap: 10 points

    b) Feeling very melancholy: 0 points

    c) Itching for a fight: -10 points

3. *Do you prefer tickets to...*

   a) The opera: 10 points

   b) *The Rocky Horror Picture Show*: -2 points

   c) A boxing match: -10 points

4. *Your Thanksgiving dinners with extended family resemble...*

   a) A Norman Rockwell all-American family painting: 10 points

   b) A group therapy session gone bad: -2 points

   c) A food fight: -10 points

5. *If you didn't like the way your aging partner loaded the dishwasher, you would...*

   a) Mentally be thankful your partner knows there is a dishwasher in the kitchen: 10 points

   b) Loudly instruct your partner on The Correct Way to Load a Dishwasher: -5 points

   c) Get loaded yourself and smash some dishes as you angrily reload the D/W: -15 points

The T & A Personality Diagnostic Assessment Results:

Score greater than 0: Let's tango! You are a "Howdy, Pardner." The fights are all his fault!

Score less than 0: Anger-prone! You are a "Rowdy Pardner." Stop tangling! Treat her like the sweetheart that she is.

CHAPTER 11. HOW TO WOMANHANDLE AN AGING HUMAN MALE: THE BASICS

Lesson 2.
Wo-mantras for Tango-ing

"Life is short. Break the rules, forgive quickly, kiss slowly, love truly, laugh uncontrollably, and never regret anything that made you smile."
—Audrey Hepburn

Practice these wo-mantras to help with your inner voice—and your outer voice—as you make a choice to tango or tangle with your AHMale. It may not feel like it at the time, but tango-ing or tangling *is a choice*.

Sometimes "good enough" is good enough. Let's be realistic here—you may be perfect, but your Boomer Buddy will never be perfect, even with your skill and talent in caring and feeding him. Sometimes your white knight in shining armor needs to be appreciated for the muddy knight in slightly tarnished, battle-weary armor that he is. Lower the bar and it will be easier for him and his tired steed to jump over it and you can all continue on your merry way.

Don't hate. Cut bait. When things start to smell fishy, cut bait and run. Better to exit a fight and leave the room so that it is easier to patch things up later and not have to apologize for the #&*@ said. It takes two to tangle.

"Shake it off." This is brilliant wisdom from pop star Taylor Swift. Life is short. Tempers don't have to be.

Junk the judgment. Try to accept this aging man as is. In all his glory or vainglory, dirty underwear and bumbling apologies. Only Boomer Chicks are perfect. Obviously.

Be humble about your fumble. Everyone makes mistakes. Admit the fumble. To quote Miss Piggy, "Who, moi?" Humble pie can be hard to make (who ever did get the knack of homemade pie crust?), but it has a sweet aftertaste.

Don't clam-up, speak up! Don't harbor those inner feelings too long or they get rancid and come out as nastygrams. Speak up, you cute crone, you!

Be sweet, don't compete. The conflict to see who's on top should only take place in the bedroom.

Rise above the storm and ride the inner wave of laughter. Just how funny is it to be fighting about THIS?!!

Ask Yourself: "Why Not?" Maybe, just maybe, there is another viable option for this power struggle. Loosen up? Try a new dance step in this tango!

"OH!" instead of "NO!" "No" can put up a wall and maybe you don't need a wall here, but some common open ground. Instead, put up an "OH!" invitation. Then just wait, be patient, and see what unfolds.

"That is an interesting point of view." No commitment and no decision gives an AHFemale —and an AHMale— time to think and feel.

Get out your Dolly umbrella! As Dolly Parton says, "The way I see it, if you want the rainbow, you gotta put up with the rain!"

Don't let anyone steal your joy! You are a good person. You are lovable. Whether he is being a curmudgeon or not, you can choose to be happy.

"Amen." The only last word you need. Grit those teeth, tighten those gluts, and let him have the last word—it really isn't the LAST word.

CHAPTER 11. HOW TO WOMANHANDLE AN AGING HUMAN MALE: THE BASICS

Lesson 3.
Womanhandling the Mansplaining: The Rebecca Rule

"Listen to everything your man says. Then do what you want." —Rebecca, Irene's Mom

Mansplaining just keeps happening and happening, ad nauseum. For those doing chapter skip-arounds or for those of us who have some short-term memory fuzzies, in Chapter 3, Lesson 2, **Rae Jean** womansplained that "Mansplaining is a simple explanation from a simple man simply looking for trouble." Rebecca Solnit observes, "Mansplaining is… the intersection between overconfidence and cluelessness where some portion of that (male) gender gets stuck… (accompanied by) that smug look I know so well." (TRUTH, *Men Explain Things to Me*, Haymarket Books, 2015.)

But what self-respecting Boomer Chick needs a definition of mansplaining? We Aging Human Females all know it when we hear it! Don't our eyes do that automatic roll-back as soon as he starts up on his soapbox?

One day, deep into a struggle in her own AHPartnership, **Irene** asked her mother **Rebecca** how she herself had survived 65 years of marriage to a man who seemed to have invented mansplaining decades before it was even a word. Her mom **Rebecca** replied without missing a heartbeat, "Listen to everything your man says. Then do what you want." **Irene** was grateful for the advice, but she wished that her mom, who was rather quiet, had given her that advice when she started dating at 16! This advice from her mom became

Irene's The Rebecca Rule when dealing with conflicts with her aging man.

As you listen to your aging man's bossy mansplaining, feel free to recite **The Rebecca Rule** to yourself. It goes without saying that women want choices and it is your choice on how to respond when an aging man is snake-bitten with the need to mansplain.

> **Rebecca** *and* **Daniel** *and* **The Rebecca Rule**
>
> **Rebecca, Irene's** mom, had always wanted a flagstone patio behind their house. Her husband Daniel said, "What do we need a patio for? We have our lawn chairs out there. Who needs all those flagstones? What a waste of money. I worked in construction that summer in high school and I saw it first hand: patios are just a money rip-off. Bad idea." **Rebecca** was silent.
>
> For the next three months, **Rebecca** quietly got estimates and plans drawn up for her flagstone patio. Then she presented the plans and estimates to Daniel and told him which patio she wanted installed. Daniel had no comment. Both she and Daniel enjoyed sitting out on their flagstone patio for many, many summers!

Antidote to Mansplaining: Water off a Chick's Tush. Sometimes speaking up is an important antidote to mansplaining and sometimes it is just a waste of breath! Sometimes remaining silent is the sanest response to mansplaining. During your Boomer Buddy's mansplaining, no need to say what you will do and no need to prove you are right—you can always prove you are right later if you need that. After the mansplaining is finished, feel free to say aloud or to yourself, "Amen," which literally translates as, "So be it." The "it" stands for your stubborn Aging Human Male, of course!

CHAPTER 11. HOW TO WOMANHANDLE AN AGING HUMAN MALE: THE BASICS

Jennifer and Jim and **The Rebecca Rule:** *Water off a Donkey's Tush*

Luckily, Jennifer and Jim belonged to the same political party, which minimized some potential conflicts, but Jim considered himself a total politico who was up-to-date on all the latest news. When they debated politics, Jim was very strident in his views and would tell Jennifer that she was wrong. Jennifer was annoyed by Jim's opinions, which he called "The Truth," and she deemed, "Opinionated Mansplaining."

When they debated the news, she made a conscious choice on whether to engage or just let the mansplaining roll off her donkey's tush. She listened. She said, "I hear you," or, "Let's agree to disagree, Hon." And then she changed the subject. Sometimes Jennifer simply ignored a simple explanation from her sometimes simple man who was simply looking for trouble.

P.S. For his birthday, Jennifer gave Jim a tee shirt that said, "Boy do I hate being right all the time." Luckily, he laughed.

The Rebecca Rule *is the Golden Rule for Silver-Haired Women*

Glue it to your bathroom mirror. Write **The Rebecca Rule** everyday in your smartphone calendar. Use it as a screensaver. Tattoo it on your forearm. Write it on your tissue box for when you grab for it after a fight. Order it custom-printed on a t-shirt. (Coming soon with the next edition of this Sassy Primer!) Quote **Rebecca** over lunch with your PODs seeking advice. Recite **The Rebecca Rule** as a morning mantra. When your AHMale talks and your eyes start to do that auto eye-roll, program yourself to think: "Listen to everything your man says. Then do what you want."

Lesson 4. Womanhandling the Boundaries: The Erma Edict

"That won't work for me." — Erma C., therapist for forty years

These five words compose a complete sentence, believe it or not.

No excuses necessary. No apologies necessary.

No need to explain or womansplain with reasons.

No need for "I'm sorry, I'm sorry, I'm so sorry."

Set this clean, clear, self-respecting limit and then stop. Take a stand and then stand strong.

And no further explanations of **The Erma Edict** are necessary —further womansplaining won't work for this womanhandling lesson!

Chapter 12.
Advanced Womanhandling: Competence, Control & Anxiety

"Women need to feel loved. Men need to feel needed."
—Rita Mae Brown

Often an AHMale in his younger years feels competent, relaxed, and in control of his own life. As life and lifestyles change, an AHMale's competence and control may be challenged by several issues that strike at a man's heart and balls: retiring often calls into question a man's identity and purpose in life. Aging is often accompanied by health concerns and financial challenges. Many of the "sure things" are not so sure anymore, leading many an older man to question his competence and control over his own life. This can cause anxiety and increase his need for control.

And don't we AHFemales know it!

So what to do about an aging man's increased need for feelings of competence and control? He may feel like The Lone Ranger hiding behind a mask of normalcy. And we may ask: "Who is this masked man?" And as we watch our male hero ride away on his white horse of aging, it can trigger puzzled feelings on how to cope. We may feel alone and not know who to Tonto—oops, turn to. The following lessons are some silver bullets to make it better for an AHMale, an AHFemale and their AHPartnership.

Lesson 1.
Caring about Competence: "Right" Questions are the Wrong Questions

"Behind every great man is a woman rolling her eyes."
— Jim Carrey

Questioning a Boomer Buddy's competence, directly or indirectly, touches on an aging man's ego and may cause anxiety, inner fears of uselessness and feelings of not being needed. This may cause unconscious hurt and subtle terror in the heart of an aging man. Competence issues are tender for an older man and need to be addressed with skill, patience, and compassion.

Why question an AHMale with a *"Competence Question?"* A *Competence Question* is any question that uses the word "right" along with a "?". Brain research by the WTF (Women's Truth Foundation) has shown that asking a question that involves "right" and "?" lights up the *Incompetence Mentis* area of an aging man's brain, which in turn activates the brain area known as *Snippyus Withmylippius*.

Examples of Competence Questions to Avoid:

1. "Are we going in the **right** direction**?**"
2. "Is that the **right** tool to use**?**"
3. "Do you know how to do that the **right** way**?**"
4. "Why do you always think you are **right?**"
5. "Is that the **right** thing to do**?**"
6. "Did you remember that **right?**"

CHAPTER 12. ADVANCED WOMANHANDLING: COMPETENCE, CONTROL & ANXIETY

The more an AHMale's competence is questioned, the more easily the *Snippyus Withmylippius* section of his brain is activated. Questioning competence is compounded, like bank interest—but is not nearly as rewarding as compounded bank interest.

Don't indirectly declare an aging man's incompetence with an AHFemale *Competence Declaration*. An AHFemale *Competence Declaration* is any sentence with the words "I" and "right" or "better" that ends with "!"

Examples of AHFemale Competence Declarations to Avoid:

1. "See, I was **right** about your parents' anniversary!"
2. "I don't always think I am **right**, but I usually do **better** than you on the Sunday crossword!"
3. "I did remember the directions to Kate and John's cabin **better!**"
4. "I knew we would have been **better** off if you had ordered those tickets to Elton John sooner!"
5. "And, YES, I do know how to balance our checkbook **better** than you!"

An additional warning note: An older woman's triumphant tone of voice can further activate an AHMale's *Snippyus Withmylippius*, which makes an aging woman fantasize about giving him a *fatlippius*.

So what is the "right" thing to say? Oops, bad *Competence Question* with a "right" and "?" Sorry, not sorry. The challenge for any aging woman is to strengthen the *Buttonmylippius* section of her brain. The more the *Buttonmylippius* section of an AHFemale's brain is activated, the larger her *Patienceisgolden* section of her brain becomes.

Patience, Precious Old Dame—it may be hard to stand there watching him use the wrong size wrench on the pipe under the kitchen sink, but better not to pipe up and cause a fight that includes everything, including the kitchen sink!

Lesson 2. Controlling Control: Five Tips

"Man does not control his own fate. The women in his life do that for him." —Grouch Marx

So your Boomer Champ's competence and anxiety issues are manifesting as control issues. How can you womanhandle his need for control that puts you back in control of your geezess self, his geezer self, and the whole geezing situation?!

Tip #1. Apply **The Rebecca Rule:** Listen to everything he says. Then do what you want.

Tip #2. Pick and choose your battles: You did this with your three-year-old, remember? It works as well with a seventy-three-year-old! Having trouble deciding if it's a worthy battle? Check out Chapter 35 offering Wo-mantras to Push-up Your Bra-very.

Tip #3. Giving choices helps reduce anxiety by giving a sense of control. The more choices, the more a feeling of control —as small as they may be.

"Do you want to leave for the party at 7:00 or 7:30pm?"

"I am wondering if we should label parts of the fridge for various items—what do you think the categories should be?"

"What would be the easiest and quickest way to hang this picture?"

"What movie are you interested in seeing today?"

CHAPTER 12. ADVANCED WOMANHANDLING: COMPETENCE, CONTROL & ANXIETY

It takes a big-hearted Boomer Babe to cede control on small issues that don't matter. Small concessions lead to big peace.

Tip #4. Re-frame "control" as predictability in your own mind. No surprises can be a good thing. If one of his control issues is that he likes you by his side—okay, so it's the left side only since that is his "good" ear—go with it!

Tip #5. Whose power struggle is it, anyway? Admit it, Boomer Chicks, we have issues of control and anxiety, too! Sometimes it is just too hard to back away from our own anxiety, and to keep our traps shut when he is clearly so wrong, or when his attitude is absolutely obnoxious, or when we are simply itching for a good fight. And who better to use as a verbal punching bag than our Aging Significant Other?! This is the time that we need to think about pursing our lips together—okay, glares allowed—and not taking the bait. Sometimes the best way to womanhandle a man is to womanhandle ourselves: be patient and breathe deeply through our own control needs. Two anxious heads are not better than one.

Here's hoping that these tips tip the balance of control in an AHFemale's favor since, to be honest, when some aging women feel their feelings getting out of control, they feel the need to control whatever and whoever is around! Watch out!

CARE & FEEDING OF THE AGING HUMAN MALE SPECIES: A SASSY PRIMER

Lesson 3.
Assuaging Anxiety: Happy 67th Birthday, Alfred E. Neuman

"What, me worry?"
—*Alfred E. Neumann, mascot 67-year-old MAD Magazine*

The Crones for Disease Control (affectionately known as the other CDC, an organization for controlling control) has recently issued a warning about a harmful virus in an important food—and, no, this time it is not about tainted meat or e.coli in lettuce. The CDC discovered that there are germs present in cake frosting, specifically with icing that reads:

"Happy ___th Birthday, _____!"

with the "*___th*" including any numbers greater than **50**, and the second _____ filled with ***John*** or ***Bob*** or ***Mike***, that is, any name common to an Aging Human Male.

CHAPTER 12. ADVANCED WOMANHANDLING: COMPETENCE, CONTROL & ANXIETY

Crones for Disease Control has declared that any birthday cake with the above icing message contains a virus known as the *D/Witis Virus.* Only AHMales are subject to this virus. This *D/Witis* causes great anguish, but only to those around the victim. The CDC states that there is no known medication or treatment for *D/Witis*... and no cure.

As indicated by recent brain research, the *D/Witis Virus* attacks the "reptilian," or "primitive" portion of the brain and causes an aging man to feel out of control and anxious, thus releasing male hormones that increase his need for control to counteract this anxiety. *D/Witis* spreads and manifests in an aging man as a need for obsessive control in any way, shape or form. The Crones for Disease Control consider *D/Witis* a serious disease of control, and these CDC gals are the experts on control, as evidenced by their name.

> ### *Mildred and Mike and D/Witis*
>
> Mildred planned a surprise birthday party for Mike. Whe Mike returned home from his usual Saturday golf game, he was wow-ed by a big "Happy 65th, Mike!" banner and his friends singing and cheering. There was lots of laughter and delicious food, topped off with a huge golf-themed cake. UH-OH on the "Happy 65th Mike!" written with gooey icing!
>
> After the party, while Mildred was cleaning up in the kitchen, Mike came in and started rearranging the dishes that Mildred had put in the dishwasher.
>
> *Mildred:* "Mike, what are you doing?"
>
> *Mike:* "I am rearranging the dishes so they will be washed more efficiently."
>
> *Mildred:* "What, you've never cared about loading the D/W before?!"
>
> *Mike:* "It needs to be arranged this way. Back off... way off. This is the way to load a D/W!"
>
> *Mildred:* (giving him a "pass" on his birthday) "Oh. Okay."

Mildred felt worried about this new D/W control issue in Mike. She was up during the night, turned on her cellphone and Googled "dishwasher control in aging men." Up popped: "The *D/Witis Virus* can occur in human males who have aged. The first symptoms of *D/Witis* man-ifest as control issues over their environment, such as taking control of how to load a D/W. There are no medical cures known to man, or an aging man." Mildred became worried.

The next morning:

Mike: "So I invited Betty and Larry over for brunch this morning."
Mildred: "What? You didn't ask me or tell me about this. I am so tired from yesterday's party!"
Mike: "Well, too late, they will be here in ten minutes."
Mildred: (no time for words, quickly opening up the fridge and pulling out leftovers.)

After Betty and Larry left, Mildred was so tired that she went to the bedroom to take a nap. She woke up worried again. She picked up her cellphone and Googled: "D/Witis Virus social plans" Up popped: "Progessive symptoms of *D/Witis Virus* man-ifest as control issues over social plans, such as unexpectedly inviting company for a meal. There are no medical cures known to man, or an aging man." Mildred became very worried.

CHAPTER 12. ADVANCED WOMANHANDLING: COMPETENCE, CONTROL & ANXIETY

Later that afternoon, Mildred decided that her PODs, her Precious Old Dames, might have better information on the *D/Witis Virus* than Google. Mildred's PODs suggested the following:

POD Home Remedies for D/Witis Virus: **The Geezer Triangle**

These are Home Remedies as in, "There is no place like home," keeping in mind that the basic **Geezer Triangle** of **Sex▲Sustenance▲Sports** defines "home" for an aging man.

Warning: Home Remedies are not "controlled substances," but are considered "substances to deal with an AHMale's feeling OUT of control."

Recommended Dosage: To be given as often as needed—and only as often as an AHFemale feels like dispensing the remedy!—for calming symptoms of anxiety and need for control in an AHMale.

Home Remedy #1. **SEX** Guided by D/W cycle options: "Normal," "Delicate," "Fast" or "Eco"

Home Remedy #2. **SUSTENANCE:** Homemade Chili Cheese Frito Pie brought into the man cave.

Home Remedy #3. **SPORTS:** Man Cave time—without any female complaining— for 24 hours.

Home Remedy #4. **S▲S▲S TRIFECTA:** Sex and Frito Pie in the Man Cave (ESPN turned low) simultaneously.

Prognosis: Relief—for the AHFemale!—is not guaranteed.

Mildred was desperate to deal with Mike's *D/Witis Virus*. She tried giving Mike one dose of the recommended **S▲S▲S** trifecta—nachos, "delicate" sex, and Monday Night Football—and it worked immediately! Mildred decided that her PODs were a lot smarter than Google!

Chapter 13.
Fire Prevention:
STOP, DROP, and ROLL

"Only YOU can prevent forest fires." — Smokey the Bear

So that "talk" with your AHMale is escalating. Smoke is starting to come out of his ears and you are ready to start spitting fiery words. Why not follow the advice of the experts in fiery confrontations—the firefighters?! Survive the smoke and flames with: *STOP, DROP, and ROLL.*

Helen's version of STOP, DROP, and ROLL: The Silent Treatment

1. **STOP** talking and…

2. **DROP** that heated conversation and…

3. **ROLL** yourself out of that room!

Helen likes Harry Truman's advice: "If you can't stand the heat, get out of the kitchen."

Rae Jean's version of STOP, DROP, and ROLL: The Violent Treatment

1. "**STOP** your bellyaching!"

2. "**DROP** any pretense of civility."

3. "**ROLL** those nastygrams off your tongue!"

Rae Jean then likes Bess Truman's advice: "Call a POD (Precious Old Dame) and complain!"

CHAPTER 13. FIRE PREVENTION: STOP, DROP, AND ROLL

This **Sassy Primer** highly recommends *Helen's Silent Treatment*—even though *Rae Jean's Violent Treatment* may feel better in the heat of the moment! Remove your a__ (a for arson, of course!) before the only thing that's left is ashes. Take space, distance, and time to douse the flames and then Air Wick™ that smoky stink. Find your safety zone and meditate. There's no place like h-ommmm-e. Ahhhhh.

You did great! You were able to blow out that flaming matchstick by giving the situation some fresh air, and, when you're ready, you will move on to attempt match-making again.

Chapter 14.
Fight Club: The Rules

"It is not so much trying to keep alive as trying to keep from blowing apart from inner explosions every day."
— May Sarton, author, poet, memoirist

Yes, no, maybe so. Every day conflicts happen; small things nudge; large decisions come lickety-splat… not enough sleep, not enough fun, not enough money, too much wine, too much dog poop on the carpet, too much arthritis. Whatever it is, fights happen. Before you know it, you are both in the fight ring, also known as the kitchen, the car, the bedroom, the restaurant table. The referee announces, "And in this corner, weighing more than she wants, is _____ and in the other corner, not even deserving to be in the same ring, room, relationship, planet, or universe as his worthy, loving, beautiful opponent, is _____." And then Round 1 begins. The audience—people present, people not actually present but present in your head as ghost people (parents, siblings, exes, frenemies)—stand up in their seats, wildly cheering and jeering as the adrenaline goes flying off your bodies like sweat and you square off in the center!

Whoa… how did you get here?! And where do you go from here?

Take several deep breaths. Sit in the time-out chair/bar/POD party of your choice and attempt to calm yourself. Here are some crucial don'ts and do's for when you step into that boxing ring and put up your dukes—and duchesses.

CHAPTER 14. FIGHT CLUB: THE RULES

Lesson 1. Don'ts

"My husband and I have never considered divorce—murder sometimes, but never divorce."
—Dr. Joyce Brothers, psychologist

Here are eight don'ts to self-referee so that Round 1 doesn't proceed to Round 2.

Don't #1. Never use "never." Always avoid "always." Why use "why?" What in the world are you doing saying, "What in the world?" How could you ever say "How could you ever…?" You are wrong to use "wrong" in the same sentence as "you."

Don't #2. Make it a point to never point. Never point out he is wrong. Never point out you are right. Never point any finger—especially the middle finger—in his face.

Don't #3. No name-calling. Sticks and stones may break someone's bones, but name-calling will always hurt… sometimes forever.

Don't #4. No yelling. Except if one of you is deaf or lost the batteries to your hearing aids.

Don't #5. No judgment. Judgment belongs in a courtroom, not real life.

Don't #6. No blame. Blame is a game that ends in shame.

Don't #7. No kitchen sink fights allowed. Statute of limitations on old complaints: two weeks. Any complaints over two weeks old stink and should be put down the garbage disposal or taken out with the trash.

Don't #8. No fight lasts longer than 36 minutes. Professional boxing matches are limited to 12 rounds—3 minutes per round x 12 rounds = 36 minutes. You and your AHMale are not even professional fighters! Any fight that lasts longer than 36 minutes is not entertaining. Take a break—someone needs to head for the showers to cool off.

Lesson 2. Do's

*"There are two theories to arguing with a woman.
Neither works."*
—Will Rogers

Here are eight do's to help you—okay, e-v-e-n-t-u-a-l-l-y help you—get to that place where you can step out of the boxing ring, both champions...

Do #1. Stay strong. Just because his bark is louder and deeper than yours doesn't make him right. His Alpha Dog doesn't define you as a Zeta Bitch. The hair on your back can raise up as much as the hair on his back. This is a hairy disagreement among equals.

Do #2. Go to bed mad if you are still feeling mad. Who wants to get or give an angry goodnight kiss? Don't stuff your feelings away. Sometimes the space and extra time can help gain perspective. Sometimes there is truth hiding underneath the anger. Give it time to emerge. Give yourself time to heal from the stress of the disagreement.

Do #3. Do a Scarlett O'Hara. Remember that "Tomorrow is another day." And let's hope that by the time the sun rises on another day, the feist in the fight has gone with the wind. And let's hope you can then say, "Frankly, my dear, I don't give a damn about that anymore."

Do #4. Try to get past the past: "What do we/you need to get past this?"

"What is the next step to help us step out of this boxing ring? Do we need to think out of the box? How can we stop acting like a___s and put this behind our big behinds? Life is too short to be bickering over…wait, I just forgot what this fight was all about!"

Do #5. "Help me understand how you think/feel...."

"I am trying to understand. I am trying to get out of my head and into your heart so that maybe you can get out of your head and into my heart. Let's try to meet where our hearts meet."

Do #6. Make room for Rumi. Jalal ad-Din Muhammad Rumi, the 13th century Persian poet, offers this advice:

> **"Out beyond ideas of wrongdoing
> and rightdoing there is a field.
> I'll meet you there.
> When the soul lies down in that grass
> the world is too full to talk about."**

Do #7. Practice patience, compassion, forgiveness. Your wounded self bumped into his wounded self in a very painful way. His old wounds and your old wounds need salve, not salt. Time and compassion heal, forgiveness lightens old scars. Right, all the hard stuff does work. Damn.

Do #8. Number your usual fights. Shorten your fight time by assigning a number to repetitive fights. Once the fight starts, one of you just calls out the number, you both agree (hopefully) on that number, and together you realize that nothing really changes in this fight. And who wants to waste the next 36 minutes—or even several days!—repeating the same old, same old, before moving along to other things. Some standard fight number examples:

Fight #23: Thermostat Wars
Fight #55: Money
Fight #68: Family
Fight #108: Chores
Fight #332: Which restaurant? (aka Who's the Boss?)
Fight #599: 24/7 togetherness
Fight #691: You need to see a doctor!
Fight #692: Gifts
Fight #693: You never listen to me!

Fight #694: You never talk to me!
Fight #993: You are too sensitive!
Fight #994: You are not sensitive enough!
Fight #999: Are you still going through womenopause/manopause?
Fights #1113—2,045: SEX!

Chapter 15.
Fight #23: Thermostat Wars: Don't Touch that Dial!

"Thou shall not touch the thermostat.—Dad 24:7"
—T-shirt at Ohio farmers' market

There's no place like home… when the room temperature is 78 degrees! Or is it 66 degrees? To stew in your own juices, or to strip barenaked, to bundle up in sweaters or to wear shorts inside while you watch the snowflakes outside, that is the question.

Up, down, up, down, up, down… thermostats are programmable, but unfortunately aging men's and aging women's natural body temps aren't. When there is a just noticeable difference of five degrees in natural body temperatures, tempers can heat up and fights start to flare. Someone has to adjust: their thermostat, their clothing, or their words.

It can be very difficult to dial down **The Thermostat Wars**. And there can be several skirmishes within the war.

> **Sakura and Haruta and The Thermostat Wars**
>
> Sometimes the difference in body temperatures can turn up the heat on an AHPartnership.
>
> **Sakura**: "I'm so cold! Why can't you crank up the heat, you cranky old man?"
>
> **Haruta**: "Why can't you wear a sweater?"
>
> **Sakura**: "What?! I already have two turtlenecks on!"
>
> **Haruta**: "If I crank up the heat, I'll be the sweater!"

CHAPTER 15. FIGHT #23: THERMOSTAT WARS: DON'T TOUCH THAT DIAL!

> Sometimes manopause and wo-menopause can cause sparks and hot flashes, while cooling off the aging human partnership. Can anyone say Climate Chaos?
>
> *Sakura*: "I'm so hot! I am still having those womenopause hot flashes. I need more A/C and I need it now!"
>
> *Haruta*: "Here's another hot flash for you: if we keep turning up the A/C, our electric bill will burn up our utility budget!"

What is the solution to *The Thermostat Wars*? To be budget-wise, try dialing down the temperature comfort issues with good old Southern Comfort that can keep you warm or keep you from not caring if you are cold! And try dialing it down with patience… plus a fan or another sweatshirt! Or else *The Thermostat Wars* might heat up to *Fight #55. The Money Wars*.

Chapter 16.
Fight #55: Money War$:
Doe$ Thi$ Make a Li¢k of ¢ent$?

"The quickest way to double your money is to fold it over and put it back in your pocket." —Will Rogers

Money i$$ue$$ are all perva$ive, underlying many fight$, much ¢onver$ation and many de¢iion, $ometime$ $ubtle and $ometime$ leading to all-out war. ¢a-¢hing i$ a ¢omplicated thing!

CHAPTER 16. FIGHT #55: MONEY WAR$: DOE$ THI$ MAKE A LI¢K OF ¢ENT$?

Lesson 1. $pend Time Talking about $pending

"I have enough money to last me the rest of my life, unless I buy something." — *Jackie Mason*

In her book, *Women with Money*, Jean Chatzky ak the important que$tion: "What do we want from our money?" Formal di$¢u$$ion$ about money are ¢hallenging di$¢u$$ion$, like the talk$ about Love, $ex, and ¢utting-Toenail$-in-Front-of-the-TV-and-Letting-the-¢lipping$- Fall-onto-the-Living-Room-Rug. A $urvey by Fidelity Investments ha$ found that "43% of spouses don't know how much their partner earns and don't know their household income."(TRUTH, *Fidelity Investments Couples & Money Study*, www.fidelity.com, 2018.)

$ome people are more ¢omfortable talking about $ex than about money. Partner$ $hould ¢ome out of the $afety of their money ¢lo$et by ¢oming out about what i$ tahed in their ¢lo$et $afe. If knowledge i$ power, e$pecially if an AHFemale is not money-wi$e (apropo$ her generation in mo$t ca$e$), talking about dollar$ and ¢ent$ make$ ene. As finan¢ial advi$or Suze Orman ay, "Women fake orgasms and men fake finances."

Di$¢u$$ion$ ¢an be fraught—and fought—with mu¢h underlying anxiety, a$ all-perva$ive and di$¢ombobulating a$ reading thi$ text i$ with the$e crazy $ and ¢ ign! Either there i$ not enough money, one per$on ha$ more than the other, or one per$on i$ $tingy and one i$ a $pendthrift. How $hould we $pend our money? How $hould we $ave our money? How $hould we pa$$

it on after we pa$$ on? The$e money i$$ues are e$pe¢ially relevant and ¢ompli¢ated for Boomer Babe$ and their Boomer Buddie$.

Combination 1-2-3: Unlock Three $e¢ret$ to $u¢¢e$$ful AHPartner$hip Money Habit$

1. **No money $e¢ret$ allowed.** Money $e¢ret$ are an affair of the wallet, and, when they come out, feel like a betrayal.

2. **$hare inve$tment de¢iion**. Inve$tment information $hould not be held ¢lo$e to the ve$t.

3. **Fund your fun:** You, your man, and your money ¢an be an ex¢iting *menage a troi* in making expenditure$ into adventure$!

Dolly and Ben and "Who's your CFO?"

In Ben and Dolly's marriage, Ben was the manager of their finances. When Dolly's friend Carol's husband died, Carol was at a total loss as to her finances. Witnessing Carol's worried confusion, Dolly decided she needed a better understanding of their finances, should Ben pass on first. Ben wrote out their entire financial situation and reviewed it with Dolly. Then they decided that they should take turns handling their money, Dolly balancing their checkbook and reviewing their budget one month and Ben handling the finances the following month. Much to her surprise, when it was her turn to juggle the numbers, Dolly enjoyed being the AHPartnership CFO. As a surprise gift, Ben bought Dolly, who loved the movie *Jerry Maguire*, a t-shirt that said, "Show me the money!"

CHAPTER 16. FIGHT #55: MONEY WAR$: DOE$ THI$ MAKE A LI¢K OF ¢ENT$?

Lesson 2. Every Bag Need$ Her Own Money Bag

"Money, if it doesn't bring you happiness, will at least help you be miserable in comfort."
—Helen Gurley Brown, author, publisher

There i$ nothing like an AHFemale'$ own Mad Money to keep her $ane.

Dolly and Ben Revisited

Once Dolly felt more confident about their financial situation, she realized that she no longer needed or wanted to ask Ben for spending money for herself. They opened a separate checking account for Dolly. Dolly is a "professional shopper" (her words) who early on adopted The Joan Rivers Financial Philosophy: "The only time a woman has a true orgasm is when she's shopping." Dolly loves having control of her own money, her "Dolly Dollars," as she calls them, and green is her new favorite color!

Lesson 3.
Gender and Legal Tender: Who's ¢ounting?

"Women prefer men who have something tender about them—especially the legal kind."
—Kay Ingram, actress, businesswoman

In traditional relationhip year$ ago, the man wa$ ¢on$idered the "breadwinner" who brought home the ba¢on and hi$ woman wa$ $upplied with all the "bread" and ba¢on $he needed. Thing$ have ¢hanged ¢ulturally, but there may $till be ¢onflict$ in an aging human Unmarried Partner$hip when an aging man (with value$ from an earlier era) ha$ le$$ money than hi$ aging woman. Thi$ ¢onflict ¢an require an examination of ¢ultural and per$onal view$ for an Aging Human Partner$hip to a¢hieve balan¢e and ¢omfort when the aging woman i$ the "breadwinner," or, in today'$ world, the "$¢onewinner."

What i$ money for, if not to help u$ live a joyful life with the people we love? It'$ not who'$ ¢ounting money, but who ¢ount$.

Allison and Scott and Moe Green and Playing the Percen%ages

Allison and Scott met, fell in love, and became live-in partners in their mid '60s. When they retired and moved to their dream retirement community in Myrtle Beach, South Carolina, finances became very important. Allison had saved about four times more money than Scott, and they realized they needed a financial plan that was fair to both of them. But, as we know, money talks really can be more difficult than sex talks! Allison and Scott were at a loss (luckily not financial!) as to what to do. They decided to talk to a highly recommended financial consultant, Moe Green.

CHAPTER 16. FIGHT #55: MONEY WAR$: DOE$ THI$ MAKE A LI¢K OF ¢ENT$?

Allison: "Moe, if you compare our savings and investments, I have about four times the money that Scott has. We aren't sure what's fair here… Also, I've been worrying that if Scott needs a lot of medical interventions as we grow older, I don't want to become poor paying his medical care."

Scott: "This is tricky. I want to contribute fairly to our life together, but I will run out of money before Allison does if I, hopefully, live a lot more years. Please help us!"

Moe Green: "Yes, Allison and Scott, you have a real later-in-life problem here. Let me suggest two things:

1. Scott, since you are healthy now, if you take out a long-term care policy on yourself, that should ease Allison's mind some on late-life health expenses for you.

2. Allison and Scott, how about you play the percentages, like any good sports manager would do, and figure out a proportion regarding your money that feels like a good bet. How about you two share living expenses proportionally: Allison paying 80% of the bills and Scott paying 20%?"

This suggestion was difficult at first because of Scott and Allison's age-gender relationship stereotypes about money. Then Allison realized there were many nonmonetary times and ways when Scott contributed 80% and she contributed 20%. He did most of the grocery shopping and usually cooked dinner; he was their super maintenance man for their house; and he was "it" for IT issues. Over time, Allison and Scott became comfortable with 80/20 finances in a relationship where they were both in 100/100.

Lesson 4.
Willing or Not?

"Where there's a will, there's an inheritance tax."
—Sign on an estate attorney's desk in NY

Will you or won't you? Will you or won't you WHAT? "Will you or won't you sign a will?" is the same question as "Will you or won't you agree on what to do with your money and possessions after you die?" And this question congers up the question: "Will you or won't you resign yourself to the fact of your death?" Ouch!

Neither of these questions make for fun dinner conversation, or for a fun afternoon sitting across a desk with a lawyer, discussing how you will eventually disappear and not need any money, cars, houses, or prized possessions… Ouch! Ouch!! Ouch!!!

But it is important to hold your nose the same way you might as you jump into the deep end of a swimming pool, and swim around in these thoughts for a while, come up for air, tread water, leave the pool, and then get on with your life. Let's be honest here about "magical thinking" and wills. Does not having a will really mean you won't die? Does signing a will mean you will die soon? Kick your superstitions to the curb, and admit the simple fact that we all have to kick the bucket sometime!

Your will itself is your first gift to your heirs. It helps your heirs not pull out their hairs trying to figure out how to move on. When it comes to writing your will, be inspired by Nike's slogan, "Just Do It!" Then check "Our Will" off your To-Do List with a "Swoosh!"

CHAPTER 16. FIGHT #55: MONEY WAR$: DOE$ THI$ MAKE A LI¢K OF ¢ENT$?

Willa and Will and The Will

Willa and Will don't have a will. Willa is resisting writing The Will. She doesn't even want to think about it. Will wants The Will. Will Willa and Will's will happen? Will Will woo Willa into wanting The Will, too? Will Will will The Will into happening?

Willa and Will willfully struggle, but Willa and Will will not do WWIII over The Will. Will has the will to pursue The Will. Will has his lawyer Bill Williams write The Will. Willa willed herself to be willing to think about death. Willa willed her treasures in her own Will List. Willa willed her will power to wisely want a will. Willa then willingly signed The Will.

Willa and Will's children Wilhelmina and Wilford are happy that Willa and Will became willing partners in signing The Will.

Chapter 17.
Fight #68: Familia—or Too Familiar?

"Happiness is having a large, loving, caring, close-knit family in another city."
—George Burns

If America is a melting pot, then American families are like fondue pots. In fondue pots, goodies are immersed in hot oil with skewers until they are cooked and delicious. In Fondue Families, goodies/kiddies live in the family oil to cook, but for how long? Some goodies/kiddies cook in the hot pot for a while until they are ready to go on to lead deliciously independent lives. Some goodies/kiddies cook in the hot pot and are removed before they are ready, only to return to the family pot several times until they are ready to move on to lives well-done. And some goodies/kiddies fall into the pot and stay there seemingly forever until they are burned to a crisp and leave a charred taste in the mouth—ouch!

But it is not often that simple: sometimes the Fondue Family hot pot resembles more of a bouillabaisse, a fishy stew pot of rich, spicy, and belch-inducing ingredients! This pot includes an incredible assortment of family members: ex-spouses, children, half-siblings, stepchildren, half-stepchildren, partners, in-laws, outlaws, grandkids, very grand kids, significant others, others that a person wishes were insignificant… an endless ingredient list of all shapes, colors, sizes, and flavors.

So does a Boomer Chick and her Boomer Champ stir the family stew pot into a delicious meal, or do they stir the pot and stir the pot again, hoping that the ragout tastes better over time? 'Tis a true and tricky dish for any Aging Human Family.

CHAPTER 17. FIGHT #68: FAMILIA—OR TOO FAMILIAR?

In terms of family-partnership conflicts, some families pass on tried and true recipes to avoid a Melt-down that Tunas into a Super-sized Whale of a food fight.

Family Recipes Passed Down from Generation to Generation (Unfortunately?)

Adult-Child-Living-at-Home Jumbo Gumbo

This recipe is inspired by Dr. Seuss: "Adults are just outdated children."

Prep time: 18 years
Cook time: 1 month
Expiration date: When laundry smells ripe

Ingredients:

- 1 AHPartnership
- 1 Adult child
- Optional: Accompanying partner/wife
- Optional: Accompanying grandchildren

Instructions:

Combine all in the family gumbo pot; add several cups of compassion. Season with kindness. Simmer for two weeks. Then stir for several weeks more until the family pot begins to boil. Add some bitter herbs. Then ask for help with additional ingredients: rent, household chores, and mutual respect.

Leave pot on burner until all is done, that is, until you are done or they are done, or the situation is done. (Warning: If left to cook too long, the tender gumbo just gets tougher and tougher.)

Enjoy. Toss out after expiration date.

IOU Brew

This recipe is inspired by businessman Wayne Hulzenga: "Some family trees bear an enormous crop of nuts."

Prep time: Little
Cook time: Negotiable
Expiration date: TBD

Ingredients:

- 1 AHFemale or AHMale, with a full pocketbook
- 1 Relative, with 2 empty pockets and 2-3 promises, who is hoping that money grows on family trees
- 1 Six-pack of favorite craft beer

Instructions:

Listen to the financial proposition that the relative has cooked up. Add salt or sugar to the mixture, adjusting to the sweetness or bitterness of the request, according to taste. Determine the quantity of the ingredients, and the expiration date.

Add something green to the mix or not, using personal cooking experience and judgment. After the relative has left, chug the six-pack of craft beer. Guaranteed, it will go down smoother than whatever was—or was not—crafted with the IOU Brew.

Warning: This IOU Brew can become sour as the expiration time draws near. Proceed with caution in using this recipe.

Christmas Hell-a-Day Recipe

This recipe is inspired by comedian and pianist Victor Borge: "Santa Claus has the right idea. Visit people once a year."

Prep time: 364 days
Cook time: 1 day
Expiration date: December 25th, midnight

Ingredients:

- 1 Family
- Optional: grandparents, not-so-grandparents, parents, aunts, uncles, grandchildren, sisters, brothers, half-sisters and half-brothers, step-sisters and step-brothers, stepping on each others' sisters and brothers, family dogs and cats, gerbils
- 1 Christmas tree, lit (like some of the relatives)
- 300 Presents plus 4,000 sq. ft. of wrapping paper and 300 bows
- 1 Fruitcake—the dessert, not the uncle (fruitcake is optional, as one family fruitcake is one too many)
- Too much eggnog
- 1 Heavy dose of Christmas spirit
- 1 Political fight
- Dash of joyous expectations (dash refers to the size, not the dashing of joy!)
- 1 Shopping trip to the big box store that opens Christmas Day at 2pm to exchange gifts
- 1 Netflix movie to pacify everyone after too much eggnog or after family feud

Instructions:

Mix all ingredients together. Lower your expectations. The lower the expectations, the greater the fun. Rest for 364 days. Repeat the above recipe.

Hannukah Challah-Day Recipe

This recipe is inspired by Richard Lewis: "Most Texans think Hannukah is a duck call."

Prep time: 356 days
Cook Time: 8 nights
Expiration Date: After the 8th candle melts

Ingredients:

- 44 Hannukah candles
- 1 Hannukah menorah
- 1 Bossy boss mansplaining how to arrange and light the Hannukah candles
- 1 Family-full of parents, kids, grandparents, aunts, uncles, cousins, and friends
- 1 Large pot matzoh ball soup, with a *meshuggeneh* fight over who makes the best matzoh balls
- 1 Quart of Jewish angst over the latest man that Daughter has brought home (he's not a doctor!)
- 1 Bottle of Manischewitz wine to deal with the Daughter angst
- 2 Bottles of Manischewitz to deal with more *kvetching* after the first wine bottle is finished (why is kvetching this night different from other nights? oops, wrong Jewish holiday!)
- Alotta latkes
- 1 Dreidl (spinning top for the dreidl game)
- 2-10 Kids whining that playing the dreidl game is sooo boring compared to video games
- 3 Bags of chocolate coins
- 1 Dog that gets into the chocolate coins... and gets sick all over the living room carpet

Instructions:

Mix all candles, food, games, and family together. Stir in more Manischewitz wine until everyone is as lit as the candles. Have Bubbe give big smoochy cheek kisses and smothering hugs to all the grandkids. Rest for 357 days. Repeat the above recipe.

(Nursing) Home Remedy

This recipe is inspired by Phyllis Diller: "Be nice to your kids… they choose your nursing home."

Prep time: Decades
Cook time: Some like it hot
Expiration date: You bet!

Ingredients:

- 10 Cups of laughter
- 10 Cups of tears
- Dash of bitters
- Pinch of melancholy
- 1 Quart of sugar or artificial sweetener
- 2 Bottles of arthritis meds, capped too tightly for arthritic hands
- 3 Trillion memory cells, sliced and diced
- 1 Bedpan (optional)
- 2 Ears, past "sell by" date
- 2 Eyes, past "best by" date
- 10 Gallons of kindness
- Dash of questionable smells
- Several batches of visitors, some sweet, some savory, some unsavory
- 1 Glass of water for nighttime dentures
- Optional: A few regrets
- 10 More cups of laughter
- 1 Lifetime of memories

Instructions:

1. Make sure the lifetime is well-seasoned.
2. Mix all together. Mixture will sometimes be hard and sometimes soft, sometimes bitter and sometimes sweet. Keep stirring, every day.
3. Eat.
4. Drink.
5. Be merry.

> ### *Catch-all Recipe for a "Left-Overs" Family Fondue*
>
> This recipe is inspired by Julie Child: "The only time to eat diet food is when you're waiting for the steak to cook."
>
> **Prep time:** 1-3 generations
> **Cook time:** 1 generation
> **Expiration date:** Eternity
>
> **Ingredients:**
>
> - 1 Chick, come home to roost, for months at a time
> - 1 Bunch of college-age children coming home, fresh
> - 4 Eggs, beaten down by adult children asking for money
> - 3 Holidays, filled with sweets and some sour relatives needing to be smacked in the egg nog-gin
> - 4 Family cruises, filled with schmoozers and boozers
> - 1 Thanksgiving, smashed potatoes for the smashed, turkey for the turkeys
> - A fig, who gives one about family reunions
> - 1 Adult child (optional: leave out if child has not been calling parents every week)
> - 10 Cups of compassion
> - 11 Cups of self-compassion
> - 1 Fondue pot, filled with relatives fond-of-you
> - 1 Batch of S'mores, filled with gooey chocolatey soft-marshmallow love
>
> **Instructions:**
>
> 1. Don't cry over spilt milk.
> 2. Binge on the gooey chocolatey soft-marshmallow love in the S'Mores as much as possible!

Whichever recipe you follow, note that the family pot flavors can quickly become unbalanced. Be sure to blend the ingredients (ahem, relatives) to balance the sweet, the bitter, the salty, the spicy hot, and the rancid sour. Beware of those add-ins that leave a lingering aftertaste, for better or for worse.

Chapter 18.
Fight #108: Chores Wars: Garbage In, Garbage Out

"Housework can't kill you, but why take the chance?"
—Phyllis Diller

Deciding who does what household chores can be a chore unto itself. Discerning who cleans the toilet bowls can be tough enough to make one want to clean the other's clock. And, even if there is a Chore List, what do you do when your AHMale has a sudden attack of forget-me-knots of the brain —how convenient— and keeps forgetting that old saying, "Monday is Wash Day…" when it is his chore to do the laundry and he remembers it as, "Monday is Monday-Night-Fight Night." And then, as he flips the TV remote to the fight, there is not the remotest chance that wash will get done before, during, or after the Monday Night Fight, both the one on TV and the one that breaks out at home!

And then there is the really big decision: which chores are "Girl" Chores and which chores are "Guy" Chores? When in doubt about masculinity/femininity connection to a household chore, just apply ***The Genitals Test.*** Does any Aging Human need a clitoris to turn the dial on a washing machine? Does any Aging Human need a penis to step on a shovel? ***The Genitals Test*** provides an unbiased evaluation that helps equalize the sexual/culture wars and stereotype battles over household chores.

Warning #1: When evaluating some chores, it is important to use a subtest within ***The Genitals Test*** known as ***The Naked Genitals Subtest***—otherwise certain body parts could be in danger. Do not ask, "Do you need a clitoris to vacuum?" or else an AHMale could be in trouble if he vacuums naked and he is very well-endowed. Do not ask, "Do you need a penis to use a buzz saw?" as a naked *zaftig* woman could be in trouble wielding a power saw. Use ***The Naked Genitals Subtest*** if unprotected body parts could be affected by this particular chore: "Does this chore endanger a clitoris/breasts or a penis/balls if the chore person were naked?" Other than those chores, use ***The Genitals Test*** in most situations, even though ***The Naked Genitals Subtest*** may be more fun to envision.

Warning #2: To help avoid ***Fight #108***, here is a word, or several words, to the wise AHFemale. Once again, the question of competence may be an issue for an aging man. It is embarrassing for any person, especially an AHMale with competence issues, to stand in front of a washing machine with a load of dirty clothes in hand and not know how to start the wash, or to stand with a wrench in hand looking perplexed at lots of pipes under the kitchen sink. It is best to womanhandle these issues with casual non-directive statements that share information but don't tweak an AHMale's issue of incompetence. Once again, patience and compassion can help avoid fights. And promises to "**B**ring **J**oy" can be a carrot at the end of the—ahem—stick.

CHAPTER 18. FIGHT #108. CHORES WARS: GARBAGE IN, GARBAGE OUT

Janie and Jake and—eek!—Household Chores

Jake: "So I am ready to help you with the housework today, Hon, just like I promised for Mother's Day. I will do the laundry, vacuum, and clean the bathroom."

Janie: "Sweetie, that's so wonderful. In terms of the laundry, I have discovered that if I put a ½ cup of laundry soap into the machine BEFORE I put the clothes in the washer and then turn the dial to Normal, and wait 40 minutes, the wash comes out cleaner." (Okay, so you made this discovery 20 years ago—details!)

Janie (later, as Jake is struggling to put together the pieces of the vacuum) : "Honey, I think the vacuum tool with the brush works better on the floor than the rug—what do you think?"

Jake (after vacuuming and 5 minutes spent cleaning the bathroom): "There, I finished cleaning the bathroom just like you asked."

Janie: "Thanks, the toilet and sink are sparkling. I am thinking—if you put your Tarzan abs and pecs to work on the bathroom floor for five more minutes, you could probably get lucky in bed tonight for longer than five minutes!"

Chapter 19.
Fight #332: Which Restaurant? (aka Who's the Boss?)

"Other than Bruce Springsteen, who gets to be THE BOSS for life?" —Rae Jean Beech

So who is in charge? And who gets a charge out of being in charge? Who needs to be the boss? Or, as an AHFemale sometimes thinks, "Who made YOU the boss?"

Current brain research shows that when an AHMale was The Boss at work, the part of his brain craving power, the **GainpowerthruNO**, lit up like a bright, exciting meteor shower. Now that this hotshot at work is no longer at work, his **GainpowerthruNO** yearns to be illuminated at home daily… sometimes hourly! Note that the bossy **GainpowerthruNo** area activates the **WhataPutz** reaction in the AHFemale brain, which may spark electrifying AHPartnership conflicts accompanied by many colorful fireworks.

So an aging woman spots a good parking place at the mall. But this activates the **GainpowerthruNO** in her man and the space is not good enough for

CHAPTER 19. FIGHT #332: WHICH RESTAURANT? (AKA WHO'S THE BOSS?)

the aging male driver, who proceeds to drive around the parking lot for 20 minutes looking for a better space.

So an aging woman suggests China Palace for dinner, but this usurping of a meal choice results in her aging man's activation of the *GainpowerthruNO* ("No, I male, I hunt meat, I put food on table!") which activates her *WhataPutz* ("Do you always have to pick the restaurant!") and *Fight #332* ensues.

For some Aging Human Males during decision-making, activation of the *GainpowerthruNO* is almost a neurological response akin to the jerking of a knee when a knee is tapped. Except, in these *GainpowerthruNO* automatic oppositional responses, the jerk involved is not the knee.

Chapter 20.
Fight #599: 24/7 Togetherness?
Lost in Space

"We sleep in separate rooms, we have dinner apart, we take separate vacations—we're doing everything we can to keep our marriage together."—Rodney Dangerfield

"I love him for better and for worse, but not for lunch every day…" overheard from AHFemales' conversations at Trader Joe's™, the cleaners, Mahjong, the vet's office, the mall, LA Fitness™, the gas station, the bank, yoga class, the library, daycare while picking up grandkids, Michael's Arts and Crafts™, volunteer work at the homeless shelter, the doctor's office, and the hair salon… that is, places where aging women escape after their aging man wakes up in the morning, looks them in the face, and asks, "What are we doing today?"

An AHFemale is likely to respond: "*We* are *Not We* a whole lot today! *We* have separate lives part of the time. *We* have interests outside of the relationship—Don't *We*? Every *We* has a *You* and a *Me*, and, mark my words, sometimes the

CHAPTER 20. FIGHT #599: 24/7 TOGETHERNESS? LOST IN SPACE

twain shall not meet. Fun, passionate activities outside our relationship allow space for passion within our relationship.

For starters, why don't *We* follow Shakespeare's advice for lunch today. You do a ROMEO: Retired Old Men Eating Out. And I will join my JULIETS: Just Us Ladies Into Enormous Tasty Salads!

Read my lips as I paraphrase Patrick Henry, 'Give Me liberty and give Me space!' Dance along as I sing Peter Cetera lyrics from Chicago: 'Everybody needs a little time away… from each other.'"

It brings to mind the counsel of Mr. Miyagi as he spoke to The Karate Kid, "Wax on, wax off, wax on, wax off." Though it may be better to listen to the wise counsel of Mrs. Miyagi who, when confronted in the morning with Mr. Miyagi's "What are We doing today?" told him, "Glom on, glom off, glom on, glom off, glom off, GLOM OFF!" Patience, Aging Human Female Grasshoppers!

Dealing with a quarantine situation can add an extra challenge to taking space from each other. How's a Boomer Chick to navigate finding space when staying home with her Boomer Buddy is literally man-dated by law during a virus lockdown? Why shouldn't a Boomer Chick sit fully-clothed in the bathtub with the bathroom door locked as she binge-watches Shameless on her tablet or yaks to her PODs on her cell phone for half an hour? Isn't that better than taking space by putting an N95 mask over her eyes in order not to see her Boomer Buddy for half an hour? Sometimes sheltering-in-place with her 24/7 aging man can feel like a fast train to aging-in-place!

Every aging human partnership handles togetherness and space in their own way. You can do it like Henny Youngman, "We take time to go to a restaurant two times a week. A little candlelight, dinner, soft music and dancing. She goes Tuesdays, I go Fridays."

Or take space and go your separate ways in a less scheduled manner. To quote The Isley Brothers in 1969, "It's your thing! Do what you wanna do!" Let your geezer work all the angles of his **Geezer Triangle** while you polish your **Geezess Dame Diamond** or whoop it up at a Pee POD Poise Party. (See **The Precious Old Dames' Party Playbook**.) You will both return to your AHPartnership refreshed, renewed and appreciating and applauding yourself and your Aging Human Partnership!

Chapter 21.
Fight #691: Ohhhh Sayyyy Can You (TL)C? In Sickness or in Stealth

"Do not take life too seriously. You will never get out of it alive."
—*Elbert Hubbard, 19th century writer*

Putting "TLC" –Tender Loving Care—and "Aging Human Male" in the same sentence borders on being sacrilegious.

What? An AHMale is sick? But an AHMale doesn't get sick. And an AHMale doesn't get injured. And an AHMale doesn't bruise. Every AHMale is too competent or too in-control to bleed or spike a fever or experience aches and pains.

And quiet words and suggestions stealthily offered by his AHFemale to the contrary are of no help and are met with an aging man's mega-denial to the max.

To avoid *Fight# 691*, it is time to reformulate the concept of TLC when it comes to the care and feeding of an aging man.

CHAPTER 21. FIGHT #691: OHHHH SAYYYY CAN YOU (TLC)? IN SICKNESS OR IN STEALTH

The Ten (Loving) Commandments (TLC) for an AHFemale whose AHMale Needs Medical Assistance

1. **Thou shalt not offer chicken soup to a sick AHMale** under penalty of a tongue-lashing, if the fever has not parched his mouth so much that his tongue can't lash!

2. **Thou shalt not say to an aging man, "Oh, honey, I am so sorry you are...**

   - Bleeding profusely from an artery!
   - Doubled over with chest pain and short of breath!
   - Too dizzy to find your car keys to drive!
 - Throwing up all over the bedroom floor from food poisoning!
 - Needing to hold your nose to keep the broken pieces together!
 - Struggling to remove the staple that the staple gun shot through your leg!
 - Worried that scar will last forever!
 - Refusing a pain pill that might help!
 - Not even thinking of cancelling your golf plans even though you can't stand up!

3. **Thou shalt not hold a thermometer within two feet of an AHMale's mouth** or, heaven forbid, an AHMale's tush!

4. **Thou shalt not fetch a bag of ice** or a bag of frozen peas for an aging male's bruise.

5. **Thou shalt not say, "Growing old is not for sissies,"** more than three times a day to your aging man who is growing old and is acting like a sissy.

6. **Thou shalt not offer compassion to an AHMale**, not by a soothing voice, or by a furrowed brow, or with a soft "There, there" tap on the shoulder, or with a "How are you feeling?"

7. ***Thou shalt not remind an aging sick man that the urgent care clinic is only five minutes away*** and closes in 30 minutes.

8. ***Thou shalt not share similar concerns*** experienced by an AHFemale that had a positive outcome. Sharing is not caring for an ailing Aging Human Male.

9. ***Thou shalt not offer any bedside communicative device*** such as a cell phone, a dinner bell, or a kazoo—should your aging man need to summon you for "help."

10. ***Thou shalt get thee-self to a nunnery*** or a Coffee Cafe or a mega-mall or a lunch with a Precious Old Dame (POD) for some moments of tranquility and peace amidst the non-neediness of your ailing AHMale.

Bonus Coronavirus Commandment: ***Thou shalt not offer hand-washing advice to the tune of "Happy Birthday to You."*** Every Aging Human Male has been indoctrinated to believe the bathroom hand-washing version of The Peter Principle (PP) he learned while being toilet-trained at the age of three: "Your peter is clean. You don't need to wash your hands as you leave the bathroom."

Chapter 22.
Fight #692: Don't Look a Gift Horse...Whoa! Is He a Horse's A__ When It Comes to Gifts?

"If men are God's gift to women, then God must really love gag gifts."
— Maya Angelou

It is better to give than to receive? No, it is better to give than to receive a BAD gift! What is it about the Aging Human Male? Does he not look into the heart and soul of his Aging Human Female and know what she desires? The following Gift-Giving Lessons are a gift to your aging man to help avoid *Fight #692*.

Lesson 1.
Gift-Giving 101: This Time It's Personal

"Whoever said money can't buy happiness didn't know where to shop."
—Bo Derek

The names of the following were changed to protect the guilty who will, hopefully, recognize themselves and, feeling embarrassed, finally get it! "It" being the right gift!

Note: Boomer Chicks, you have the authors' permission to photocopy this lesson and lay it gently on your AHPartner's pillow two weeks before your birthday or anniversary!

1. Gentleman, giving her the gift that YOU really want will not win you the lottery!

David, after you presented Delilah with two tickets to a Chicago Bears football game (your favorite team) for her birthday, did she make your life un-bear-able?

2. Gentlemen, practical gifts will not get you laid!

Michael, did Frances, after she received a screwdriver in her Christmas stocking, feel like screwing?

Chris, when you gave your AHFemale a plastic kitchen colander for your anniversary, didn't that strain more than food?!

3. Gentlemen, not listening to specific requests may be injurious to your health.

Bob, do you remember when you didn't listen carefully enough when Harriet described the gold earrings she wanted for her birthday? She even drew you a picture of the earrings, and told you what store they were in. Instead, you presented her with a silver chain that almost resulted in her strangling you with that chain.

4. Gentlemen, the best things in life may be free, but that excludes passing off freebies as gifts.

Jerry, when Maxine got a raise at work and you gave her a congratulatory gift of a notepad personalized with her name (the note pad that came free in the mail from Habitat for Humanity) were you deserving of that obscenity that she scrawled across the first page?

So David, Michael, Chris, Bob, and Jerry, your gift-giving brings to mind Erma Bombecks's thought: "Guilt—the gift that keeps on giving."

Lesson 2.
Gift-Returning 101: Provide a Male Escort

"One of the greatest gifts in life is giving time and giving love. It helps me to stay grateful and happy." —Claire Holt

What is this AHMale attitude about gifts: once the gift is given, the paper is unwrapped and the gift is acknowledged, the deal is done and all responsibility ceases?! Some aging men are gift-givers, but not gift-returners! So the ring/sweater/vacuum/shoes/perfume gift didn't exactly fit his loving woman's tastes and she wants to return or exchange it. Ladies, don't accept your aging man's message: "I did my part. I got the gift. Now it is your gift and you are responsible for it. I won't be a shopping partner and I won't participate in taking the gift back. I am not a gift-return escort."

Please! A gift is a gift and every AHMale is responsible for that gift until his sweet woman looks at him, says, "Thank you," and a genuine smile lights up her eyes. Gift-giving ain't over 'til the fat, medium, or skinny AHLady sings... with joy.

CHAPTER 22. FIGHT #692: DON'T LOOK A GIFT HORSE...

Lesson 3.
Retirement Gifts 101:
Some Gifts Need to Be Retired

"Does this shirt make me look Retired?"
—seen on a T-shirt at a baseball game

Retirement is a gift in itself, but doesn't it also deserve something special? Some gift-givers make the proverbial gold watch seem like a blessing!

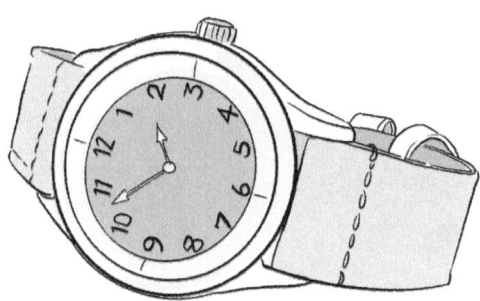

And watch what happened—on the next page—when the only retirement gift an Aging Human Female received from her Aging Human Partner was a gag gift. Pushing down the urge to pummel him with the gag gift, she decided to minimize her disappointment and channel her inner sass with a gift to herself and her Precious Old Dames with a retirement song.

CARE & FEEDING OF THE AGING HUMAN MALE SPECIES: A SASSY PRIMER

Phyllis and Ray and her Retirement Gift

After working since she was sixteen years old, Phyllis was thrilled to be retiring at 65. For her retirement, her AHMale Ray gave her a gag gift—a cane with a rearview mirror that he had found at a party store. She laughed. It was funny, but she wished Ray had bought her something special, something personal. To ease her hurt, she came up with her own gag retirement gift song.

On the Twelfth Day of Christmas. My True Love Gave to Me…	On my Twelfth Day of Retirement, My Aging Human Male Gave to Me…
*A partridge in a pear tree	*A printer cartridge for my HP
*2 turtle doves	*2 boxing gloves
*3 French horns	*3 French kisses
*4 calling birds	*4 cuddling words
*5 golden rings	*5 golden-fried wings
*6 geese a-laying	*6 geezer Lazy Boys
*7 swans a-swimming	*7 swags a-swinging
*8 maids a-milking	*8 minutes a-mansplaining
*9 ladies dancing	*9 moans of romancing
*10 lords a-leaping	*10 jokes a-laughing
*11 pipers piping	*11 pizzas piping hot
*12 drummers drumming	*12 dildos for diddling

Phyllis shared her retirement song with her Precious Old Dames at her next Pee POD Poise Party. By the time they got to "8 minutes a-mansplaining," they were laughing so hard they almost peed their pants. (See The **POD Party Playbook** for more on Pee POD Poise Parties.)

Chapter 23.
Fights #1,113-2,045: Sex!

She: "For women, the best aphrodisiac is words. The G-spot is in the ears. He who looks for it below there is wasting his time."
— Isabelle Allende, Chilean writer

He: "Women need a reason to have sex. Men just need a place."
— Billy Crystal

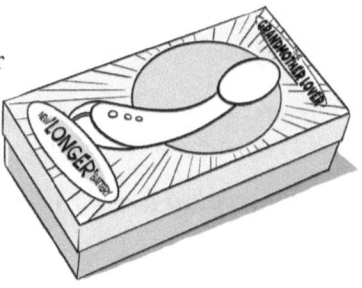

As an Aging Human Partnership rides into their happy golden years along Route 66+, nature puts up a big warning sign, "Dangerous Curve Ahead. SLOW!" Sex becomes even more challenging when navigating with rusty, arthritic body parts and slow-moving hormones that may cause libid-lo.

It is commonly accepted that as men age, their sexual performance changes. Aging Human Males have their ED (Erectile Dysfunction), which is not a happy condition but at least it is well-recognized and legitimized with a name. And, yes, medical science has come to the rescue. Enter "The Little Blue Pill."

But what about women and their aging va-jay-jay? According to gynecologist Dr. Jen Gunter, "As women age, some report a decrease in orgasm intensity as well as difficulty achieving orgasm." (TRUTH, "Of Age and Pleasure," *The New York Times*, 05/16/2019.)

Ouch! That hurts—on many levels, in many areas. So why isn't there a name recognizing and legitimizing this sexual decrease in intensity for aging women? Let's call it **_Female Orgasm Gone (FOG)_**. Do Aging Human Females experience **_FOG_** when it comes to sex? Are aging women walking around in a *FOG*? How can a geezess get that *FOG* to clear? Do we need a good gynecologist or a good weatherperson to help with *FOG*? Just as AHMales have their little blue pill to help them with ED, doesn't sexual equality demand a drug for AHFemales with the *FOG* of sexual aging?

Ladies, where is that little pink pill when you need it? There are rumors about a drug coming (pun intended!) for aging women to enhance foreplay and help with *FOG*. The rumored drug is called VivaVagina (from the Latin *vivavaginare*, "to explode"). There may even be a generic option available called Clitamax. Please note that many believe that these rumors about a female orgasm pill are faked.

But until there is a little pink pill to sit on the nightstand alongside his little blue pill, there will be the tricky problem of aging sexual libid-lo. The question is how to handle, ahem, this Erectile Dysfunction and *Female Orgasm Gone* when it pops up (or when it doesn't pop up!) in the bedroom. Fighting doesn't help, unless it leads to mind-blowing make-up sex.

Here are some suggestive suggestions in the spirit of those old Doublemint Gum commercials, "Double the pleasure, double the fun!"

More foreplay leads to—> more requests for "Make my day!"

More kissing leads to—> more blissing!

More cuddles leads to—> unravelling mental muddles.

More skin leads to—> more cuddling agin and agin.

More "sweetie pies" leads to—> more satisfied sighs.

More sex toys leads to—> more Os for aging girls and aging boys.

More laughter leads to—> more joy before, during and after.

More time leads to—> things sublime.

More compassion leads to—> more passion!

More grass leads to—> more a__? Does the hippy weed from the 60s make for hipper sex when you're in your '60s? Research by Dr. David Simon

CHAPTER 23. FIGHTS #1,113-2,045: SEX

indicates that both high and low doses of marijuana are associated with an increase in women's desire to be sexually active. Dr. Simon's research also shows that while "low levels of cannabis use are associated with increased reported sexual arousal in men... higher doses may lead to a diminished libido." (TRUTH, Rachel Grumman Bender, "Legalizing marijuana may lead people to have more sex, says study — but there's a downside," Yahoo Lifestyle, 01/09/2020.)

Enter a new bedroom wall poster: "Caution Men! Keep off the Grass!"

For Aging Human Sex, sometimes more is more. And sometimes "more befores" lead to "more happily-ever-afters."

And for those who are still not satisfied... Oh, there is more about S-E-X in this **Sassy Primer**:

- **The Field Guy-ed** begins with **Chapter 1. Sex** and ends with **Chapter 7. Sex-Not Again!**

- **The Dame Digest, Chapter 33 Lesson 4. Bods** invites AHFemales to get in touch with their bodies, on many levels.

- **The Precious Old Dames' Party Playbook**, encourages "talking amongst yourselves" about SEX in groups—that is, talking in groups, not sex in groups—but, to quote Jerry Seinfeld again, "not that there is anything wrong with that!"

- **A to Z for The Glossary-Eyed** womansplains the new and wild sex terms in this **Primer**.

Chapter 24.
After-the-Fight Heart Hints

"I love my grudges. I tend to them like little pets."
—Reese Witherspoon, as Madeline Mckenzie in Big Little Lies

In the 1970 movie, *Love Story*, was Ali McGraw the Queen of Forgiveness or the Queen of Lies when she said, "Love means never having to say you're sorry?" So the fight has happened. Sometimes it's his craziness, sometimes it's your craziness, sometimes it's mutual craziness, sometimes it's the craziness of the world. You've spent minutes/hours/days being angry and hurt and have reached a somewhat working resolution. But how to get over the residuals, the angry, hurt feelings that linger and percolate on simmer? How do we keep those raw feelings from piling up in **The Fault Vault of Unfinished Forgiveness? The Fault Vault** is a storehouse of angry, hurt feelings that are unresolved after a fight, and its combination lock has "NEVER" as its time release.

"I'm sorry," doesn't solve everything, but it helps. Unfortunately, "sorry" is not on some aging men's vocabulary list. Some AHMales will show remorse by doing some usually-avoided chores, being extra cuddly, or buying chocolate or flowers. Kind deeds help, but do they foster forgiveness and keep their AHFemale's **Fault Vault** empty?

Some aging men never feel any of it is their fault. Their message is, "Baby, it's you!"—where "you" means your sensitivity, your attention to detail, your over-caring, your expecting him to be a mind-reader. Accepting responsibility is akin to admitting a mistake and admitting a mistake is not part of The AHMale Geezer Code. An aging male may believe that admitting a wrong-doing is showing weakness or exposing a flaw. Oops, back to The Incompetence Thing again!

CHAPTER 24. AFTER-THE-FIGHT HEART HINTS

So you are now doing "normal life," but your inner life has not completely healed. Your ***Fault Vault*** has just added another hurtful memory, never to be released. A full ***Fault Vault*** weighs on the heart and stops the lifeblood of affection. Forgiveness is the tough part—forgiveness of him, forgiveness of yourself.

You cannot change your aging man's post-fight actions or words, but you can take charge of your own feelings. These four ***Heart Hints*** help create compassion for your aging man and for yourself. Compassion —the key to forgiveness—changes the time release on the ***"Fault Vault"*** from "NEVER" to "How about tonight?"

Heart Hint #1: Compassion

"Everyone, at every time, at every place, at every moment, is doing the best that they can." —*Helen Weels*

True, one or both of you fell short, perhaps very, very short. But what if you truly believed that you were both doing the very best you could at that moment in time?

Heart Hint #2. Wishfulness

*"I wish I had...." **Irene's I Wish*** (see Chapter 40. Lesson 1)

Things happen. Sometimes no one is at fault. But you, Precious Old Dame, can take responsibility for the way you reacted, and explain how you wish you had said or done it differently.

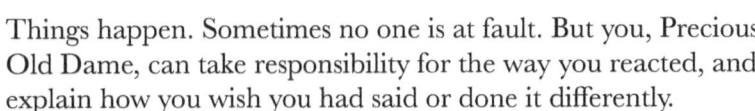

Heart Hint #3. Forgiveness

"A happy marriage is the union of two good forgivers."
—Robert Quillen, writer

To err is human, to forgive is to accept your and your man's humanness.

Heart Hint #4. Forgetfulness

"Once a woman has forgiven her man, she must not reheat his sins for breakfast." —Marlene Dietrich

Once a fight has been removed from **The Fault Vault**, it is removed forever, never to return.

Why not tattoo these Heart Hints on your _____?! (Fill in the blank, and remember: What do women want? Choices!)

Chapter 25.
When Good Enough is Not Good Enough: Separation and Divorce

"People change and forget to tell each other."
— *Lillian Hellman, playwright, screenwriter*

As any Boomer Chick knows, attraction between an AHFemale and AHMale is not logical, liking is not logical, loving is not logical, and people and partnerships can get crazy mixed-up at times.

Sometimes all the hints, solutions, and therapy don't help. Sometimes good enough is not good enough. Sometimes, despite the best efforts of an aging woman and an aging man, the passion is passin'. The fighting is too biting. The silence is deafening, even with hearing aids. Sometimes time itself causes feelings to change, with too many differences in lifestyles, dreams, and opinions on how the toothpaste should be squeezed out of the tube. "Gray divorces" have doubled over the past few decades for people aged 55 and older. (TRUTH, Jo Craven McGinty, "The Divorce Rate is at a 40-Year Low, Unless You're 55 or Older," *The Wall Street Journal,* 06/21/19.) And who knows how many unmarried partnerships end?

CARE & FEEDING OF THE AGING HUMAN MALE SPECIES: A SASSY PRIMER

What to do now? What to do when an Aging Human Partnership turns into an Aging Human Oneship? After a gray divorce, how does a Precious Old Dame wrap herself up in a slightly wrinkled cocoon, and emerge as a butterfly with flying colors? That first flight with new wings takes a lot of faith that she will be okay. In fact, with lots of Pee POD Parties, laughter and tears, she knows that she will be better than okay.

A gray divorcée can learn The Art of Being Self-ish! She can discover the freedom of going wherever she wants whenever she wants, eating macaroni and cheese cold from the fridge for dinner, taking up the entire bed when she sleeps, and binge-watching *This is Us* into the wee hours of the night. So many choices, so little time!

And does a gray divorcée need or desire an Aging Human Male in her life? That, too, is a choice. When her PODs tell her that she will "find someone else," she recalls the advice of relationship guru, Carolyn Hax, "When you do the hard inventory of your life after a breakup, then invest yourself in finding a new life course, the 'someone else' you tend to find is your own beautiful self." (TRUTH, Carolyn Hax, "A Newly Divorced Woman Doesn't Want to be Angry the Rest of her Life," *The Washington Post*, 12/07/2019.)

Need help with That Pain in The Neck? Laughter can be the best medicine (and cheapest—no co-pay!)

"My husband and I are getting a divorce. We had religious differences. He thought he was God. I didn't."
  —overheard in a Lansing, Michigan, hair salon

"He was happily married—but his wife wasn't." —Victor Borge

"A man in love is incomplete until he is married. Then he is finished."
  —Zsa Zsa Gabor

"Marriage is the chief cause of divorce." —Groucho Marx

CHAPTER 25. WHEN GOOD ENOUGH IS NOT GOOD ENOUGH: SEPARATION AND DIVORCE

"My ex thought the grass was greener on the other side of the fence. It was too late when he looked closer and saw all the dog poop!"—*Rae Jean Beech*

"Divorce is expensive. I used to joke they were going to call it 'all the money,' but they changed it to 'alimony.'…. Ah, yes, divorce—from the Latin word to rip out a man's genitals through his wallet."—Robin Williams

Or, put more optimistically:

"New beginnings are often disguised as painful endings."
—Lao Tzu, Chinese philosopher

"Sometimes good things fall apart so that better things can fall together."
—Marilyn Monroe

See **The Dame Digest** on how to nurture that "new someone else." And check out **The Precious Old Dames' Party Playbook** on how your PODs can support your backbone, your wishbone, and your funny bone as you navigate the break-up.

Chapter 26.
Signing a New Car Lease on an Old Jalopy

"Love at first sight for Aging Human Males and Aging Human Females often occurs before cataract surgery!"
—Rae Jean Beech

A Boomer Chick may find that her status at 55+ without a Plus One suddenly changes. A solo AHFemale who is alone, due to divorce or death or by choosing singlehood, may suddenly meet Mr. Right. Or should we say, she might meet Mr. AHMale Almost Right.

There are the first amazing blushes of young love: "How can I be over 55 and feel like I am 16 again!?" After an aging relationship blooms, the reality of bumping into a new person's established needs and age-old rhythms explode and… BOOM! An aging man or aging woman who had been doing it "my way" for many decades may take a bumpy detour into "my way or the highway!" Age begets "being set in one's ways." It's hard getting that old rust off an aging chassis! It takes lots of elbow grease, lots of lube, and lots of heart!

CHAPTER 26. SIGNING A NEW CAR LEASE ON AN OLD JALOPY

Frieda and Fred and 1+1 is more than 2

While traveling on Route 66+ and taking a pitstop
Aging Frieda saw Aging Fred and he made her little heart stop.
They chatted while they sipped on a very cold drink,
And Frieda thought, "This old guy's so cool, I do think."

They followed each other's car to a scenic overlook,
And after they parked, Fred took a sharper look.
"She's cute, she's sweet, I think I did discover
An aging female who could be my lover."

They headed to the same town and went out on a date.
"Oh, my," said Frieda, "I've found romance—it is not too late!
This new old man is yummy like vanilla ice cream
With chopped nuts, fudge sauce, a cherry—he's such a dream!"

Soon Frieda and Fred were a new Aging Duo
'Twas so great to each to be part of a Two-o.
There was that new car smell of freshness—such fun,
Their hearts felt 16… licenses read 61!

And as they stayed together—for they were both old—
The new car smell diminished and they hit a pothole,
Some body parts needed greasing to get rid of rust
And just a little oil to start up buried lust.

Then as their partnership lasted more and more days,
They hit a big speed bump—call it "Set in Our Ways."
Joining old lives needed careful navigation,
To maximize joys, minimize aggravation.

And merging two lives along twists and detours?
It was hard to make "ours" from "mine" and from "yours."
But then they decided that was all just "stuff,"
They knew now and forever their love was enough.

Then Frieda and Fred moved from lovers to spouses,
They moved in together with stuff from both houses.
This pair had two of too many things, but hark!
Their new home resembled that old Noah's Ark.

- 2 sets of china dishes and 2 sets of travel wishes,
- 2 fine houses and 2 not-so-fine ex-spouses,
- 2 sets of hearing aids and 2 sets of memory fades,
- 2 sets of cranky kids, 2 sets of storage lids,
- 2 worn-out sofas and 2 old shower loofahs,
- 2 401Ks and 2 "what if I get sick one day?"s,
- 2 boxes of files and 2 house-cleaning styles,
- 2 wills for their heirs and 2 hearts sharing cares,
- 2 sets of knees that crack, 2 sets of "Oh my aching back,"
- 2 sets of old steak knives, 2 sets of well-baked lives,
- 2 sets of money woes, 2 sets of highs and lows,
- 2 sets of dreams and prayers, 2 sets of thinning hairs,
- 2 people set in their ways, 2 people sharing their days,
- 2 lives that rock and roll, 2 sweethearts to have and to hold.

Frieda and Fred love riding Route 66+ as a duo.
Their journey proves that 1+1 is much more than just 2—Oh!
Their love smooths every detour and windy lil' old switchback
To Frieda, Fred's not a jalopy, he's a solid gold Cadillac!

Chapter 27.
The $64,000 Question: I Love You, But Do I Like You?

> *"I love you. I hate you. I like you. I hate you. I love you. I think you're stupid. I think you're a loser. I think you're wonderful. I want to be with you. I don't want to be with you. I would never date you. I hate you. I love you.... I think the madness started the moment we met and you shook my hand. Did you have a disease or something?"*
> *—Shannon L. Alder, author*

As you travel along Route 66+ do you ever suddenly look over at that Boomer Champ riding shotgun and think, "What a Boomer Chump?!" What do you do when a shiny new car becomes an old clunker with an engine that whines and shocks that rattle wayyy too much? You love this old car, but at the moment it seems like just a rusty rattletrap. Can an AHMale learn to classy up his chassis?

What happened to that sweet AHMale that made breakfast in bed on your birthday and gazed lovingly into your eyes when he told you he loved you? When was he kidnapped and replaced by his three-year-old self having a major meltdown when he couldn't have his dessert before dinner?!

Do things always have to be his way? Why can't he learn to actually talk, rather than grunt? Why can't he change the toilet paper roll when it's empty? Shouldn't he know by now that his aging sweetheart doesn't like olives in her salad? And when, without your knowing, did your AHMale get initiated into The Curmudgeon Club and turn into someone deserving of, "I don't like you very much." (And —full disclosure— maybe, just maybe, an AHFemale is also very rarely worthy of, "I don't like you very much.")

Does a Precious Old Dame need to downshift her expectations? Hopefully she learned to drive a stickshift in case she needs to stick it to her man!

Is it him? Can an old fart learn new smarts?

Is it her? Can a Precious Old Dame change her game?

Who changes? Who changes who? Who changes at all?

Who can change their behavior? Who can change their attitude?

And does a change in behavior or a change in attitude provide the ultimate answer to the question, "I love you, but do I like you?"

Checking in with a pit crew of wise crones—both past and current generations—might provide some additional man-ual advice to help steer a loving, but not liking, AHFemale past this ugly pothole in the road.

The $64,000 Questions in 1955

Remember that very popular weekly 1955 quiz show *The $64,000 Question*? Each contestant was put in a small soundproof room like a telephone booth (remember telephone booths?) where they wore large earphones to hear the questions and the front glass panel of the booth was see-through only from the audience's side. If the contestant answered a challenging question correctly, they progressed to the next monetary level the following week, with $64,000 being the final Big Prize.

Let's time travel to 1955 and put some very wise women in the booth and see how they answer these age-old big-money questions:

Week 1 Question: "Can old farts learn new smarts?"

Week 2 Question: "Can a Precious Old Dame change her game?"

Week 3 Question for the Grand Prize: "I love you, but do I like you?"

CHAPTER 27. THE $64,000 QUESTION: I LOVE YOU, BUT DO I LIKE YOU?

> **Helen's** *Grandma Molly, who immigrated from Ukraine in 1921 and was married 50 years, would have answered these questions in 1955:*
>
> "So your grandpa Ben is an old man with beautiful blue eyes who cares about me and who works in his laundry shop seven days a week and who puts food on the table and sits in his comfy chair in his slippers and he doesn't talk too much and he only complains a little. What's not to like?"
>
> *Molly's* Man-ischewitz wine glass is half-full. *Molly's* answers:
>
> "Can old farts learn new smarts?" "*No.*"
>
> "Can a Precious Old Dame change her game?" "*Yes.*"
>
> "I love you, but do I like you?" "*Most of the time.*"

> *Rae Jean's Grandma* **Pauline**, *who immigrated from Poland in 1919 and was married 55 years, would have answered these questions in 1955:*
>
> "You modern women with your non-sticky frying pans, your plastic cards that are like money, your mini-wavy ovens, and your Dear Abby gossip! What good are they? You've still got your crotchety old man who never talks, who is always out doing whatever, who is always scratching his balls, and who doesn't help with housework. You have a right to mutter under your breath and complain."
>
> **Pauline's** Man-ischewitz wine glass is half-empty. Her whine glass is overflowing. **Pauline's** answers:
>
> "Can old farts learn new smarts?" "*No.*"
>
> "Can a Precious Old Dame change her game?" "*No.*"
>
> "I love you, but do I like you?" "*On a good day.*"

The $600,000 Questions in 2020.

Allowing for inflation, $64,000 is worth $600,000 in 2020 dollars! And, for many Boomer Chicks, who may be more economically independent from an AHMale (which may not have been the case in Grandma *Molly*'s and Grandma **Pauline**'s day) the questions about loving your Boomer Buddy versus liking him (and staying versus leaving) may be less of an economic decision.

> ### *Helen answers The $600,000 Question: "I love you, but do I like you?"*
>
> *Helen* had a HUGE, No-Holds-Barred, No-Words-Unsaid fight with her Aging Human Male. They were partners for nine years. *Helen* sent this text to her best POD:
>
> *Helen:* " I think the hard, painful, scary question I ask myself is why I am putting up with him. Sometimes I justify my answer, thinking it's due to my age, not wanting to be alone. Sometimes it's because I just know he is a really good man who I care about. Sometimes it's because I think either I can change or he will change. I guess now I am realizing that while I wish for a better relationship, it's good enough, particularly since I am free to do whatever I want… It's a tough call when a woman like me is older….And sometimes just venting like this about our struggles helps me put the negatives behind me and focus on the positives in our relationship. And I do think he is doing the best that he can."
>
> *Helen's* can of soda water is half-full and bubbling with realistic resignation. *Helen* answers:
>
> "Can old farts learn new smarts?" "*Sometimes.*"
>
> "Can a Precious Old Dame change her game?" "*Sometimes.*"
>
> "I love you, but do I like you?" "*Lots of days.*"

CHAPTER 27. THE $64,000 QUESTION: I LOVE YOU, BUT DO I LIKE YOU?

> *Rae Jean answers The $600,000 Question: "I love you, but do I like you?"*
>
> *Rae Jean:* "I didn't know the true meaning of the word 'ambivalence' until I woke up one morning next to this guy who had morphed into one of the Aging Human Male species. We rarely fight, but when we do it's a doozie! Sometimes I let my anger at my ex leak into feelings about this guy, but this guy's not perfect either. When we fight I think he would rather be right than be in our relationship. And I ain't gonna hear 'I'm sorry' more than once in a blue moon. But I can be a tough cookie, too, so maybe we are evenly matched. And he has supported me to the max in my cancer surgeries and, even though he doesn't do a lot of things *with* me, he does a lot of things *for* me (like all the grocery shopping—YAHOO!) We are far from perfect, so I spend a lot of time just doing my own thing!"
>
> *Rae Jean*'s bottle of craft beer is half-full and lukewarm. *Rae Jean's* answers:
>
> "Can old farts learn new smarts?" *"No."*
>
> "Can a Precious Old Dame change her game?" *"I wish. I try."*
>
> "I love you, but do I like you?" *"Enough days."*

It's not easy answering The $64,000/$600,000 Questions and all the questions in-between. Real life is not a game show and there are no right answers.

An Aging Human Female can always follow Stephen Stills advice, "Love the one you're with!" Especially when you yourself are also "the one you're with."

If you are having one of those bumpy travel days where you love your AHMale but your Like Tank is empty, either stop and give your AHMale gas about his behavior or downshift to the next rest stop to buy a Snickers bar labelled "DISGRUNTLED." You choose: grousing or chocolate —or both— to the rescue!

Chapter 28.
Burma-Shave Road Signs Along Route 66+

"When you come to a fork in the road, take it." —Yogi Berra

Note for the "younger" aging man and the "younger" aging woman: From 1925-1963 Burma-Shave advertised their shaving cream with fun roadside signs. Each line of the rhyming jingle was posted on a separate sign along the road every several hundred feet. These signs helped drivers and passengers smile and laugh as they zipped along the interstate. Here are some roadside signs to add fun to your journey with your Aging Human Partner.

CHAPTER 28. BURMA-SHAVE ROAD SIGNS ALONG ROUTE 66+

You promised to love
'Til death do you part
Hottie or Old Fart
Embrace him with heart.
Burma Shave

Aging Human Males
Worry and control,
When things get fiery,
Just stop, drop, and roll.
Burma Shave

Stop any fighting
And be sweet instead
And if you bicker
Resolve it in bed.
Burma Shave

Happy trails to you
Over hill and dale.
Love to you and your
Aging Human Male.
Burma Shave

> "Stop worrying about the potholes in the road and enjoy the journey."
> —*Babs Hoffman, Girls' Pro Baseball League Player*

The Dame Digest

"It's not vanity to love yourself, it's sanity." —Helen Weels

The Dame Digest. offers nourishment and encouragement to perfecting the art and craft of aging well as a female. As an added bonus, a happy Aging Human Female makes for a happier Aging Human Male. Shine, baby, shine!

Intro.
Yes, Arethra, R-E-S-P-E-C-T!

"Your butt can't be kicked if you are proud of your butt."
—Rae Jean Beech

Let's be honest here, ladies. An AHFemale's perspective on life with her AHMale depends largely on what's going on inside of her. If an older woman is fulfilled in her own life, she is happier dealing with her older geezer's crankiness. And that is just one reason why self-care is at the top of the To-Do List. In fact, good self-care changes the To-Do List to the TA-DA List!

As she embraces her aging, a geezess realizes that each and every day she had best be doing what she really wants to be doing. To be herself and to be her happiest self, ah, that is the question, before anyone says, to paraphrase Hamlet, "Goodnight, Sweet Princess." But let's put aside these morbid metaphors…

Good self-care and self-reflection bring joy, health, and sparkle into a Boomer Chick's *Dame Diamond* life.

Chapter 29.
Follow Your Heart, Not His Fart

"In life there is no real safety except for self-belief."
—Madonna

"Follow your heart, not his fart," is a wise adage with a simple meaning: make sure that you are not too close behind his behind. If you follow your aging man too closely, things start to smell. And we are not talking about Chanel No. 5!

For a change, why not let him follow you? Easier for him to follow you anyway, since Real Aging Women don't Fart! And, besides you're going to be going your own way, stubborn you. Take **The Rebecca Rule** to heart: "Listen to whatever your man says. Then do what you want!"

The Geezess's Guide to an Easy, Febreze™-y Life

1. **Strike out on your own path**, away from his fart. If you get lost, you can machete a new path or backtrack and take the road not taken. Sometimes getting lost is the best way to find yourself.

2. **Trust your instincts**. They don't stink. What? Back to odors again!

3. **Recall those faint voices from your childhood dreams.** Turn those voices into your own special song.

4. **Close your eyes and remember five things that made you laugh** so hard that you cried—or peed—and do those things again!

5. **Recall your past loves**—people, activities, thoughts, hopes—and reconnect or re-create these.

6. **Think of morning farts as wake-up calls**. Every morning, ask yourself: "How can I bring joy to me this day?"

Chapter 30.
The Dame Diamond: Feelings ◊ Revealings ◊ Bods and PODS

"Above all, be the heroine of your life, not the victim."
—*Nora Ephron*

Just as every Aging Human Male has his **Geezer Triangle** of needs (**Sex ▲ Sustenance ▲ Sports**), every Aging Human Female has her geezess geometric shape of needs, and that shape is the multi-faceted, shining jewel: ***The Geezess Dame Diamond.*** As Carol Channing sang in the 1949 movie Gentlemen Prefer Blondes, "A diamond is a girl's best friend."

CHAPTER 30. THE DAME DIAMOND: FEELINGS ◊ REVEALINGS ◊ BODS ◊ PODS

But what is *The Dame Diamond?* Every Precious Old Dame (POD) has her four-faceted diamond of needs to be fulfilled: *Feelings* ◊ *Revealings* ◊ *Bods* ◊ *PODs.*

Feelings: An AHFemale has strong emotions and spiritual needs.

Revealings: An AHFemale has her passions and reveals her inner self to the world through diverse interests, actions, and creations.

Bods: An AHFemale connects with her body through her body image, body choices, health TLC, clothes and sex.

PODs: An AHFemale survives and thrives on friendships with her Precious Old Dames (PODs), both one-on-one and through Pee POD Poise Parties. (See **The Precious Old Dames' Party Playbook**.)

And all four facets of *The Dame Diamond* need occasional polishing to max out on the sparkle!

Chapter 31.
The Dame Diamond: Feelings

"Never apologize for showing your feelings. When you do, you are apologizing for the truth."—Jose N. Harris, psychologist, author

An aging woman is a wonderland of emotional energy, often feeling moods connected to family, friends, lifestyles, endeavors, nature, animals, spirit, and, to be honest, connected to all matters over time and space.

An aging man might say his woman is "all over the map" with her "mood swings," even after womenopause should have shut down PMS. Silly man, an aging woman never loses her emotional gifts!

Important Aside: "Womenopause," commonly called "menopause," is derived from the French phrase for "moon cessation," although during and after womenopause, no self-respecting woman ever loses her ability to moon a deserving man!

Many aging men are unaware that after womenopause, AHFemales transition from *PMS* to *PMMS: Prized Mega-Maturity Status*, a graduate degree in *PMS* awarded by Emotions University, with a diploma that bestows upon its graduates the right to own all their feelings and display them with pride. An aging woman carries her *PMMS* status with honor, and with a moody swing of her hips. In the words of Marilyn Monroe, "I am not a victim of emotional conflicts. I am human." Flaunt those feelings, dear POD!

 ***Polish the Feelings:*** How can you honor all facets of your feelings, your emotional needs, and your spiritual needs? Here, my Precious Old Dame, is how to polish your emotional diamond to an exquisite shine.

Nourish yourself first. Take the flight attendant's safety advice at the beginning of a plane trip: if the oxygen masks fall, put on yours first so

CHAPTER 31. THE DAME DIAMOND: FEELINGS

that you can help others. What type of oxygen do you need? Feeling overwhelmed? Tired? Angry? Lonely? Sad? Bored? Hangry? Think about returning yourself to your OM-base of calm. Breathe!

Don't let anyone steal your joy. No one can make you feel like a bad person if you truly believe you are a good person.

Own and honor your feelings. Your feelings are your feelings. There are no right or wrong feelings. No one can tell you how to feel.

Take time for yourself with a walk in a park or soak in a steamy bath with a really steamy book.

Find a physical space, a "womb of your own," be it a "she-shed," a room, a desk, a chair, a park bench, or lakeside grass that belongs to you and only you (although perhaps shared with a beloved dog, cat, bird or squirrel).

"Lose that Unloving Feeling!" (Shout-out to composer Carole King) Choose a feeling or attitude that you no longer want. Is there a sell-by date on this feeling? Did that feeling expire years ago? Time to put it in the trash and take that garbage can to the curb for an immediate pickup. Stock your emotional pantry with a new feeling that nourishes a fresh new attitude!

Be your own good mother to yourself. Hug yourself. Love yourself. Feed yourself chocolate. Perhaps Virginia Woolf was thinking of self-love—and chocolate— when she said, "One cannot think well, love well, sleep well, if one has not dined well."

Doing nothing is doing something special. Stare at the trees. Play *Solitaire*. Soak in a hot Epsom salt bath. Binge watch *Grace and Frankie*. Take a nap. Mindlessly search *Zillow* for your dream villa in Italy. Apply a facemask and lie in bed doing nothing for 30 minutes as it hardens.

Your Precious Old Dames are female oxygen. Your PODs are the ultimate polish for supporting, affirming, and sustaining your feelings. Depend on one POD or a Pee POD Poise Party for many breaths of fresh air.

Honor your heart. Your feelings are your heart and, in the words of psychologist Belleruth Naparstek, "Our heart is the seed of our strength and the home of our spirit."

Chapter 32.
The Dame Diamond: Revealings

"The most powerful weapon on earth is the human soul on fire." —
Ferdinand Foch, French General in WWI

Every AHFemale desires to create, nurture and reveal her passions through such diverse interests as: knocking on doors for a political party, baby-sitting grandbabies, fostering shelter dogs, writing her memoirs, kayaking the intracoastal waterways, portrait painting, studying physics, raising carrots and tomatoes in her home garden, training for a marathon, delivering Meals-on-Wheels, stretching into yoga, researching financial investments, or volunteering at the local hospital. Often these passions involve the healing of others and, in healing others, AHFemales often heal themselves. Revealing passions can heal an aging women in the wounded times, and bring additional wonder in the smoother times.

It is a basic need of a woman to express her inner life by revealing and nurturing her passions. One of the joys of becoming an Aging Human Female is becoming clearer about one's passions. And how wonderful it is to have faith that there is always another passion waiting to be revealed just around the next corner!

Polish the Revealings: As they sang "Dream a Little Dream of Me," The Mamas and The Papas uncovered those long-buried childhood yearnings of "sweet dreams that leave all worries behind you." Let your young girl passions reveal your aging woman adventures. Need help recapturing the most joyous times of your childhood?

Ask Yourself:

> ***What activities brought a joyous smile to your young face?*** Look at your childhood photos. Were you ice skating, baking cookies, walking

CHAPTER 32. THE DAME DIAMOND: REVEALINGS

in nature, hanging with friends, drawing, collecting stamps, learning new things, dancing, shopping, playing with your baby brother, being a girl scout, doing science experiments, playing soccer, solving puzzles, reading, knitting, watching movies, hugging your dog, working with your friends, making music, spending time alone in your room, getting dirty, being at school, babysitting, making things with your hands?

What events, holidays, and gatherings were the most anticipated?
Was it your birthday, family celebrations, holidays, county fairs, school sports days, visits with grandma and grandpa, attending religious services, wandering through museums, checking out the library?

Try the self-reflection activities in The Precious Old Dames' Party Playbook, Chapters 48-50 to jiggle and joggle your memory. When you can recall these joyous childhood moments you can recreate a long-lost "Dream A Little Dream" map to discover a treasure trove of joy!

Amanda and Her Revealings

When Amanda was single, she was passionate about her career as a pastry chef, her two close friends Jess and Tara, and the dozen houseplants in every room in her house that she lovingly tended every day. After her marriage, Amanda down-sized to working part-time and her life centered mainly around her husband Mike, her son Brad, and her daughter Katy.

Once the kids were grown and off on their own adventures, she decided to revisit her childhood fantasies of being a writer and an artist. She is now writing a western romance novel and taking oil painting classes. After forty-five years, Amanda revelled in the reveal-ation of her dreams coming true as an aging woman.

Betsy and Her Revealings

Betsy worked as a computer analyst for **IBM** and later taught math in high school. She always loved to read and write poetry (remember her fave: e.e. cummings?), and this passion brought her to her partner Scott, whom she literally stumbled upon in a bookstore (remember those?) while browsing through the poetry shelves.

Since retiring from forty years of teaching, and moving to Asheville, NC, with Scott, Betsy now enjoys writing poetry, and, lo and behold, her poetry is often published in her community's newsletter. Betsy was an only child and never had children of her own, but her heart is filled with her volunteer work with the teens at the local **YMCA** Shelter. Betsy's lifelong inner wishes lead to her reveal-ation of writing poetry and having what she calls a "beloved patchwork" chosen family of shelter teens and a sisterhood of **PODs** in her retirement community.

Chapter 33.
The Dame Diamond: Bods

"Even I don't look like Cindy Crawford in the morning."
—Cindy Crawford

Is there an Aging Human Female alive who has not spent many, many moments of many, many many days worrying about, critiquing, dressing, feeding, lifting, plucking, appreciating, oiling, shaving, examining, exercising, criticizing, depriving, wining, whining about, posing, doctoring, satisfying, soothing, bemoaning, massaging, and loving her body???

Lesson 1.
Body Image: Is This a Funhouse Mirror?

"We have to break the mirror to be ourselves." — May Sarton, author

Get real! At 21, most of us didn't have the body of Bo Derek in the movie *Ten*, so why should we have a Bo body after decades of rubber on the road? As Aging Human Females, our changes in our bodies can be somewhat startling and our changes in our body images can be even more challenging.

There are many times in our long lives that we don't have choices about changing our bodies. Most aging women have experienced required medical additions, deletions, replacements, adjustments, scars, repairs, alterations, realignments, downsizes, upsizes, removals, replacements, supplements, and/or rehabilitations. Whoa! That is a lot of body work, and most of us know, deep down inside even after all the physical alterations, that we still have a classy chassis!

Our feelings about our bodies affect us on the inside. Our positive emotions can fortify our heart and cause our skin to glow. (TRUTH, Chai Woodham, "Healing Your Skin with Your Mind," *U.S. News and World Report*, May 27, 2015.)

And our feelings on the inside affect our skin on the outside. As psychologist Charlotte Ferguson, founder of "Discipline Skincare," explains, "using expensive skincare products won't help your skin if you're stressed or anxious." (TRUTH, Olivia Cassano, "5 Ways your Mental Health is Affecting your Skin," *Metro*, 12/29/2017.)

And our emotions can take a toll on our health and physical aging. Worries about old what-ifs can cause eye bags, tit tilt, saddle bags, butt drop, jelly

CHAPTER 33. THE DAME DIAMOND: BODS

belly, knee notches, cellu-heavy, vari-not-cozy veins and crappy creepy crepe-y skin. Baggage causes saggage.

Note to the frugal among us: This Sassy Primer is cheaper than any rejuvenating lotion or potion in your friendly drug store aisle!

Polish Body Image with Re-framing: Strut your attitude of gratitude! That's not a pimple, it's a reverse dimple. It's all about Today 'Tude. Today you are alive and cooking, baby, even when you are not in the kitchen!

Be gentle with yourself. Channel the Gentle Goddess of Bodies, who whispers in your ear as you look in the mirror, "This is the youngest you will ever look for the rest of your life. Enjoy!" (And no muttering, "That is supposed to be the good news?!")

So as you look in the mirror, rather than breaking the mirror ala May Sarton, reframe your inner thoughts and words.

Strip down naked—of course you may turn the lights down low to a soft glow if you wish—and do a body scan, starting from the top. Re-frame your body language—that is, the language you are using to describe your body in the mirror—making use of your funny bone to change your inner dialogue, as needed.

Here are some positive reframing suggestions for renaming mirror images and appreciating the body that is uniquely yours at this age:

Grey hair color: A silver crown, a silver lining, wisdom highlights, tiara tresses.

Eyelid droop: That sultry come-hither look?!

Crow's feet: Derived from so many amazing in-"sights."

Lip lines: Just like frequent flier miles, they are "frequent smile miles."

Face wrinkles: Character lines, read your fortune.

Neck: Extra folds from bravely sticking your neck out frequently, kudos to you!

Boobs: Lowering the bar—er, bra—helps.

Waist: Your mom had you finish your plate because children were starving in China. You're such a good daughter!

Hips: You were a hippie in the last century and you are hippy this century, too! Cool!

Thighs: Cellulite, no! Cellu-heavy, yes! You are a powerful heavyweight in life

Knees: Don't knock them.

Calves: Moo-ve just fine.

Ankles: Need an ankle brace-let to keep up.

Feet: A little buniony, and corny, but fun to shop for. No one ever asks: "Do my feet look fat in these shoes?"

Toes: Only body part where the word "piggy" is cute!

CHAPTER 33. THE DAME DIAMOND: BODS

> *Barbie and her New Doll of a Body Image:*
>
> Barbie was born on March 9, 1959. Barbie struck terror into the hearts of many young mothers whose daughters begged for a Barbie Doll. Moms feared that their daughters would want to look like Barbie of "The perfect, but unachievable, *Ten*" with her perky boobs, cinched-in-body, chiselled thighs, and stiletto-shaped feet." Barbie represented a cultural "icon" body that was more realistically an "I-was-conned-because-I-can't-ever-have-that" body.
>
> Barbie now rocks 60+! If she were a Boomer Chick Barbie today, what would she look like? Short blue-gray hair? Crow's feet and lips lines? Crepe-y neck? Saggy boobs? Muffin top? Un-waxed? Cellulite thighs? Orthopedic shoes instead of stilettos? Would flowered muumuus, hearing aids and a walker be included in her package at no extra cost? And would she be sitting in her rocking chair in assisted living instead of driving her pink Corvette to her townhouse?

The above image of Boomer Chick Barbie is as much a false stereotype of an aging human female as the 1959 Barbie was a false stereotype of a younger woman. Female body image stereotypes—young or old—are challenging to change!

Real aging women have the freedom of breaking the aging body stereotype. Every Boomer Babe can look in the mirror and feel comfortable with her body's shape and her natural hair color, and break that aging stereotype with a joyous smile. Move aside, Barbie. Just like Carol and Jean and Jeannette in the anecdotes that follow, every AHFemale is a living doll!

> ## *Carol and Carly Simon and Meat Loaf*
>
> When Carol was getting out of the shower she fell and twisted her ankle. At the urgent care center, a young, cute, Tom-Selleck-look-a-like doctor examined her leg and told her, "Your ankle is just sprained, not broken." What a relief! But then this cute doc had to add, "And, by the way, you have varicose veins. You should be wearing compression stockings all day, and especially when you play tennis." Suddenly young Tom Selleck didn't look so cute anymore!
>
> Carol was shocked. She couldn't believe she was "of a varicose-vein age" and she couldn't picture herself wearing compression stockings "in public," especially at tennis, for everyone to see how old and infirm she was! As all these thoughts bounced around in her head, Carol heard Carly Simon singing in the background, "You're so vain!" but with the new lyrics, "You're so varicose-vein!"
>
> Carol only wore her compression stockings at home. Her partner Rodney gently teased her about how "sexy" they were and he bought her gold lame compression stockings as a joke, but even his efforts couldn't lighten up the impression the compressions made on her self-esteem.

Carol's compressions were her "Yes, I-am-old-and-yes-I-am-so-vain-about-this" secret. Was her vanity insanity?

Doesn't every Boomer Chick have at least one little/big special "aging thing?" To paraphrase Meat Loaf, "I will do anything for (self) love (and aging), but I WON'T DO THAT!"

CHAPTER 33. THE DAME DIAMOND: BODS

Jean and Stewart and her Post-Mastectomy Body Image

When Jean was diagnosed with breast cancer and had a double mastectomy, she worried about how her partner Stewart would feel about her sexually. Stewart lovingly reassured her, "When we make love, I am not making love to your breasts, I am making love to you." Jean almost cried as she embraced Stewart, her lover who embraced her whole self, not just her nipples, her lover who cherished her heart as well as her body.

Jeannette and her Silver Question

In her poem "Silver," to be included in her book of poetry publishing in Spring 2021, Jeannette Encinias asks the question: "How many years of beauty do I have left?"

This is her poetic response: "...you have decades of learning and leaving and loving sewn into the corners of your eyes... your children come home to find their own history in your face... your beauty began there beneath the sweater and the skin, remember?... Your beauty is breathtaking."

Lesson 2. Body Choices: So Many Decisions, So Little Time

"I keep thinking, 'Georgie O'Keefe wouldn't have had Botox.'"
—Gloria Steinem

Aside from aging and medical body changes, modern science and cultural trends have presented aging women with many body "fixes." In the '50s, Dinah Shore sang of "Buttons and bows..where they love a gal by the cut o' her clothes." The modern version might be loving a Boomer Chick for a medley of botox and boobs, bushiness and brows.

Polish Body Choices by Reframing: Body choices have pros and cons… some need to be performed by pros and some seem to be cons. Before you inject, let this **Primer** protect both your looks and your pocketbook with the following observations.

Botox: The un-wrinkler that wipes that furrow off your forehead and hopefully doesn't mess with your brain.

Boobs: Pierce your belly button so your belly button ring can help hold up your bra.

Bushes: The survey skinny on that most tender skin is that 84% of American women prefer pubic bare or pubic flair over natural pubic hair. And there is a higher percentage of younger women than older women who wax—guess waxing wanes as a woman ages. (Annie Tomlin, "Turns Out 84 Percent of Women Groom Their Pubic Hair," *Self*, 06/30/2016)

CHAPTER 33. THE DAME DIAMOND: BODS

Enhanced lips: Who wants to look like someone gave them a fat lip?

Face lifts: The best and cheapest face lift is a smile.

Tummy tucks: Easier to just hold your breath and suck in your stomach for photographs. Why do you think tunic tops and SPANX were invented?

Cosmetic genital surgery: Any man who complains about the way your vulva looks doesn't deserve to go down that path!

> ### *Helen and Body Choices*
>
> Yes, I have a hard time deciding what to do about improving my aging body. I want to look good because then I feel better.
>
> I've tried botox on my forehead, but I recently read research that botox restricts your facial muscle movements, and facial muscle restriction limits your feelings, which worries me.
>
> I dye my hair so that I don't look so old.
>
> I had my first mani-pedi when I was 60 and it makes me feel clean from head-to-toe, so I love those. And I love using sparkly toenail polish as a breakout fashion statement with my Florida flip-flops.
>
> I shave my legs and underarms with a razor, bringing back wonderful memories of when I was a teenager preparing for a date.
>
> Waxing my genital area hurts SO much... But a clean bikini line is so lovely at the pool.
>
> Tummy tucks and facelifts scare me because of the anesthesia during surgery. Only really rich movie stars end up with face lifts that don't scream Ms. Plastic Face!

Rae Jean and Booty Choices

Okay, so I am an all-natural woman. Also kind of lazy about my looks.

Hair is only trimmed—on the top of my head!—once a year... My mane is absolutely not dyed. I can't stand the thought of sitting in a chair for three hours having people fawning over me. No mani-pedis either.

No botox for me either—who wants a needle where a man's sweet lips should be?! No puffy lips, deplore that Angelina frog-lips look.

I don't like my wrinkles much, but then I don't look in the mirror much.

I tweeze my eyebrows myself when my two brows start to form a unibrow—love you Frida Kahlo, but a little separation is a good thing. I never tried de-threading brows—maybe because "de-threading" brings back the bad memory of my having to rip out an entire bad seam on the apron I was trying to sew in seventh grade home economics class.

I have a big tush naturally, which was so not cool when I was a teenager—I was teased mercilessly—but now I am lucky that I don't have to pay to get that big-butt crazy Kardashian look!

And that v-jay-jay surgery—are you kidding me?! Men are the ones with the weird-looking junk, not us cutesy women!

I love tye-dyed clothes and hole-y jeans, though I refuse to do bellbottoms a second time.

Guess I'm still stuck in the '60s, though I do wear a bra now or else my boobs would rest on my muffin top. As Faith Hill sings, "Take Me as I Am."

Lesson 3.
Health TLC: Ten-der Loving Commandments

"The word 'Aerobics' came about when the gym instructors got together and said, 'If we're going to charge $10 an hour, we can't call it 'Jumping Up and Down.''"—Rita Rudner, comedian

"Tender Loving Care (TLC)" and "Boomer Chicks" in the same sentence feels repetitive, as most Boomer Chicks have been dispensing TLC to others throughout their entire lives as easily as if TLC were PEZ™ candy! Ah, but for that self-caring on health issues, an Aging Human Female may need some reminders.

Note: These Ten Commandments differ from the Ten (Loving) Commandments for the AHFemale whose AHMale Needs Medical Advice (aka How Not to Nag your Boomer Buddy When He Really Needs It. See Chapter 21.) These Ten-der Loving Commandments are self-nudges for Boomer Chicks to encourage self-bodylove.

TLC: Ten-der Loving Commandments for an AHHFemale (Aging Healthy Human Female)

1. **Thou shalt whine with wine to thy PODs** about the aches and pains and fears and frets and feel total empathy in a way impossible for the AHMale Species to understand.

2. **Thou shalt take extraordinary care of thy beautiful self** by shining thy bod with exquisite self-care. As Sophia Loren said, "Nothing makes a woman more beautiful than the belief that she is beautiful." And doesn't fruit-scented body lotion sweetly add to thy shine and thy feelings of being beautiful?

3. **Thou shalt get thee to any and all doctors as needed and remember that thou is the best specialist** and expert on thine own body and thou deservest to ask any and all questions and get all the answers even after the fifteen minute specialist appointment has ended.

4. **Thou shalt be faithful to chocolate** in any emergency situation. Break glass or break open that candy bar?

5. **Thou shalt never cry or freak out over online medical research results**, especially online medical articles showing horrific red and purple photos of unidentifiable diseased body parts or articles containing the words "cancer," "immediately to a hospital," or "terminal."

6. **Thou shalt explore and honor "alternative healing practices" as "ancestral practices"**—not "woo-woo practices"—as these practices, over the past 200,000 years, have healed thy mothers, grandmothers, great-grandmothers, and thousands of AHFemales with low libidos, stiff fingers, night sweats, flaky skin and dry vaginas. Perhaps what is called "woo woo" can help thou, too! Why not get verbal about herbal? Why hesitate to meditate? Why not get flaky about Reiki? Why say "Ach!" about acupuncture? Why not tie one on with Tai Chi? Why not heal thyself as thou develops synergy feelings about energy healings!?

7. **Thou shalt honor thy PODS** as essential to thy physical, spiritual, emotional health and well-being by renaming "girls' lunch" as "therapy," as in, "Honey, I am going to my JULIETS therapy session now." (And

CHAPTER 33. THE DAME DIAMOND: BODS

JULIETS, Just Use Ladies Into Enormous Tasty Salads, Therapy is at least $300 cheaper than a shrink therapy hour—even including the waitperson's tip—and a whole lot yummier!)

8. ***Thou shalt honor thy biological connection with thy mother and thy grandmother.*** "Did you know that your grandmother carried part of you inside her womb? But how? Well. A female fetus is born with all the eggs she will ever have in her lifetime. So when your Grandmother was carrying your Mother in her womb, you were a tiny egg in your Mother's ovaries. The three of you have been connected for a very long time." (TRUTH, The Minds Journal, TheMindsJournal.com, July 15, 2019.) An amazing thought, but also possibly complicated by the current state of thy relationship with thy biological mother and grandmother, a relationship that can be unknown/known, close/distant, complex/estranged. Genetics may link thee/thy mother/thy grandmother eggs-istentially, but may eggs-agerate relationship ties.

9. ***Thou shalt honor thy body with healthy choices—in moderation.*** Eating well is a form of self-respect for thy body. But french fries with gobs of ketchup is self-respecting thy soul, right? Whatsagirltodo? Moving thy body is a gift, even with a walker or a cane. But isn't binge-watching romcoms on thy comfy couch easier on thy tush? Whatsagirltodo? Listening to thy body's needs and thy soul's needs feels like a non-ending tug-of-war. Isn't it time to negotiate thy truce, a truce without thy guilt? If not now, when?

    "If I had my life to live over again,
    I'd dare to make more mistakes next time....
    I'd relax....
    I would eat more ice cream and less beans."
    —Nadine Stair, poet, 85 years old

10. ***Thou shalt love thy body for better or worse, in sickness and in health, til death do us part.*** Thy body is thy oldest friend and has been there for thee even before thy first breath and will be there for thee until thy last breath at the very end. How cool is this: thy best buddy is thy best body?!

Lesson 4.
Clothes: How's It Hanging?

"I like my money right where I can see it... hanging in my closet."—Carrie Bradshaw, Sex and the City

Remember when, in your younger days, there were visions of grannies wearing knee-high white gogo boots and rocking it on the disco floor? Well that granny was happy with her wild mini-skirt wardrobe, so why shouldn't you be happy with whatever floats your mumu? Try on retro clothes—wear those bell-bottoms yet again? Or go modern and wear those yoga pants wherever—the latest fad for women in business, even if the image in the mirror of your thighs elicits sighs! Dressing for success means being comfortable inside and out! Go for it, girl—er, granny!

Polish Clothes by Ironing Out the Wrinkles: As Marie Kondo says, "If you can say without a doubt, 'I really like this!' no matter what anyone else says, and if you like yourself for having it, then ignore what other people think." The upside of the "invisibility" of older women is that no one will notice what you wear—except your PODs, and they love you for who you are inside your skin, not what's on it! Whatever feels good, wear it!

And as to "ironing out the wrinkles," who even owns an iron, or an ironing board, anymore!?! Wash and wear, baby!

CHAPTER 33. THE DAME DIAMOND: BODS

Lesson 5.
Sex: Yet Again?!

"It's work having a vagina. Guys don't think that it's work but it is. You think it shows up like that to the event. It doesn't. Every night it's like getting ready for its first Quinceañera, believe me." —Amy Schumer

Sex: Remember when you read the shocking first edition of *Our Bodies, Ourselves,* and bent your body into a pretzel to use a mirror and look at your genitals for the first time? And, can you recall reading Erica Jong's *Fear of Flying,* and learning to talk about the unmentionable taboos of our sexuality?

As an AHFemale, it is time to make peace with your current sex drive. Do you have libid-lo or libid-OH?! Do your sexual needs see-saw with your inner mood, your AHMale and how things are going with him, what you have been watching during screen time (movies, TV, iPhone, iPad), what you have been reading? It's time to know your sexual stimulants, or lack thereof, and put them out there for yourself and for your trustworthy partner. Time to polish sex with fewer inhibitions, more trust, and more trusty sex aids!

Polish Sex with Fewer Inhibitions: You sexy crone, you, may find yourself feeling sexually freer as you age. You are more accepting of your body and have come to truly believe that you are good enough, you look good enough, and your turn-on is good enough...no GREAT enough! You are more comfortable expressing your physical needs, either with a partner, or with a vibrator, or with both at the same time... ménage à trois with The Rabbit?! As the vagina gets drier, the sex can get wryer—isn't this about having fun and closeness and not about performance? Isn't this about having a sensual sexual sense of humor? What do you have to lose—other than inhibitions?

Polish Sex with More Trust: Trust and sex... when do you hear those words put together? Rita Mae Brown's advice, "Loving's pretty easy. It's letting someone love you that's hard" would be a great title for a country western song that could become an earworm for you as you let down your guard and learn to further trust your aging man in bed (and out of bed). Trusting your sexual desires and trusting your partner's eases sexual expectations and takes the pressure off. Opening up to possibilities without judgment, yours or his, involves trust. Opening up to your aging man's tongue as he kisses you, even when you were too tired to even have sex on your radar five seconds ago, involves trust: trust you can get warmed up or trust you can enjoy just that kiss and trust that, either way, all will be okay with both of you. Ah, that makes it all, Okay, with a capital O!

Polish Sex with A Trusty Toy Box of Gadgets for your Box:

Kegels: A kegel is legal, just a pain in the v-jay-jay to do them every day-day.

The Rabbit: Rabbits are masters of procreation and The Rabbit is a master of creation of Os. Just listen to Grace Slick's high and mighty, or mighty high, advice as she sings in "White Rabbit," or as, ahem, we AHFemales sing in the shower with our waterproof toys, "Go ask Alice, I think she'll OOOOOHHHH!"

Pube Lube: Oil for the goil.

Vibrator: With all due respect to Carole King, hopefully the earth will move in places other than under your feet; and why not try out a purple vibrator "Ménage à Moi" ala Grace and Frankie?

Ben Wa Balls: For women who are wa-wa over not having orgasms. (**Note:** These balls are not the same as an AHMale's balls!)

Porn Movies: If you want to learn how to fake it even better!

Porn on Kindle Fire: As The Doors sang, "Come on, baby, light my fire!"

CHAPTER 33. THE DAME DIAMOND: BODS

Still wanting more sex? For your reading pleasure…

The Field Guy-ed begins with **Chapter 1. Sex** and ends with **Chapter 7. Sex—Not Again!**

The Roadmap describes Chapter 23. **Fights #1,113-2,045** about sex in an AHPartnership.

The Precious Old Dames' Party Playbook encourages "talking amongst yourselves" about sex in Pee POD Poise Parties.

A to Z for The Glossary-Eyed womansplains the sex terms in this **Sassy Primer**.

Chapter 34.
The Dame Diamond: PODs (Precious Old Dames)

"I get by with a little help from my friends."—The Beatles

Our Precious Old Dames are our female oxygen—the breath that helps us balance our lives. Our PODs are essential to our well-being. In fact, research has shown that a good network of close women friends is essential for both our mental and physical health. Scientific research attributes the difference in women's longer lifespan than men's lifespan to women's relationships with their gal pals outside of their marriage. (TRUTH, Melissa Healey, "Science Confirms that Women Reap Health Benefits from Friendships" *The Seattle Times*, 06/15/2005.)

Let's break down the art and science of POD chemistry: Oxytocin, commonly called, "The Love Hormone," or "The Happiness Drug," is the hormone that surges like wildfire through a woman when she gives birth, breastfeeds, has sex, pats her dog, or talks with her girlfriends. When stress happens, oxytocin levels decrease. When lower levels of oxytocin interact with estrogen, females seek the company of others. In other words, women "tend and befriend" when they need help. When women's oxytocin levels are high, women even heal faster and better from wounds. (TRUTH, Healey, 2005.)

It turns out sister friends are the best drug your doctor and those pesky TV ads will never mention! As Healey says, "For women, friendship not only rules, it protects. It buffers the hardships of life's transitions, lowers blood pressure, boosts immunity and promotes healing... Researchers think that the hormone oxytocin is, for women especially, the elixir of friendship and, by extension, health." (TRUTH, Healey, 2005.)

And what a great drug! With PODs, there's no fighting with insurance companies over co-pays, no child-proof bottles to struggle with, and no cautions about dizzy side effects if you drink alcohol. Finally, a drug that is free, available immediately with one phone call, and comes with a smile and a hug, real or virtual! Plus, your POD, never asks, "Would you take a survey at the end of this conversation?"

So instead of feeling guilty about those long conversations and fun whine-y, wine-y lunches, acknowledge that PODs are an essential part of your health program. Exercising your jaws with your besties is great exercise! For our health and our well-being, gals' chatter truly matters!

Polish Your PODs: Every time you connect with a gal pal, pat yourself on the back (but don't pull a back muscle!) for doing something good for your health. We aging women hold our BFFs close, like peas in a POD. Embracing aging sisterhood is our survival—for richer, for poorer, in sickness and in health, til death do us part—though we'll be laughing all the way out the door!

This **Primer** offers a kickass party-hearty guide to gathering with your PODS. **The Precious Old Dames' Party Playbook** offers gab guides and (drinking!) games as you "talk amongst yourselves," chick-chatting and schmoozing as you and your Boomer Chicks laugh and cry so hard that you Depend on your Poise should you pee your pants.

Chapter 35.
Wo-mantras to Push-up Your Bra-very

"No one can make you feel inferior without your consent."
—Eleanor Roosevelt

Even with a sparkling **Dame Diamond,** an Aging Human Female sometimes needs a boost. Here are some womanly wo-mantras to up your strength and lift your spirits, if not your boobs and butt!

"No" is a complete sentence. "It's given me this tremendous sense of power. I'm a little bit drunk on it," says Anne Lamott about "No" being a complete sentence. (TRUTH, @ANNELAMOTT.) "No" to another may be honoring "Yes" to ourselves. Appeasing another does not outweigh displeasing ourselves.

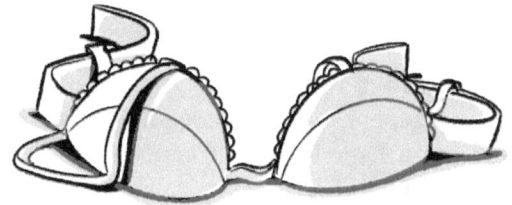

"That won't work for me." *The Erma Edict* rides again. No excuses, no apologies, no womansplaining.

I want what I want. If you don't ask, you'll never know. As Madonna said, "A lot of people are afraid to say what they want. That's why they don't get what they want."

No permission needed. Pamela Anderson gives you permission not to need permission: "Eventually you just have to realize that you're living for an audience of one. I'm not here for anyone else's approval." (TRUTH, *Esquire* interview, January 2005.) Don't ask and you won't be told. Go for it!

CHAPTER 35. WO-MANTRAS TO PUSH-UP YOUR BRA-VERY

"Be a badass with a good ass." Rae Jean lives her wo-mantra, and she believes it is worthy of being tattooed over every AHFemale's heart… or perhaps another part of her anatomy.

Take me as I am. According to actress Kaitlin Foster, "There are parts of me that will always remain untamable, messy and reckless; but I refuse to apologize for it anymore."

"Think like a queen." And, the final wo-mantra every AHFemale needs on her fridge or keyring or computer screen comes from Oprah who says: "A queen is not afraid to fail. Failure is another stepping stone to greatness."

Chapter 36.
You are "A-OK Boomers!"

"Don't let aging get you down. It's too hard to get up."
—John Wagner

"OK, Boomer!" is the latest ageist salvo that youngsters have fired on oldsters in the War Against Ageism. (And what Boomers really need is salve, not salvos!) Boomers were the generation that invented "Don't trust anyone over 30!" Good job to the current youngsters following that old advice, but that phrase hurts now that we are the "over 30s."

A-OK, Boomer

Let's remember Billy Joel's ode to ongoing generational struggles and troubles: "We didn't start the fire!" And let's hear it for "A-OK, Boomers!"

A-OK

CHAPTER 36. YOU ARE "A-OK BOOMERS!"

Lesson 1. Age-honoring

"When I was young I was called a rugged individualist. When I was in my fifties I was considered eccentric. Here I am doing and saying the same things I did then and I'm labeled senile." —George Burns

Age-shaming or ageism, discriminating against and promoting stereotypes of "The Old, " is the only -ism that will eventually affect everyone—at least those lucky enough to live long! In her book, *Ending Ageism or How Not to Shoot Old People,* Margaret Morganroth Gullet says that, "Compared to sexism, racism, or transphobia, ageism is the last censure, the most acceptable and unnoticed of the cruel prejudices." (TRUTH, Rutgers University Press, 2017.)

Ageism is so "prevalent and insidious" that in 2016, The World Health Organization (WHO) invested half a million dollars in research to investigate ageism and build a Global Campaign to Combat Ageism. (TRUTH, Bulletin of the World Health Organization, April 2018, who.int)

And, as we A-OK Boomer Chicks well know, with aging comes sagging—oops, saging. Saging is the art of accumulating wisdom and courage, along with Lipitor and a drooping butt. Striving and surviving until older age, with body and spirit and mind (well, maybe semi-mind) in place should be honored and respected.

Isn't it up to us to flip "OK, Boomer" into "A-OK, Boomer" (but careful on that flip with that aching sacroiliac)? Isn't it up to us to turn age-shaming into age-honoring, to change stereotypes of oldsters creaking in their rocking chairs into the reality of Boomer Hipsters having a flipping good and productive life?

Age-shaming is subtle and occurs everywhere—in the workplace, in the hair salon, on the street, in the subway, at a party, in a doctor's office, at the sex store, on the highway. Isn't it time to promote age-honoring and recognize age discrimination for what it is?

It is up to geezers and geezesses everywhere to set the record straight with some of these younger "whippersnappers," as that old cowboy Gabby Hayes used to call Gen-Alphabetters!

Age-honoring is respecting an AHFemale's brilliant work experience, physical ability, spirit, and humanity. And it can be done with the flip of a sentence.

Jan, Arlene, and Candy and Flipping Age-shaming into Age-Honoring

Age-shaming in the Workplace: Jan was a 55-year-old mechanical engineer at the same firm for 25 years. Her CEO Carl introduced Jan to her new boss Brian.

> ***CEO Carl:*** "Jan, This is Brian. He is fresh out of college and I am sure that he can help an old hand like you learn some new engineering tricks."
>
> ***Jan:*** "Nice to meet you, Brian. And having engineered here for 25 years, I would be glad to share my tricks, too!"

Age-shaming on the Street: Arlene was 77. As she waited to cross a busy street, a 30-something gentlemen offered to hold her elbow to help her cross.

> ***Gentleman:*** "Young lady, let me help you across the street."
>
> ***Arlene:*** "I know you mean well, but it is demeaning to call me a 'Young lady' when you know I am clearly old. And, by the way, this old lady ran a 5k last week, so I would be glad to help you cross the street!"

CHAPTER 36. YOU ARE "A-OK BOOMERS!"

Age-shaming in the Hair Salon: 65-year-old Candy hadn't had a haircut in over a year and she went to see a new hairdresser, Frederick. She sat in his chair, he greeted her and then started checking out her hair.

Frederick: "I believe that women 'of a certain age' shouldn't have long hair past their shoulders because it makes everything on their face look dragged down."

Candy: "Thank you for the suggestion, Frederick, but my face is my face, draggy or not. My long hair makes me feel sexy."

Frederick: "Oh!" and turning slightly red, perhaps at the thought of an AHFemale feeling sexy? He trimmed up his concept of whether "older women" could be sexy, and then only trimmed the split ends off her hair.

Harriet and Dawn and Self-Age-Honoring with "Focuspocus"

Harriet, at the ripe young age of 74, bemoaned looking in the mirror and seeing her aging father's eye bags and her aging mother's wrinkles staring back at her.

Harriet noticed that her daughter Dawn, even from an early age, smiled when she looked at herself in the mirror. Harriet decided to smile into the mirror and she liked what she saw.

Harriet changed the focus of her reflection in the mirror. This changed her self-talk and her self-image, almost like magic: "Hocuspocus, you now look great in the mirror." Or call it "focuspocus," the magic of poking the focus from the negative to the positive. This is an aging mirror version of "What you see is what you get" or what you focus on can bring you down or magically lift you up, without the face lift!

Why not be self-age-honoring by respecting one's own steadfast perseverance, strength, and spirit? And it can be done with the flip of a focuspocus!

Aging Women Warriors never age; Aging Women Warriors bring on the sage!

Lesson 2.
Own Your Crone

"Age is an issue of mind over matter. If you don't mind, it doesn't matter."—Mark Twain

With old age often comes bold sage. With walkers comes wisdom. With arthritis comes I-am-usually-right-is. With diminished hearing comes deeper listening. With weakening sight often comes strengthened insight. With fewer teeth come more spoken truths. With open heart surgery comes an open heart.

Time to own your crone! It should please us to be a Geezess! Isn't it foxy to have Boomer Moxie?! We crones can be on the front lines to end ageism and honor sageism.

Why not celebrate what some Aging Human Females refer to as The Third Act? The third act of a play consists of a resolution of dramatic questions posed, where players enjoy a strong sense of what they have accomplished and who they really are. And who doesn't want an earth-shattering climax?! Bring on the rave reviews and the Lifetime Achievement Awards!

Saging woman advocate Ann Kreilkamp shares, "For the first time in history, enormous numbers of women are traveling through the gate of menopause and looking forward to a lifespan of some 30 more years… We women have a certain hard-won wisdom, gleaned through consciously processing the experiences of our long and fruitful lives." (TRUTH, Ann Kreilkamp, *Crone: Women Coming of Age Magazine,* cronemagazine.com.)

If there are b'nei mitzvot, quinceañeras, and Sweet Sixteen Parties to celebrate young thirteen-, fifteen- and sixteen-year-old girls, isn't it time for Boomer Chicks to celebrate aging into the grey-atness of our 50s, 60s or 70s by owning our cronehood? Get inspired by many ancient civilizations, and some contemporary societies, who have revered and honored an older woman's healing ability, power, and wisdom.

Why not celebrate yourself as a WOW, a <u>W</u>oman <u>O</u>f <u>W</u>isdom, with your Precious Old Dames?! Sounds like an Own Your Crone Party!

Cordelia and her Own Your Crone Party

Cordelia's 70th birthday was coming and she was wondering how to celebrate this milestone. She hadn't had a birthday party in years because she didn't want to face her "advanced number." She decided that the time to own her crone was now, while she still had her health and her wits about her! She saw an article in *Pink Magazine* that described how she could give herself a crone party. (TRUTH, Elizabeth Millen, itsallpink.com/features/item/crone-power). Cordelia decided to plan a party combining a spiritual ceremony honoring how she had come to this place in her life, who she was now, and where her life journey was taking her.

The Invite

Hear Ye! Hear Ye! (Yes! Put on those hearing aids!)

You are invited to Cordelia's *Own Her Crone Party* for her 70th Birthday!

Cordelia is owning her CRONE: Cute Raunchy Oldster with Never-ending Expertise!

For Cordelia's rite of passage, please help her shine her Dame Diamond by bringing one of the following:

Feelings: Bring a wish or hope for Cordelia.

Revealings: Bring an old photo, an adventure story, a memory of Cordelia.

Bods: Bring your favorite advice about keeping your body strong, healthy, and sexy.

PODs: Bring what you love about your friendship with Cordelia.

Dress code: Fun and Funky!

The Party

Eight of Cordelia's Precious Old Dames tap-danced their way into her party, wearing their sparkly outfits. After hugs and kisses, and some bubbly and nosh, Cordelia's PODs formed a circle for the "Own Your Crone" ceremony. Cordelia's best POD Rhonda placed a crown of tea rose flowers on Cordelia's head. Rhonda handed a single birthday candle to each woman in the circle and placed Cordelia's Raspberry Chocolate Mousse birthday cake in the center.

Rhonda opened the circle with a toast to Cordelia:

"Let's raise our glasses as we honor Cordelia in this rite of passage to becoming a crone! We toast to you Cordelia for the light that shines within you, and the light you shine upon us. We honor your strong backbone, your soulful wishbone, and your outrageous funny bone. As I place this crown of crone upon your head, Cordelia, may you own your crone. You are hereby a WOW, a Woman Of Wisdom!"

Then the group sang a few choruses of "She's Got The Whole World in Her Hands," inserting their names instead of "sister" as they went around the circle including everyone's names.

Then Rhonda brought out her talking stick (a clear magic wand with glitter that floated to the bottom when turned vertically) for the crone blessing ritual. (When the glittery goo inside the wand swirled to the bottom of the wand, it was time to place a candle on Cordelia's cake and pass the wand to the next POD.)

Each gal placed a birthday candle on Cordelia's cake and offered a gift to polish the facets of her Dame Diamond:

Feelings: Karen shared a wish for Cordelia's continued good health.

Revealings: Beatrice shared a photo from her camping trip last summer with Cordelia showcasing their tent that had collapsed on them during the heavy rain their first night out. Beatrice complimented Cordelia on how she pursues her passion of nature, even when the weather doesn't cooperate!

Bods: Arlene shared her favorite morning meditation and stretch routine that helped her start her day in a calm, relaxed mood.

PODs: Wendy shared how much she loved laughing with Cordelia and had everyone laughing with some of their favorite puns.

Then the group sang a few choruses of "She's got the whole world in her hands" again.

Rhonda then lit a match to light all the wish candles on the crone cake.

"As we light these candles we are reminded of the light Cordelia brings to our world and of all our bright wishes for her strength, fulfillment, health, and joy in her passage to cronehood. Join me in singing Happy Cronehood to You." As Cordelia blew out the candles, she wished for all the wishes to come true!

Inspired to plan you or your best POD's OwnYour Crone Party? Check out Chapter 48, Chick Chat #2.

Chapter 37.
Gender Benders

"Language exerts hidden power, like the moon over the tides."
—Rita Mae Brown

Words have power. Words affect thought. Words are magic—the phrase "abracadabra" means, "As you speak, you create." Here are some common phrases that level the playing field between genders. Words can equalize womanpower and manpower.

Ballsy = Ovarian: *Adjective.* Powerful, gutsy. "That was so ovarian of her to ask for that raise."

Big Balls = Big Ovaries: *Noun.* Courage, strength. "She did THAT?! WOW! She has big ovaries!"

Blue Balls = Crimson Clit: *Noun.* Unfulfilled, non-orgasmic female sexual pleasure. "That make-out session left me with a crimson clit."

Boner = Pulsar: *Noun.* In astronomy, a pulsar is the pulsed emission of a highly magnetized star. In other words, female sexual arousal. "I took one look at him and I felt a pulsar in my vagina."

CHAPTER 37. GENDER BENDERS

Family Jewels = Wonderwomb: *Noun.* Reproductive organ. "Since menopause, my wonderwomb is heroically super calm."

Grow some Balls = Grow a Vagina: *Verb.* Get tough. "Why do people say 'grow some balls'? Balls are weak and sensitive. If you want to be tough, grow a vagina. Those things can take a pounding."—Sheng Wang, comedian

Hard-on = Wet-and-set: *Adjective.* Sexually aroused. "He looked dreamily into her eyes and she knew she was wet-and-set."

Man Up = Woman Up: *Verb.* Get strong. "She put on her big girl panties and woman-ed up."

Menopause = Manopause: *Noun.* Change of life for an Aging Human Male. "The hot flashbacks, the muffin bottom, the extra wrinkles on his penis, the brain sag—he is definitely showing the symptoms of manopause."

PMS = GMS: *Noun.* G̲eezer M̲oodiness S̲yndrome. "He's so Moody Blues-y—it must be GMS!"

Womenopause: *Noun.* Commonly called "menopause," derived from the French for "moon cessation," although during and after womenopause, no self-respecting AHFemale loses her ability to moon a deserving AHMale! "When she began womenopause, she liked to think of her hot flashes as flashes of inspiration. At other times, they felt like flashes of anger and she let it all hang out!"

According to Robin Williams, "No matter what people tell you, words and ideas can change the world." Be sure to check out A to Z for the Glossary Eyed for more game-changing words and concepts.

Chapter 38.
Love Your I Love Lucy Episodes: Self-Compassion

"If I don't do two or three stupid things in a week, I must be dead."
—Callie, 87 year old AHFemale

Crazy situations seem to just happen more and more often, especially when our AHFemale brains are just not multiprocessing or even single-processing the way they used to! It's sometimes embarrassing, especially when there are other people around, especially younger people, to witness these brain burps, brain hiccups, and brain farts!

One way to put goofy happenings into perspective is to think of them as *I Love Lucy* episodes! Who doesn't remember the episode where Lucy and Ethel worked on the candy factory line wrapping chocolates, stuffing extras into their mouths and pockets to keep up? Remember laughing out loud at Lucy, who was prepping for an Italian movie, climbing into a vat of grapes and stomping as she do-si-doed around her grape partner? And then there was Lucy getting drunk on Vitameatavegamin tonic as she downed spoonful after spoonful during many takes for the commercial!

You are not alone in your best laid plans turning into disasters. And why not ditch your embarrassment and have a great laugh when you eventually get up the nerve to share your episodes and brain farts at your Pee POD Poise Party?!

CHAPTER 38. LOVE YOUR I LOVE LUCY EPISODES: SELF-COMPASSION

As *Helen Weels* says, "To err is human, to self-forgive is divine... to share is funny!"

> ### Annie and Her "Lucy and her Cell Phone" Episode
>
> Annie was in Sears looking for a purse. She had chosen Sears because they had dozens and dozens of purses within her budget. She wanted a purse with a zipper pocket on the outside that was big enough to hold her cell phone, so she decided to try out one purse she liked by putting her cellphone in the pocket to make sure it fit. Then she tried her phone in another purse, and then she saw another cute purse, and another cute purse, and then... she realized that she didn't remember which purse she had last put her cell phone in!
>
> Annie looked through a dozen purses and couldn't find her phone! She panicked. Feeling mighty stupid, she went over to a salesperson, who looked all of 16 years old, and explained the situation. The salesperson then shared this with another salesperson, who also looked all of 16, and, needless to say, they both looked at Annie like she was a little nuts. The first salesperson took out her cell phone and called Annie's phone, but Annie's phone was on silent mode, so nothing happened. Finally, after a few minutes, they saw a purse shaking and vibrating on the shelf and Annie went and got her cell phone out of that purse.
>
> She was so embarrassed! (And yes, she did buy that purse!) It took her a few weeks before she shared this with her PODs, whereupon an avalanche of laughter cascaded through the room.
>
> And Annie's story started an avalanche of *I Love Lucy* episode-style stories from her PODs...

Brenda and Her "Lucy and Her Boob" Episode

Brenda loved to play tennis. One Tuesday, she went to her indoor tennis club to play with a male friend, and as she unzipped her sports jacket, she looked down and saw… OH, NO! Brenda had had a mastectomy several years before and used a prosthesis on her left side and she had forgotten to put her prosthesis in her bra! She was a 38D on her right side and, without the prosthesis, a 38A on her left side!

Brenda panicked, and then had an idea: she ran into the ladies' room, pulled out her spare pair of sport socks from her gym bag, and shoved them into her bra. Whew! She was good to go!

After recovering from her embarrassment, she later laughed with her girlfriends at her Pee POD Poise Party over the new meaning of the saying, "Put a sock in it!"

Georgette and Mark and Her "Lucy and the Soap Suds" Episode

Georgette spilled an entire bottle of liquid laundry soap on the floor of her laundry room. She "tsk, tsk"-ed herself as she mopped up the soap with towel after towel. She threw the towels in the washing machine and then went to fix lunch.

After lunch she went to put the towels into the dryer, and was shocked to see a mountain of soap suds completely hiding the washing machine, and spread out over the entire laundry room floor. Her loud, "OH, NO!" brought her partner Mark into the laundry room. Soon their dismay turned into belly laughs. Mark videoed her *I Love Georgette* episode so she could share it with her with friends at her Pee POD party. Then Georgette began her second mop-up of the day, with help from her beloved Mark.

CHAPTER 38. LOVE YOUR I LOVE LUCY EPISODES: SELF-COMPASSION

Lillie and Her "Lucy and the Sexy Postmaster" Episode

Lillie always liked to send snail mail birthday cards to family and friends and put special celebratory birthday cake stamps on the envelope. She went to the post office to buy some stamps and, as she was waiting in line she checked out the postmaster, who was definitely eye candy. His good looks got her musing about her love life.

When Lillie got to the counter, she asked the postman for some "celibate stamps." He looked at her quizzically. She repeated, "I would like some celibate stamps." He looked over to his counter colleague and loudly asked, "Do we have any stamps commemorating celibates?" That postman looked puzzled for a minute, then said, with a smile on his face, "Do you mean celebration stamps?" Lillie began blushing and stammered, "Yes, something for birthdays!" Then she quickly paid for her birthday-cake-themed stamps, grabbed them, and ran out the door, as the people still waiting in line chuckled. Sharing this story at her Pee POD party prompted many amusing celibate-themed cards from her PODs on her next birthday!

Chapter 39.
Be Your Own Best POD: Self-Kindness and Self-Forgiveness

"I never loved another person the way I loved myself." — Mae West

Every Aging Human Female has decades and decades of living, sometimes challenging living. Anger arises, fights are fought, words wound, bitterness bites, sadness succumbs, accidents abound, plans pouf out, and right intentions go awry. As Frank Sinatra sang in "My Way," "Regrets, I've had a few," and especially after having had a few too many.

In *The Self-Compassion Skills Workbook*, Tim Desmond offers: "Self-compassion is the recognition that no matter what is going on in our lives we are lovable… We can embrace our own suffering like a mother holding a newborn baby." (TRUTH, W.W. Norton & Company, 2017.)

After bearing your chest to your best POD, what would she say to make things more bearable? Okay, she may scold you at first with a "Tsk, tsk," and shake her head a little in disbelief. But then your best **POD** would say, "You did the very best you could. Hold your bruised heart with kindness and tenderness. Heal your heart with compassion."

CHAPTER 39. BE YOUR OWN BEST POD: SELF-KINDNESS AND SELF-FORGIVENESS

Marcia and Emily and Self-Kindness

Sixty-five-year-old Marcia had a complicated relationship with her depressed mother for her whole life. When Marcia's mother developed Alzheimers, Marcia moved her into a memory care facility and, amidst her busy work schedule, Marcia visited her mother almost every day. At first, it felt healing to offer her mother the loving nurturance she herself had never received.

However, after several months, Marcia dreaded visiting her mother, who was often angry and regularly forgot who Marcia was. Marcia felt ashamed for being reluctant to visit her mother.

Marcia confided to her best friend Emily about her guilt around these visits. Emily said, "But Marcia, some daughters would hate to visit their mother and wouldn't go. You feel what you feel, and, despite those feelings, you show up. You are there for your mother as best as you can be."

Marcia felt relieved. Emily added, "The key is to be kind to yourself, to believe in your heart that you are doing the *very best* that you can." Marcia started to cry. Emily was her best POD who supported her and loved her no matter what.

Emily gave Marcia a hug and offered, "This is all so tough. You need some loving mothering yourself! How about I treat you to dinner at Barney's tonight, and we'll top it off with a gooey Hot Fudge Brownie Mountain—with two spoons!" For the first time in a while, Emily smiled, a big, big smile.

Chapter 40.
Your-Self-Healing through Your-Self-Reflection

"Time spent in self-reflection is never wasted—it is an intimate date with yourself."—Paul TP Wong, Canadian psychologist

Forget about looking at your reflection in the mirror, especially in the morning! How about imagining what an inner mirror of your heart would reveal? Certainly there are some bumps and bruises, some sparkly places, and some inner yearnings within your heart. Polish your *Dame Diamond* to a sparkly shine with self-reflection.

Feelings: Instead of asking what you want to do with your life, ask yourself how you want to feel. What will bring more of those feelings into your life?

Revealings: What new passion is just around the corner waiting to be revealed to you?

BODs: Your body is like the Timex™ watch in that old commercial. Remember when John Cameron Swayze used to retrieve the Timex from a tank of water, hold it to his ear, and say, "It takes a licking and keeps on ticking!" How can you best honor your body, your oldest friend?

PODs: You can never attend too many Pee POD Poise Parties! Your female friendships put joy in your heart and, literally, add years to your life!

CHAPTER 40. YOUR-SELF-HEALING THROUGH YOUR-SELF-REFLECTION

Lesson 1.
I'm Sorry that I Said "I'm Sorry:" Irene's "I wish"

"Never ruin an apology with an excuse." —Anonymous

In the 1970s movie, *Love Story,* Ali McGraw told Ryan O'Neal that "Love means never having to say you're sorry." Was she right or wrong? Sometimes bad behavior warrants an apology, but sometimes life just happens out of our control. Chances are most AHFemales have an overabundance of the words "I'm sorry" in their vocabularies, especially for events that just happen.

Things happen! Life HAPPENS! The Universe HAPPENS! And we will feel better about ourselves for acknowledging our lack of control for so many of the *"oops-es"* in life. We women of a certain generation and a certain age need to adopt this thought: Stop apologizing for the universe! "I'm sorry the dishwasher broke." "I'm sorry it rained on our picnic." "I'm sorry the dog threw up on the rug." "I'm sorry that I am always saying 'I'm sorry!'" It is embarrassing to count how many times in a day we Boomer Babes mutter, "I'm sorry."

Irene's *"I wish:"* Don't apologize for Life or for The Universe. Happenings happen. Turn events beyond your control into wishes. Turn "I'm sorry" into *"I wish..."* Changing apologies to wishes goes beyond words of regret to transform the spirit in the connection.

Irene's *"I wish"*... to Change Life's Happenings

"I wish I could have been on time. My neighbor's cat ran under my car and I couldn't get her out!"

"I wish I could talk longer on the phone but I have the hiccups."

"I wish we had a cooked turkey for Thanksgiving, but both our oven and microwave broke!"

"I wish I understood you better, honey, but I just don't and I am thinking I never will!"

"I wish that I could say *'I wish'* more often rather than 'I'm sorry'!"

And then there are things within our control that are sorry-worthy.

"I'm sorry" for My Own Happenings

"I'm sorry that I rear-ended your car. I was singing along with The Beatles and got distracted."

"I'm sorry that I forgot your birthday. Can I take you out for a special lunch soon?"

"I'm sorry, honey, but I was distracted and wasn't listening to you."

"I'm sorry that I have such a lifelong habit of apologizing!"

The *Aging Human Female Serenity Prayer* saves the day:

Grant me *Irene's "I wish"* for the things I cannot change,

"I'm sorry" for the things I can,

And the wisdom to know the difference.

CHAPTER 40. YOUR-SELF-HEALING THROUGH YOUR-SELF-REFLECTION

> ### *Rochelle and Sharon and "I'm Sorry"*
>
> Rochelle flew cross country to take care of her aging mom Sharon, who was hospitalized for emergency back surgery. Sharon was so regretful that her daughter's whole life was upended that Sharon kept apologizing and apologizing to Rochelle.
>
> ***Sharon:*** "I'm so sorry that you had to interrupt your life to spend days with me at the hospital."
>
> ***Rochelle:*** "Mom, it's not your fault. It's okay."
>
> ***Sharon:*** "Well, I still feel so sorry that this happened."
>
> ***Rochelle:*** "Mom, I wish you would stop apologizing. You were rear-ended and hurt your back. Not your fault."
>
> ***Sharon:*** "I'm just so sorry."
>
> After several days, Sharon left the hospital, but she didn't leave her "I'm sorry"s behind. Sharon apologized for her empty refrigerator, the lumpy mattress on Rochelle's bed, and for Rochelle needing to get up during the night to give her pain meds. After a week, Sharon was feeling much better.
>
> ***Rochelle:*** "Mom, I gotta tell you, I wish you would stop apologizing for things you can't control. It makes me feel guilty and it makes you feel bad. Sometimes things just happen."
>
> ***Sharon:*** "I'm sorry. I didn't realize I was apologizing so much."
>
> ***Rochelle:*** "You just apologized again! And you apologized because you couldn't get out of bed to make the morning coffee and because you didn't have my favorite coffee on hand… Hmm, let's have a contest. Whoever says, 'I'm sorry,' the least today gets her choice of Ben and Jerry's tonight."
>
> ***Sharon:*** "Sounds good to me! But I'm sorry that you'll have to run out to the store to get it."

And the story continues…

> *Rochelle:* "MOM! Stop apologizing! Now your Sorry Count is 1!"
>
> After dinner...
>
> *Rochelle:* "Mom, the Sorry Count is Rochelle 3, Mom 13."
>
> *Sharon:* "I really wanted to win. But I said 'I'm sorry' about a fraction of the times I usually do!"
>
> *Rochelle* (with a wink): "Mom, you just jacked your Sorry Count up to 14!"
>
> Rochelle smiled all the way through her pint of Cherry Garcia, which she shared with her mom, who was a super fan of The Grateful Dead.

(Too bad that there is no Ben & Jerry's flavor named after singer Connie Francis, who sang "Who's Sorry Now?"!)

Lesson 2. Gender Discrimination and The Erma Edict

"You may not control all the events that happen to you, but you can decide not to be reduced by them."—Maya Angelou

Remember back in 1968 watching on TV as angry women at the *Miss America* contest in Atlantic City outed their feminist rage by burning their bras? Remember consciousness-raising groups, women discussing their lives and the men in their lives and calling themselves "feminists," a shocking epithet at the time? Remember embracing the thought that "the personal is the political," from Carol Hanich?

Fast forward to the 21st century. So we women burned our bras in the '60s. Now we need to continue by burning our SPANX. Gender equity issues are still prevalent, despite the greater social acceptance of "house husbands" (but still, who really cleans the bathroom in most households?!) and the rise of the #MeToo movement.

The Women's Truth Foundation (WTF) has identified a silent disease that causes queasiness and muteness in Human Females when confronted with improper sexual words and actions by a Human Male.

GDQD: Gender Discrimination Quease Dis-ease. *Noun.* The queasiness, or dis-ease that a female feels in her stomach when a situation involves sexual inappropriateness, be it sexual discrimination, sexual politics, sexual intimations, or sexual acting out. This queasiness may not be consciously experienced until after the incident has passed.

So we've all been there. A male makes an inappropriate comment—sexually provocative or sexually demeaning or gender stereotyping—and we feel that queasiness in our stomach. How to respond? Sometimes this comment comes out of the blue (no pun intended). We are caught off-guard, and unsure how to react. We may feel a slight upset in our stomachs, some heated anger in our chests, or a blush of shame in our cheeks. Our bodies know, but our brains aren't tuned in quickly enough to activate our mouths. We remain silent, give a weak smile, or offer a grimace. Oftentimes, we don't have a strong and true response until later, and the moment has passed.

Is there a Pepto-Dismal that can transform a Gender Discrimination Quease Dis-ease interaction into a healthy situation? It helps if a woman is prepared. She can premedicate and strengthen herself by practicing and internalizing *The Erma Edict.* Recall how saying, "That won't work for me," worked with your AHMale?

Refresher on The Erma Edict:

"That won't work for me!" are five simple words that set the limit. No apologies, no excuses!

It's time to tweak The Boy Scout Motto, "Be Prepared," to fit an Aging Human Female Motto: "Be prepared with *The Erma Edict.*" Why not practice it while doing some morning tummy crunches? And why not rehearse it before an upcoming situation where you anticipate a quease in your tummy —when discussing a raise with your boss, at a party where things may get raunchy, or in a unisex steam bath at the gym where some jokes from men have seemed inappropriate before. The more "That won't work for me!" is practiced and used, the more it will work for you!

(See Chapter 11, Lesson 4, Womanhandling the Boundaries.)

CHAPTER 40. YOUR-SELF-HEALING THROUGH YOUR-SELF-REFLECTION

Helen and GDQD

Helen graduated from college in the '60s with a B.S. degree in computer science, which was unusual at the time since women comprised only 2% of science majors at her school. She applied for a job at a small computer start-up and knew she was the only woman among dozens of male applicants. *Helen* decided to wear her cranberry miniskirt and pink semi-transparent blouse to her job interview. During the interview, the man who would be her future boss asked her if she had plans to get married, if she planned to have children and if she would then stay at home with them. *Helen* answered the questions with a firm "No." *Helen* got the job.

Helen excelled as a computer systems designer. After several months on the job, *Helen* was asked to attend a meeting of computer analysts who were several levels above her job designation, which was counter to company guidelines, but the team needed her expertise. The men asked her to take notes to justify her presence and called her a "secretary."

After her yearly review, *Helen* discovered that her annual raise was less than her male counterparts. When questioned, her boss said, "These men are paying a mortgage and have wives and kids to support. You don't." She felt a sudden bout of GDQD and thought she might lose her lunch, but retained her composure and her soft smile.

Years later, in retirement, *Helen* spent time reflecting on her younger career experiences in a male-dominated environment. She wished she had spoken up more, but also had compassion for her younger self and embraced her pride at what she had accomplished. She remembered how she had experienced GDQD when wearing sexy clothes to a highly competitive job interview, and she was glad things were different for her daughter. When a man asked *Helen* to take notes at her annual Homeowners' Association meeting, she happily invoked the ***The Erma Edict*** and replied in her AHFemale strong voice, "That won't work for me."

Lesson 3.
Move Past Your Past

"There are no regrets in life, just lessons learned."
— Jennifer Aniston

Of course it is difficult to put challenging, even traumatic, events out of your mind and not have them gnaw at you in your waking hours or in your sleep. You want to move on from that painful hurt, intense anger, deep sorrow, and shocking betrayal, but the truth is that some of these challenges replay in your mind. Why not try these two very different healing exercises, one involving **Helen** and one involving **Rae Jean**?

Move Past Your Past Exercise #1: Helen's Loving Arms

Helen occasionally ruminated about her senior year in college and how her best friend cheated on her with her longtime boyfriend. **Helen's** Reiki teacher Corinda helped her move past her old pain with this exercise.

Corinda spoke calmly to **Helen:** "Sit quietly. Take a deep breath. Picture that moment when you found your best friend and your boyfriend in bed in each other's arms. Breathe. Picture someone coming up behind you and putting loving arms around you, hugging you. That person says, 'You are lovable. You deserve so much love.'"

Corinda continued, "Feel your body relax into those loving arms. Breathe. Those loving arms and loving words have changed your feelings and your past experience. They have soothed your old wound. The scar is fading. The pain in your heart is easing. Healing your heart in the past has helped heal your heart in the present. Breathe… Relax… Breathe."

Helen's mind quieted, her heart softened. **Helen** calmly thanked Corinda.

CHAPTER 40. YOUR-SELF-HEALING THROUGH YOUR-SELF-REFLECTION

Move Past Your Past Exercise #2: Rae Jean's Kickass Action

Rae Jean's cousin Jamie kept mentally reliving what she called "That Restaurant Debacle," the time when her partner of 15 years, Trey, told her in a Thai restaurant that their relationship was over. She asked for help from her cousin **Rae Jean**, who had survived a wicked relationship breakup.

Rae Jean suggested that Jamie move past her past by rewriting that restaurant scene as a scene from a Jamie Bond movie, with Jamie herself as the Super Shero and her ex, Trey, as a devious lover-villain-spy.

Rae Jean: "So, Jamie, you are British undercover agent 36-24-36 for M50+. You and your lover Trey are eating at a Thai restaurant on the Thames, enjoying your meal, casually sipping sexy Thai cocktails from coconuts decorated with those little umbrellas. Then suddenly, as Trey reaches for the bottle of soy sauce, his shirt sleeve slips up his arm and you see the faint tattoo of a Silver Snake on the underside of his wrist! The Silver Snake is the symbol of the spy gang you are pursuing.

You are enraged at Trey's betrayal. You, as Super Shero Jamie Bond, grab Trey's wrist and flip him up into a twist. He lands flat on his back on the table. His eyes are aghast as you bop him on the head with your coconut, dump drunken rice noodles all over his face, put chopsticks up his nostrils, and pour hot sauce down his pants. In a final act of revenge, you insert the purple drink umbrella between his lips.

You call for back-up: 'Trey is a traitor. His good fortune has crumbled like a fortune cookie. Come and get him!' As your M50+ POD arrives to haul him away, you stand over him, hands on hips, triumphant in your stiletto heels, as you give him the Goldfinger!

There, doesn't that feel better, Jamie? As they say in James Bond movieland, 'Live and let old pains die.'"

Jamie laughed and laughed. And Jamie invited her dear cousin **Rae Jean** out for an all-expenses-paid Thai meal.

Lesson 4.
In Ourselves Do We Trust

"All the world is made of faith, and trust, and pixie dust."
— J.M Barrie, Peter Pan

Our quarters say, "In God We Trust." But what is written on our hearts? Do we trust ourselves and our strengths? Do we acknowledge all that life has thrown at us, and that we are still here and standing—with or without a cane, but we are still here. Our spirits have been tested and we are proudly WISER Aging Human Females.

We are **WISER:**

Women of...

Intelligence: Okay, so all those years of mistakes have to have taught us something!

Spirit: Take pride in your steadfast faith and strong heart!

Experience: Let's do the math: 365 days x 66 years = 24,090 days. Then add in 2,555 days (for those teen years, which count double) +16.5 leap days for a grand total of 26,661.5 days. Wow, that is a lot of experience!

Resilience: Your skin is now so tough you might want to Oil of Olay your face three times a day!

Once we honor all of our triumphs, amidst the tribulations, we can embrace the wisdom of baby doctor Dr. Benjamin Spock, who instructed us to, "Trust yourself! You know more than you think you do!" (TRUTH, Benjamin Spock,

CHAPTER 40. YOUR-SELF-HEALING THROUGH YOUR-SELF-REFLECTION

The Common Sense Book of Baby and Child Care, first sentence, Duell, Sloan and Pearce, 1946.)

As you have aged, you have become WISER, a true Women of Intelligence Spirit Experience and Resilience!

> ### *Bob and Carol and Ted and Alice*
>
> Bob and Carol were married for 33 years when Bob walked out and filed for divorce. At the divorce hearing, Bob admitted to having had an ongoing affair with his secretary for ten years. Carol was devastated.
>
> At 66 years of age, Carol had to rearrange her entire life. After five years of being single, and five years of therapy, Carol met Ted and they really hit it off. But Carol was scared.
>
> "How can I trust Ted after what happened to me?" Carol asked her best friend Alice.
>
> "It's not a matter of trusting Ted," Alice advised. "It's trusting yourself and knowing that you will be fine no matter what happens with Ted."
>
> Carol decided to give her trust issues and her relationship time. After all, it's not easy adjusting to an aging relationship when an aging man and an aging woman are both set in their ways. Carol trusted her friend Alice's advice and also heeded Maya Angelou's advice: "Have enough courage to trust love one more time and always one more time." Carol and Ted have been partners, albeit sometimes struggling partners, for over ten years now and have pledged to always be together, but they still take it one day at a time. At last, Carol trusted in herself.

Lesson 5.
Have a Latte with Your Younger-You

"Youth is a gift of nature, but age is a work of art."
—Stanislaw Jerzy Lec, Polish poet and philosopher

Think of yourself at 21. Try to recall a photo of you at that young age. Keep that photo of your Younger-You in your mind. Imagine you and your Younger-You have each ordered a latte at Cafe Cocoa and are sitting across the table from each other. Your Younger-You says, "You seem to have survived many challenges and enjoyed many adventures. C'mon, please share your wisdom with me?!"

Ease into the conversation. Take your time. What joys and sorrows, challenges and triumphs, hurts and revealings will you share? What regrets and great decisions will you re-live? What advice will you give your Younger-You? You and your Younger-You are two BFFs sharing coffee talk.

CHAPTER 40. YOUR-SELF-HEALING THROUGH YOUR-SELF-REFLECTION

Helen and her Sweet Sixteen

Helen meets with her 16-year-old Younger-You for coffee. She smiles at her bubble haircut and her madras skirt and saddle shoes. "Hi, sweetie, sit down. It's so good to see you. You don't know it now, but you are very lovable and very cute. You don't know how many challenges you will face and how strong you will be. You don't know all the joys that will fill your heart for decades. Let me offer you some advice from the future:

1. Honor humor—it eases the heart and allows love to flow in.
2. It's all good.
3. Always Depend on your Poise.
4. Be open to all the twists and turns in life. I've been a computer scientist, teacher, wife, mother, entrepreneur, child advocate, retiree, mentor, artist, writer, partner, best friend. Who woulda thunk it?
5. Is it bad news or good news? I fell while playing racquetball and broke my wrist. Bad news? The stranger on the next court helped me up and became my lifelong partner. Good news!
6. You can do this. You really, really can. Trust in yourself! You are so strong!
7. Loving yourself is necessary, but not always easy.
8. When you open your heart to a man, make sure your eyes are wide open, too.
9. Don't waste time worrying. I wasted so much time worrying!
10. Check in with your heart as often as you check yourself in a mirror.
11. Stop thinking you know where you're going. You don't. Start appreciating where you are.
12. Lifelong friends hold your history in their heart.
13. Be kind.
14. Love nature.
15. Vote.
16. A tender heart saves the day.

I wish you so well!"

Rae Jean and her Sassyass Sixteen

Rae Jean meets with her 16 year-old Younger-You at The Corner Pub. She checks out the skirt that is two inches above her knee (that will earn her two hours detention after school) and the cocky smile on her face. "Hey, babe, good to see that you are doing your own thing. Who needs those rules, anyway? You are one tough cookie. I know you will struggle to remove that protection around your heart, but go for it. Here are some of the hard knock lessons that may soften some blows:

1. Be a badass with a good ass.
2. Nike is my spiritual inspiration: Just do it!
3. When raising kids, know that two heads are **NOT** better than one when it comes to head lice.
4. Psychologists talk about "closure." But when it comes to deep losses, "closure" is BS.
5. Feelings just get in the way of fun.
6. It's the curves, hills, potholes, bumps, and rockslides that make mountain biking exciting!
7. Every day of my six weeks of cancer radiation, after the treatment I rewarded myself with a mini Baby Ruth candy bar. I am five years cancer-free. Who knew that Baby Ruths cure cancer?
8. True courage is experiencing **EVERYTHING** as an adventure.
9. Once I walked through a graveyard and realized that no tombstone had the weight of the dead woman written on it.
10. Love makes the world go round, but if love's twelve rounds of boxing matches, it's not worth it.
11. When it comes to adult children, keep an open heart and a closed wallet.
12. The true test of friendship: When you are comfortable farting with that friend!
13. Blaming the family you grew up with has an expiration date of twenty years.
14. Don't let the a__holes get you down.
15. My cardiologist says that the best way to a man's heart is through his groin area.
16. A warrior heart conquers all.

And remember to whoop it up!"

CHAPTER 40. YOUR-SELF-HEALING THROUGH YOUR-SELF-REFLECTION

Lesson 6.
Have a Heart-to-heart with Yourself

"My therapist told me the way to achieve true inner peace is to finish what I start. So far I've finished two bags of M&Ms and a chocolate cake. I feel better already." –Dave Barry

As The Byrds sang, quoting *The Old Testament*, "To everything, turn, turn, turn… there is a time for every purpose under heaven." Sometimes it's fun and supportive to share feelings and experiences with our Precious Old Dames at a Pee POD Poise Party. Sometimes it is special to do that Dave Barry chocolate thing alone, with a mug of chamomile tea—okay, add a shot of whiskey if it's been that kind of day! Spend some precious girl time alone with your favorite girlfriend, yourself, asking yourself some amusing, introspective questions in the privacy of your own room, your own womb and your own heart.

One question to start your self-reflection. Is the glass half-empty or half-full? ***Rae Jean*** gives you permission to forget half-empty/half-full and make this self-reflection a full-on whine experience!

If you want to add some structure and fun to your me-time, flip to **The Precious Old Dames' Party Playbook**, which is chock full of checklists, questions, games, quotes, and imaginary scenarios. Choose to Schmooze with yourself for a special Pee POD Poise Party of One. As *Saturday Night Live*'s Wayne says, "Party On, Dude!" Or in this case, "Party On, Dudess!"

Chapter 41.
Good Morning, Glory

"There are two ways of waking up in the morning. One is to say, 'Good morning, God[dess,]' and the other is to say, 'Good God[dess], morning!" — Bishop Fulton J. Sheen, Catholic bishop

Morning rites and rituals can either jumpstart or jump-stop your day, especially in retirement when you have nothing to do and all day to do it! Knowing your morning rhythm, be it waltz or cha-cha-cha, can help you with the first steps in your daily dance.

Finding mornings that fit your own rhythm may require some tricky tap-dancing if your AHFred Astaire is be-bopping to a different tune. You may be hiding your head under the sheets if he starts the morning scratchily singing "Oh, What a Beautiful Morning" from *Oklahoma!* Or maybe you're snoring blissfully in bed if he snuck out for an early morning bike ride. Each morning can be quite a dandy dance when you are rubbing elbows at the sink with your leftie as you both brush your teeth, or are doing the shower jig together, his tempo "cold as ice" and yours "hot as Hades!"

But let's assume that, given time, you and your AHMale are partially swaying to the same morning beat and no longer stepping on each other's toes. Why not focus on your own morning rhythm?

CHAPTER 41. GOOD MORNING, GLORY

Helen and Her Glorious Morning Waltz

Helen wakes early each morning, usually up before dawn around 5:30am. It's a slow but grateful "Good morning, Goddess!" She does some morning stretches in bed and stays in bed reading her current fave book for a bit and WhatsApp-ing her grown children on their many travels. Then she grabs a robe and goes to get her morning paper.

Helen loved the teenage summers that she spent with her favorite, very dear Aunt Thelma and cousins on Long Island. Aunt Thelma loved gardening and around her backyard porch she planted morning glories whose blue-white blossoms opened each morning. Breakfast was usually served on the back porch and Aunt Thelma was always there to greet ***Helen*** with a sweet, "Good morning, Glory."

When ***Helen*** retired to Florida, she planted a long row of blue morning glories along her front walkway. Now, as she goes out to get her paper, blue flowers greet her and her memories of her Aunt Thelma warm her heart.

Helen fixes a big breakfast of pancakes for herself, quietly pan-flipping her cakes to the Bobby Lewis '60s hit "Tossin' and Turnin." While getting juice from the fridge, ***Helen*** reads Maya Angelous's affirmation on the fridge door: "Nothing can dim the light from within." ***Helen*** waltz-starts her day with quiet connections, a full belly, and a mellow heart.

continued on next page ➡

Rae Jean and her Glorious Morning Jitterbug

For **Rae Jean** the morning jumpstarts at the ripe hour of 8am. She's rarin' to go and wants to rev up to higher gears by 8:15am. It's always a "Good Goddess, morning already and I haven't accomplished anything yet?!" As soon as she salsas out of bed, she rushes into the kitchen for her drug of choice, coffee. She likes her caffeine with caffeine! Above the coffee-maker is **Rae Jean's** inspirational quote from Helen Keller: "Life is either a daring adventure or nothing at all."

While the coffee-maker is doing its thing, **Rae Jean** is doing her thing, singing and rocking to her favorite radio station while making notes on her smartphone of To-Dos, To-Calls, and Groceries-To-Buy. Breakfast is another something to check off the list as she grabs a bagel, shmears it with cream cheese and wraps it in a napkin to take with her in the car on the way to her volunteer morning at the animal shelter. **Rae Jean** jitterbug-starts her morning with hot coffee, long lists, cold breakfast on the run and a be-bop in her hips.

What is your morning music? To each her own. An AHFemale can ground herself with coffee grounds or grounding yoga postures, or both. Whether in a slow dance rhythm or a samba sway, every morning ritual can be orchestrated to make it a "Singin' in the Rain" kind of day, no matter what the weather.

Chapter 42.
Yes!

"i imagine that yes is the only living thing."
—e.e.cummings, poet

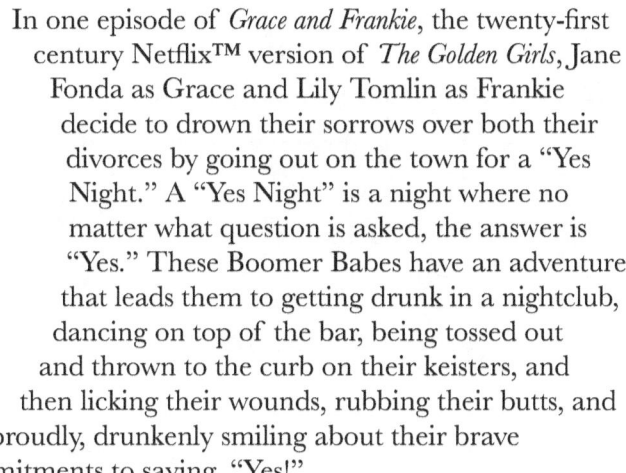

In one episode of *Grace and Frankie*, the twenty-first century Netflix™ version of *The Golden Girls*, Jane Fonda as Grace and Lily Tomlin as Frankie decide to drown their sorrows over both their divorces by going out on the town for a "Yes Night." A "Yes Night" is a night where no matter what question is asked, the answer is "Yes." These Boomer Babes have an adventure that leads them to getting drunk in a nightclub, dancing on top of the bar, being tossed out and thrown to the curb on their keisters, and then licking their wounds, rubbing their butts, and proudly, drunkenly smiling about their brave commitments to saying, "Yes!"

Many Aging Human Females have a lifelong cultural tendency to say, "Yes," to be the "Good Girl" who goes along to get along. For many Boomer Chicks, inner growth is in the struggle of learning to say, "NO, Dear!" rather than, "Yes, Dear!"

However, when an AHFemale feels really free to make a choice, sometimes fear can raise its scary head, leading to a quick and safe, "NO!" Fear can mess up any Boomer Chick's head. **Rae Jean** advises a knee-jerk response to that fear: "'Yes!' is a screaming, laugh-out-loud Boomer Babe affirmation telling Lady Life, 'Bring it on!'"

And what about the consequences? Have faith! As Tina Fey says, "Say yes and you'll figure it out afterwards."

Your mission, Aging Human Female, if you choose to accept it: Say "YES!" to exploring strange new adventures. And be sure that the video self-destructs afterwards!

It takes a good POD to urge you to your "YES!"

And it takes a great POD to be by your side while you are "YES"-ing together!

> *Rae Jean's YES! LIST for Helen*
>
> *Helen*, say Yes to sushi.
> *Helen*, say Yes to leaving the house without makeup.
> *Helen*, say Yes to stepping on the scale only once a month.
> *Helen,* say Yes to anger and not feeling guilty about it.
> *Helen,* say Yes to doing nothing.
> *Helen,* say YES to faith in yourself!

> *Helen's YES! LIST for Rae Jean*
>
> *Rae Jean*, say YES to binge-watching *This is Us*.
> *Rae Jean*, say YES to buying flowers for yourself.
> *Rae Jean*, say YES to drinking more water than craft beer.
> *Rae Jean*, say YES to telling me in words how much I mean to you!
> *Rae Jean,* say YES to buttoning your lip (not shooting from the hip).
> *Rae Jean,* say YES to faith in yourself!

Chapter 43.
Out Your Outrageous YOU!

"I think the reward for conformity is that everyone likes you except yourself."—Rita Mae Brown

Remember how in high school all the popular "in" girls tried to dress way cool, same matchy-matchy skirts and tops? All the "in" girls had one cool hairdo, short and teased, and all the "in" guys had one cool Fonzie phrase, "HEYYYYY!!" Then, all of a sudden, things went all topsy-turvy. The Rolling Stones couldn't get any satisfaction; The Beatles wanted to hold your hand while giving cultural norms the finger; and Bob Dylan claimed that the answers were blowing in the wind but there was no way to keep the usual kite afloat.

Now, decades later, why not, once again, throw convention aside and embrace even more invention. Why not just be yourself? Time to cue that small whispery voice: "Am I okay with me? I only need to satisfy myself!"

Lesson 1.
Who Do YOU Want to BE?

"Remind yourself that you cannot fail at being yourself."
—Wayne Dyer, psychologist

In her book, *At Seventy: A Journal*, May Sarton says that as we age, we become more and more ourselves. "We have to dare to be ourselves, however frightening or strange that self may prove to be." (TRUTH, W.W. Norton and Company, Inc., 1987.)

Isn't it time to give up the image your parents have of you, the image your siblings have of you, the image your high school cronies or college roommates have of you, the image your exes have of you, the image your AHMale has of you? It's time to embrace the you that you now want for yourself. You *and only you* define yourself.

Now, stop right here. Take a deep breath. There are no roadblocks to your thinking! Who do you admire—a celebrity, a heroine, friend, family member, historical figure? What qualities do you like and respect and envy in them?

Now picture yourself saying those words, doing those activities, wearing those clothes, performing those deeds that you admire. Why not try on one of those much-respected qualities, actions, or ways of being?

For a fun activity on outing your outrageous you with your gal pals, see **The Precious Old Dames' Party Playbook**, Chapter 50, Flow and Tell #5, Re-version Yourself.

CHAPTER 43. OUT YOUR OUTRAGEOUS YOU!

Suzanne, Patricia, Vi, Bettye, Sandy, Iris, Ginny and Ernestine Outing their Outrageous Selves

"Reinvention after 50: Many Women Wait Decades to Fulfill Their Dreams" is an exciting series of interviews collected by Jenny Rogers. (TRUTH, *The Washington Post*, 06/09/2019.) Here are some snapshots of Aging Human Females from that article who dared to follow their dreams… and you can too!

Note: "yy" = "years young," as in the Rolling Stones, "Get your ya-ya's out!"

Suzanne, 57yy, became a doctor twenty-five years after being accepted to medical school.

Patricia, 57yy, became a stand-up comedian after retiring from her teaching career.

Vi, 68yy, was elected to her city council after working for the City of Charlotte, VA.

Bettye, 73yy, sang for Barack Obama's Inaugural Ball after being an unknown singer for decades.

Sandy, 85yy, came out as lesbian to her two children and three grandchildren.

Iris, 63yy, became a well-known author after retiring as a full-time lawyer.

Ginny, 77yy, started a shoestring nonprofit after working in corporate finance.

Ernestine, 82yy, became a champion bodybuilder after long avoiding exercise.

What might your next dream challenge be? Use this handy Mad Lib to get you dreaming and scheming:

_____, _____, became a _____ after _____.
(Your name) (Your age)   (Your dream)   (Your past life experience)

Lesson 2.
What Do YOU Want to DO?
Your Luna List

"Nothing is impossible. The word itself says 'I'm possible.'"
—Audrey Hepburn

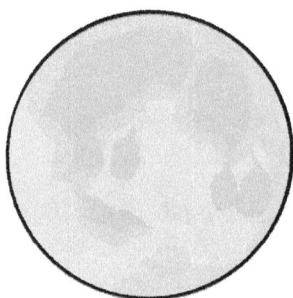

Why not tap into your wildest fantasies? After all, dreaming is free!

Try making a **Luna List**, from the Latin word *luna* or *lucere*, meaning "to shine." What activities will have your smile beaming from sea to shining sea? What three things have you always wanted to do?

Note: This is *not* a Bucket List! Buckets bring up images of a mop and bucket and the last thing you have always wanted to do is mop the kitchen floor!

Teresa, Andrea, Jeanie and Cecelia and their Luna Lists

Teresa, Jeanie, Andrea, and Cecelia always carpooled together to their first-Friday-of-the-month Pee POD Poise Party. At one gathering, the PODs chose to schmooze about their *Luna Lists*. (See **The Precious Old Dames' Party Playbook**, Chapter 49, Choose to Schmooze #9.)

After several glasses of bubbly and some gnashing on pencil erasers, they shared their *Luna Lists* with each other and pledged to do one thing on their *Luna List* within six months and share their progress and success at a future Poise Party.

Teresa's Luna List #1. The Rose Bowl Parade

While growing up, Teresa's brothers always watched the Rose Bowl in Pasadena on New Year's Day. Teresa was always mesmerized by the flowered floats at The Rose Bowl Parade. At age 70, she arranged to fly across the country to be a participant in The Rose Bowl Parade by adding roses to the floats. She loved her time with the floats and flew home with some roses that she dried and put in a vase on her dining room table to remind her of her *Luna List #1* come true.

Andrea's Luna List #1. Ice Skating

Andrea loved watching figure skating on TV. She had always wanted to learn to ice skate. Andrea signed up for a beginner's class, where she was the only skater over 35. After some wobbling and falling on her butt, she got steadier and loved sailing over the ice. Andrea even learned to skate backward, with a big smile on her face!

Jeanie's Luna List #1. Italy

In high school, Jeanie's family hosted a foreign exchange student, Aurora, from Italy and Aurora sparked Jeanie's interest in all things Italian. After the Poise Party, Jeanie spoke with her three sisters and they rented a 200-year-old farmhouse on a hilltop in Umbria, Italy, from which they ventured out daily to visit nearby charming Italian villages. And there was a special bonus— after 45 years, Jeanie reunited with her dear friend Aurora, who invited the sisters over for a delicious Italian dinner, topped off with homemade tiramisu.

Cecelia's Luna List #1. A Birthday Party

Cecelia had never, ever had a birthday party. At age 60, Cecelia decided it was time for her to give herself the party of a lifetime. She invited all of her friends, decorated her rec room with sparkling streamers, bought her favorite six-layer vanilla cake/caramel cheesecake, rented a jukebox, and learned The Electric Slide. Cecelia and her PODs had a blast! Thereafter every Pee POD Party included a finale with The Electric Slide.

What's on your *Luna List?* Here's a template to get you started.

My Aging Human Female Luna List

1. *Luna List:*

2. *Luna List:*

3. *Luna List:*

And, as all Aging Human Females know, life is short and, if the list is long, time to get crackin'—er, shining! Shine, Boomer Chick, shine!

Chapter 44.
What in the World are You Doing?

"[S]he's got the whole world in her hands."
— Song written by Obie Edwin Philpot, 1927,
sung by Laurie London, 1957

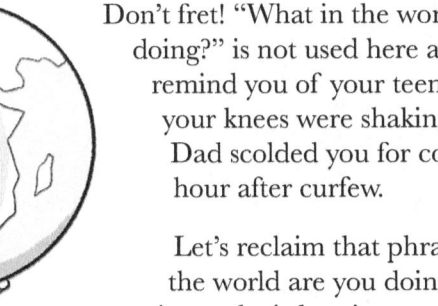

Don't fret! "What in the world are you doing?" is not used here as a phrase to remind you of your teenage days when your knees were shaking as your Mom or Dad scolded you for coming home an hour after curfew.

Let's reclaim that phrase, "What in the world are you doing?" to bring our joy and wisdom into our communities. How can we, Precious Old Dames, help our towns, our county, our world that is desperately in need of help? Is it time for a **Community Luna List** or a **World Luna List?**

In the '50s and '60s, many "women's magazines" were about good housekeeping and the value of supportive pantyhose. Now in your 50s and 60s yourself, you may be concerned about good planet-cleaning and supporting the butt out of cultural values.

What bigger-than-me thoughts keep you reaching for your Ambien at night? Perhaps your concerns include this laundry list that requires Tide Power Pods—or power PODs such as powerful Precious Old Dames—to clean up these community and global messes:

- Education
- Health Care
- Clear Water
- Clean Air
- Homelessness
- Animal Cruelty
- Artificial Intelligence and Jobs
- Teen Addictions
- Infectious Diseases
- Food Banks
- Climate Change
- #MeToo
- Big Pharma
- Gender Equity
- Immigration
- Corporate Greed
- Racism
- Species Extinction
- Poverty
- Hunger
- **LGBTQIA** Rights
- Nature Preservation
- Terrorism
- Crime
- Gun Violence
- Privacy
- Cyber Bullying

To paraphrase Thomas Paine from his pamphlet, *The American Crisis, 1776*, "These are the times that try [wo]men's souls." (TRUTH.) Isn't it time the 1950s Hostess with the Mostest is replaced by the twenty-first century Hostess with the Protest? Aging Human Females are desperately needed to march—slip on those compression stockings, ladies—with the younger generations.

Good self-care also embraces caring for other selves in the world. Why not out your outrageous you by creating your ***Community Luna List?*** Here are some ideas to get you started:

- Knocking on doors during a political campaign
- Volunteering at a homeless shelter
- Planting vegetables at an inner-city community garden
- Working on fundraisers for the cancer wing at your local hospital
- Participating in a beach Loggerhead turtle nesting surveillance
- Volunteering for Meals on Wheels

CHAPTER 44. WHAT IN THE WORLD ARE YOU DOING?

Your *Luna List* may also include a ***World Luna List:***

- Volunteering for UNICEF
- Welcoming refugees into your community
- Teaching English to immigrants
- Marching to support action on climate change
- Volunteering for the Sierra Club
- Hosting a foreign exchange student
- Volunteering for The Red Cross after a natural disaster

Time to rise up, Boomer Chicks, and bring joy into the world by doing what brings you yourself joy! And if there is power in numbers, why not encourage a ***Community & World Luna List*** project for your PODs at your next Pee POD Poise Party?

CARE & FEEDING OF THE AGING HUMAN MALE SPECIES: A SASSY PRIMER

Chapter 45.
Baby, It's You, Finally

"Life is a movie, and you're the star. Give it a happy ending."
—Joan Rivers

Sad—but true—everything does come to an end, including this **Sassy Primer**.

You read this book wanting to know how to care for and feed your Aging Human Male, but here's the twist: One of the best ways to take care of your Aging Human Male is to take tender care of yourself. You and your Boomer Buddy can nurture each other best when his **Geezer Triangle** of **Sex ▲ Sustenance ▲ Sports** is fulfilled *and* your **Dame Diamond** of **Feelings ◊ Revealings ◊ Bods ◊ PODs** is sparkling. Partners support each other best when they support themselves well. (Okay, maybe a knee brace can help a little, too.)

Another way we Boomer Babes can find the strength and courage not only to survive our Aging Human Partnerships but to thrive with our Boomer Buddies is through whine-y, wine-y lunches with our PODs, our Precious Old Dames. In the bonus section, **The Precious Old Dames' Party Playbook**, invites us to gather at fun Pee POD Poise Parties for sharing hilarious and thought-provoking games and gab sessions with besties.

This final formal chapter in this **Sassy Primer** ends with an essay question, ahem, a "yes-say" question. This yes-say question is an open-primer, self-graded final exam and, as always in life, help from our Precious Old Dames is encouraged. Why not carry this question—and possible answers—into your next Pee POD Poise Party?

In her poem "The Summer Day," Mary Oliver asks this yes-say question that invites your innermost TRUTH:

> *"Tell me, what is it you plan to do with your one wild and precious life?"*

The Precious Old Dames' Party Playbook: Pee POD Poise Parties

"Any time women come together with a collective intention, it's a powerful thing. Whether it's sitting down making a quilt, in a kitchen preparing a meal, in a club reading the same book, or around the table playing cards, or planning a birthday party, when women come together with a collective intention, magic happens." —Phylicia Rashad

The Precious Old Dames' Party Playbook is a study guide (ahem, party) that womansplains how our survival with our AHMales (and within ourselves) Depends on our Precious Old Dames (PODs). We PODs whoop it up at Poise Parties where we share joys and jolts, tips and tribulations, all while crying and laughing so hard that we PODs may pee in our pants.

Intro.
Like Peas in a POD

"For women, friendship not only rules, it protects. It buffers the hardships of life's transitions, lowers blood pressure, boosts immunity and promotes healing… and health."
— Melissa Healey, journalist

Our Precious Old Dames (PODs) are our female oxygen, the breath that helps us live, love, enjoy, feel and balance our lives. Our PODs are essential to our well-being: research has shown that a good network of PODs is essential for both our mental and physical health. In fact, research shows that one reason women live longer than men is precisely because of women's friendships with others outside their marriage! (TRUTH, Melissa Healey, "Science Confirms that Women Reap Health Benefits from Friendships," *The Seattle Times*, 06/15/2005.)

So instead of feeling guilty about our girlfriend time, we need to realize that exercising our jaws with our PODs literally strengthens our hearts. Melissa Healey reports, "Oxytocin, 'the love hormone,' spreads like wildfire through the veins of a woman when she gives birth, has sex, pats her dog, and shares with her girlfriends."

Our Pee POD Poise Parties are integral to our self-care, not only for our hearts, but also for our spirits and our brains… and our bladders! Our PODs are with us through thick and thin, for richer, for poorer, in sickness and in health, 'til death do us part… as we laugh together all the way out the door!

Chapter 46. What is a Pee POD Poise Party?

"To succeed in life, you need three things: a wishbone, a backbone, and a funny bone."
—Reba McEntire

Lesson 1. What is a POD?

A POD is a gathering of Precious Old Dames.

Precious. *Adjective.* Has great value and is well-loved, such as precious gemstones like sparkling diamonds.

Old. *Adjective.* Used affectionately to describe both "old" as in aging and "old" as in longtime friends. Sometimes the bond is only minutes old; connections happen fast when time is precious!

Dame. *Noun.* As in "Mae West was a Dame… an ambitious woman of authority—one that pushed the limits without fear… [a] confident, desirable, and witty woman with mischievous sexuality." (TRUTH, Ash Pariseau, "Dames That Know," damesthatknow.com.)

We Aging Human Females hold our Precious Old Dames close, like peas in a pod.

Lesson 2.
What is a Pee POD?

Like peas in a pod, a Pee POD is any gathering of two or more Precious Old Dames who laugh so hard they pee their pants.

Lesson 3.
The Pee POD Mission Position (NOT Missionary Position!)

> We hold these truths to be self-evident, that all Aging Human Males and all Aging Human Females are created equal. They are endowed by their Creator/Spirit/Goddess/Source with certain unalienable Rights, among these are Life, Liberty and the pursuit of Happiness, even with Crow's Feet, Muffin Tops, and Hair Loss. We mutually pledge to each other our shared Wrinkle Cream, our Medical Apparatus and our Memories, as well as our Wise Support and our Sacred Compassion. We gather as Precious Old Dames to sanctify our commitment to strengthen our wishbones, backbones, and funny bones.

Lesson 4.
What is a Pee POD Poise Party?

A Pee POD Poise Party (affectionately referred to as a Pee Party) is a scheduled gathering of Precious Old Dames—old friends and new acquaintances—who laugh so hard they pee their pants. A Pee Party is centered around sharing survival strategies about life with AHMales, and sharing stories that nourish hearts and souls. Just like *SNL*'s Mike Myers (aka Linda Richman), Pee Parties encourage PODs to "Talk amongst yourselves." Feelings abound, laughter happens, tears and cursing are welcomed! Throughout it all, every Precious Old Dame "Always Depends on her Poise."

Lesson 5.
Party of One, Anyone?

These Pee Party activities can be used by the lone she-wolf, solo flyer, shy-pie, or off-the-grid gal in a self-contemplative mood wanting her own private laugh, cry, or inspiration. Enjoy your Party of One.

Chapter 47.
Bring It On: Let's Party!

*"Here's to the nights we don't remember
and the friends we won't forget."*
— Lee Brice, from the song, "Friends We Won't Forget"

Here's your ultimate step-by-step guide to hostessing your Pee Party.

> **1. Prepare to Party**
>
> ***Hostess tips:*** Pick a date. Pick a time when your AHMale will be out of the house. Pick up pencils and paper or sticky notes.

CHAPTER 47. BRING IT ON: LET'S PARTY!

Here's a blank invite to help.

****

Frustrated with Your Aging Human Male Partner?
Join us for Complaining, Womansplaining & Talking Amongst Ourselves

Pee POD Poise Party*

When: _____

Where: _____

Dress Code: *No pantyhose, girdles, SPANX allowed; bras optional*

BYOB: *Bring Your Own Bubbly*

Bring Retro Snacks: *Fritos, spinach dip in a bread bowl, jello mold...*

Bring: Care & Feeding of the Aging Human Male Species, A Sassy Primer, *by Irene Shere*

R.S.V.P.: _____

*What is a Pee POD Poise Party? *A Pee POD Poise Party is a group of two or more Precious Old Dames (PODs), gathered together like peas in a pod, who laugh so hard they pee their pants, while Always Depending on their Poise. Pee Parties strengthen aging funny bones, backbones, and wishbones.*

****

2. Bring it On!

Time to PAR-TAY! PODs are arriving, carrying this Sassy Primer in one hand and a bottle of bubbly in the other. Coats and shoes off, purses strewn on the floor, hugs all around, name tags on, pencils and paper at the ready, glasses filled, giggles happening. There is a snap, crackle, pop in the air and it ain't from Rice Krispies; it's from Precious Old Dames breathing in the female oxygen that is the lifesaver that keeps us from turning into Fruit Loops! (Ok, ok, maybe some of the snap, crackle, pop is those aging old bones as Aging Human Females sit on the floor!)

3. Open with a Toast

"We honor our mothers, grandmothers, and all maternal ancestors that met in Pee POD Poise Parties of times past while fetching water at the well, foraging for herbs in community gardens, selling wares at the town square, stitching in quilting bees, and tending children in play groups, always sharing joy, hope, insanity and sanity to further their survival in support of each other. (All are invited to name ancestors or mentors to honor.)

We raise our glasses in a toast as we gather to cut the ties that bind (including tight bras and SPANX) and to strengthen our ties with each other. We share our challenges and triumphs as we become better manthropologists and mengineers, crafting the art of aging well with our Aging Human Males. To you, to me, to us, and to the circ-us of life!"

4. Choose a Topic from Cheat Sheet on Page 286

What do women want? Choices! So many topics in Chapters 48, 49, and 50, so little time. Start out with conversation lite in *Chick Chats,* slide into pithier (pissier?) topics in *Choose to Shmooze,* or delve deeper in *Flow and Tell.* How to decide what to gab about?

Plan ahead: Someone chooses a specific topic, such as *Chick Chat #11,* beforehand.

Vote: A choice is made at the Pee Party by a vote.

Call out a number: Someone randomly calls out a topic and a number: 1-11 for *Chick Chats,* 1-11 for *Choose to Schmooze* or 1-6 for *Flow and Tell.*

Choose a subject: Someone chooses a subject and finds a matching topic.

Go fish: Choose whatever floats everyone's boat!

CHAPTER 47. BRING IT ON: LET'S PARTY!

5. Stop Talking Amongst Yourselves Already, and Choose the Damn Topic!
Yes! There is always so much to share, but let's pretend there's some structure here!

6. How to Party

POD Pong: Every time a POD says, "Can you believe he does that!?" everyone takes a chug of their bubbly.

POD Sorry!™: Every time a POD says, "I'm sorry," she has to change it to "I wish" with a wish of her choice. (See Chapter 40, Lesson 1.) Then everyone takes a chug.

Talk amongst yourselves: Discuss or explore each topic as presented. And if talking goes all *Thelma and Louise*—off the road and over the cliff—that's okay!

Charades: Act out your answers—especially fun for sex topics and *Lust Lists!*

POD Pictionary™: Draw your answers, especially fun when topics involve body parts or *Luna Lists.*

7. Party Time
Share. Laugh. Cry. Eat. Blush. Blubber. Drink. Pee. Confess. Empathize. Pee. Whine. Eat. Hug.

8. Thank You Toasts (See Chapter 51)

9. The Grand Finale: Close with a Group Selfie + Group Toast
(See Chapter 52)
Share your selfies with each other, and send them to *Helen, Rae Jean* and *Irene* at Irene@SassyPrimer.com.

Once everyone is out the door, enlist your Aging Human Male in helping wash the dishes with a promise of eating the leftover Fritos when the dishes are done.

Cheat sheet for Discussion Topics

Chick Chat Topics (Chapter 48)

Chick Chat #1. Aging Human Female Whine List

Chick Chat #2. Own Your CRONE Game (Chapter 36, Lesson 2)

Chick Chat #3. I Feel (Blankety-Blank) about my AHMale

Chick Chat #4. Oh, My Aching (Blankety-Blank) (Chapters 30,33)

Chick Chat #5. His **Geezer Triangle: Sex ▲ Sustenance ▲ Sports** (Chapter 1, Lesson 2)

Chick Chat #6. *Your Dame Diamond* (Chapters 30-34)

Chick Chat #7. Household Chores, Clothed or Naked (Chapter 18)

Chick Chat #8. Sweet and Sour, Pass the Sauce Please

Chick Chat #9. Wo-mantras to Push Up Your Bra-very (Chapter 11, Lesson 2 and Chapter 35)

Chick Chat #10. You've Come a Long Way, Baby! (Chapter 40, Lesson 2)

Chick Chat #11. Name that Tune

CHAPTER 47. BRING IT ON: LET'S PARTY!

Choose to Schmooze Topics (Chapter 49)

Choose to Schmooze #1. SEX, A Hot Topic (Chapters 1, 5, 7, 23, and 33 Lesson 5)

Choose to Schmooze #2. Show Me the Money (Chapter 16)

Choose to Schmooze #3. My Blankety-blank Family (Chapter 17)

Choose to Schmooze #4. 24/7 Togetherness?! (Chapter 20)

Choose to Schmooze #5. 24/7 Apart: Break-ups and Divorce (Chapter 25)

Choose to Schmooze #6. Changing PODs (Chapters 30 and 34)

Choose to Schmooze #7. Yes, Arethra, R-E-S-P-E-C-T (Dame Digest, Intro)

Choose to Schmooze #8. Give Your-Self-Forgiveness (Chapter 39)

Choose to Schmooze #9. Your Luna List (Chapter 43, Lesson 2)

Choose to Schmooze #10. Burning Bras (or Spanx): Community & Global Luna Lists (Chapter 44)

Choose to Schmooze #11. Gender Discrimination Quease Disease (Chapter 40, Lesson 2)

Flow and Tell Topics (Chapter 50)

Flow and Tell #1. The Goddess's Prayer

Flow and Tell #2. Your Lust List (Chapter 1, Lesson 5)

Flow and Tell #3. Talk to Your Inner *Helen* and Your Inner *Rae Jean*

Flow and Tell #4. Talk to Your Younger-You (Chapter 40, Lesson 5)

Flow and Tell #5. Re-version Yourself (Chapter 43, Lesson 1)

Flow and Tell #6. Your One Wild and Precious Life (Chapter 45)

Chapter 48.
After Some Laughs: Chick Chat

"It is more fun to talk with someone who doesn't use long, difficult words but rather short, easy words like 'What about lunch?'"
—A.A. Milne, Winnie-the-Pooh

Chick Chat #1. Aging Human Female Whine List

Because every wine deserves a little whine!

1. Do you often shake your head in amazement at the stubborn streak on your AHMale's back?
2. Do you sometimes grit your teeth to keep a nastygram from being delivered from your mouth?
3. Do the words, "Who says?" often want to escape your lips?
4. For tonight, are you hoping that SEX isn't on the table—literally and figuratively?
5. Do you carry excess baggage in your midsection *and* in your heart?
6. Do you feel like you do the compromising 80% of the time? 90%? 110%?!
7. Why can't he just hear what you are saying?!
8. What are your favorite fine old whines?

CHAPTER 48. AFTER SOME LAUGHS:CHICK CHAT

Chick Chat #2. Own Your CRONE Game (See Chapter 36, Lesson 2)

Crone: 1. A cruel or ugly old woman (TRUTH, *Merriam-Webster Dictionary*), 2. A WOW, a Woman Of Wisdom.

Unfortunately, for many, the word "crone" has the derogatory first definition. Use the acronym C-R-O-N-E to formulate your own definition of CRONE, be it positive (on a good day, a WOW, a Woman of Wisdom) or negative (on a rough day, WOW, a Woman Of Woe).

Check out these examples and share the one you create.

CRONE: Cute Randy Open to Nearly Everything

CRONE: Crotchety Raggedy Oldie Nearing Extinction

CRONE: Clever Ribald Oxygenated Niceness Expert

CRONE: Creative Resilient Optimist Nearing Enlightenment

C_____ R_____ O_____ N_____ E_____

Now that you have defined yourself as a crone, is it time for your own Own Your Crone Party?

Chick Chat #3 . I Feel (Blankety-Blank) about my Aging Human Male

1. I love it when my AHMale _____.
2. I hate it when my AHMale _____.
3. I feel embarrassed when my AHMale _____.
4. I so appreciate it when my AHMale _____.
5. I count to 10 when my AHMale _____.
6. I get impatient when my AHMale _____.
7. I want to hug him forever when my AHMale _____.

Chick Chat #4. Oh, My Aching (Blankety-Blank)
(See Chapters 30, 33)

1. My least favorite body part is my _____.

2. My most favorite body part is my _____.

3. My most changed body part(s) over the years is/are _____.

4. When it comes to grooming, my least favorite task is _____.

5. When I look in the mirror, what surprises me most is _____.

6. My AHMale would say this about my face: _____.

7. My AHMale would say this about my body: _____.

8. I would say that I worry about my health _____.

9. When I can't remember things as I used to, I feel _____.

10. I feel _____ years younger/older than my chronological age.

11. My basic attitude about aging is _____.

CHAPTER 48. AFTER SOME LAUGHS: CHICK CHAT

Chick Chat #5. His **Geezer Triangle: Sex ▲ Sustenance ▲ Sports**

Read Chapter 1, Lesson 2. **The Geezer Triangle** aloud.

1. Does **The Geezer Triangle** describe your Aging Human Male's basic needs?

2. Talk about your Geezer's sex needs. Do your needs match? What's a girl to do?

3. Talk about your Geezer's sustenance needs—food and drink. Do your appetites match?

4. Talk about your Geezer's sports. How many sports can one Aging Human Male have? And when will he actually play one?

5. Does his **Geezer Triangle** limit you or set you free? How?

Chick Chat #6. Your **Dame Diamond** (See Chapters 30-34)

Refresh your memory on **The Dame Diamond** of *Feelings* ◊ *Revealings* ◊ *Bods* ◊ *PODs*.

Polish your diamonds, gals! Talk about each facet. How do you sparkle? What needs shining up?

Chick Chat #7. Household Chores, Clothed or Naked

Read Chapter 18. Fight #108. Chore Wars: Garbage In, Garbage Out aloud.

1. Compare the household chores you and your AHMale do. Ratio: Yours ____% : His ____% How do you feel about this ratio? What would be your *ideal* chore ratio?

2. What is your least favorite household chore? Have you asked him to do it? If yes, what was his response? If you haven't asked, what is holding you back from asking?

3. If you were a millionairess, what chores would you hire out? Are there any chores you would still like doing?

4. As an Aging Human Female, there are so many chores and so little time. Decide which chores you want to do a "Scarlett O'Hara" on and say, "Be gone with the wind!" for "Tomorrow is another day!" Why not put off that chore? And it's okay if you laughed at "Why not!"—nobody's watching, not even your PODs!

Chick Chat #8. Sweet and Sour, Pass the Sauce Please

Sometimes it is hard to have to take the sour along with the sweet.

1. "If only he'd just do/say this *less* often…"

2. "If only he'd just do/say this *more* often…"

3. What is the sweetest thing your AHMale has said recently?

4. What is the sweetest thing your AHMale has done recently?

CHAPTER 48. AFTER SOME LAUGHS:CHICK CHAT

Chick Chat #9. Wo-mantras to Push Up Your Bravery

Read the wo-mantras in Chapter 11, Lesson 2, and Chapter 35.

Which of these mantras work for you? Do you have others to share with your PODs?

Chick Chat #10. You've Come a Long Way, Baby (See Chapter 40, Lesson 2)

Remember that sleek-looking woman in the Virginia Slims™ cigarette commercial who said, "You've come a long way, Baby!" 'Tis true that women's rights, social roles and societal expectations have changed tremendously in the past decades… and that there is still a long path to true equality with men.

When you were younger, did you ever…

1. …not raise your hand in class because you didn't want to seem smarter than the cute guy next to you?
2. …get the "girls' chores" in your home, like cooking, cleaning, vacuuming?
3. …think that science and math were for boys?
4. …feel shy talking about menstruating, even with girlfriends, and call your period "having your special visitor," or "being on the rag?"
5. …believe that the only "acceptable" career choices were teacher, nurse, secretary, or mom?
6. …have your credit card application rejected because you weren't married?
7. …receive less pay than the men you were working with?

> *Chick Chat #11. Name that Tune*
>
> Songs can hold important memories and feelings in our hearts, and can generate a dynamo playlist for your post-party dancing in the sheets with your Aging Human Male!
>
> 1. What is your and your partner's "special song?" Where were you when it became "your song"? What were you doing—both during the song and after?
>
> 2. What song best describes your relationship today? Here are some suggestions to get you humming. Feel free to break out in song— with or without air guitar—if so inclined!
>
> I Wanna Hold Your Hand... Heartbreak Hotel... Peaceful, Easy Feeling... Feelin' Groovy
>
> You've Lost that Lovin' Feelin'... If I Had a Hammer... You are so Beautiful to Me
>
>
>
> Shake It Off... Total Eclipse of the Heart... Happy... Just Another Manic Monday
>
> Can't Get No Satisfaction... Ain't Too Proud to Beg... Try a Little Tenderness

Chapter 49.
After Some Tears:
Choose to Schmooze

"Of course your man can't fulfill all of your needs. That's what your girlfriends are for." —Bea L., Helen Weel's therapist for 30 years

---

Choose to Schmooze #1. Sex, A Hot Topic

Sex—so much to say about it! Talk about the following chapters. Giggling allowed!

Chapter 1. Sex, Lessons 1-5: Pills, Triangles, Beds, Love, Lust!

Chapter 5. Lesson 2. It's My Body and I'll Cry If I want To: H.E.R.S. versus H.I.S.

Chapter 7. Sex—Not Again!

Chapter 23. Fights #1,113-2,045: Sex!

Chapter 33, Lesson 5. ***Dame Diamond***, Bods, Sex

CARE & FEEDING OF THE AGING HUMAN MALE SPECIES: A SASSY PRIMER

Choose to Schmooze #2. Show Me the Money (See Chapter 16)

Research has shown that 80% of partners are not aware of their money situation and how much their partner contributes to expenses.

1. Do you and your AHMale talk about money? Do you fight about money?

2. What was your mother's attitude about money? Your father's attitude?

3. How much of your AHMale's money attitude comes from his mother and his father?

4. If you won $1,000,000 in the lottery, what would you do with it? What would your AHMale do with it?

Choose to Schmooze #3. My Blankety-blank Family (See Chapter 17)

1. My family is really crazy when it comes to _____.

2. To be honest, I (___) would (___) would not have chosen the family I was born into.

3. My partner would describe my family in one word: _____.

4. I would describe my partner's family in one word: _____.

5. **Helen's** bro Ron: "The best thing you can give your adult children is a lobotomy." (___) I agree. (___) I disagree.

CHAPTER 49. AFTER SOME TEARS: CHOOSE TO SCHMOOZE

Choose to Schmooze #4. 24/7 Togetherness?! (See Chapter 20)

"It seems to me that southern Europeans are just more intimate socially, whereas I like a lot of personal space—like, a mile from the nearest person is fine for me."—Peter Steele, singer, musician

Where are you and your partner on the "Peter Steele Scale?"

1. How do you and your AHMale navigate the physical space you each need?

2. How do you and your AHMale navigate your different needs for activities, noise levels, socializing, conversation, food and meals, medical issues, quiet time, travel?

3. Do you have a physical *Room of One's Own* as espoused by Virginia Wolff? A She-shed? If not, what would be your dream physical space? Where would it be? What would it be filled with? What would you use it for? Who, if anyone, would be allowed in?

Choose to Schmooze #5. 24/7 Apart: Break-ups and Divorce (See Chapter 25)

Thinking about exes? When the past calls, sometimes it's best to let it go to voicemail. But sometimes it helps, and is more fun, to schmooze about it with your PODs! Okay, Precious Old Dames, choose your quote and go at it!

"Women leave their marriages when they can't take anymore. Men leave when they find someone new."
—J. Courtney Sullivan, from the book, *Commencement*

"They say marriage is made in heaven. But so is thunder and lightning." —Clint Eastwood

"There are two sides to every break-up —yours and shithead's!"
—A Hallmark Greeting Card

"It's hard being in a relationship and it's hard not being in a relationship." — Lee S., a 73 year old AHFemale who was divorced 25 years ago after a 25-year marriage

Choose to Schmooze #6. Changing PODs
(See Chapters 30 and Chapter 34)

"We are travelers in the wilderness of this world, and the best we can find in our travels is an honest friend."   — Robert Louis Stevenson

How have your female friendships changed over the years?

What is the glue that holds your oldest friendships together?

What friendships didn't last? Do you know what happened?

How are your friendships changing as you are aging?

How do you cope with the passing of your friends?

What qualities do you most enjoy in your friends?

Choose to Schmooze #7. Yes, Arethra, R-E-S-P-E-C-T
(See The *Dame Digest,* Intro)

How do you feel about respect? Is it a given or is it earned? Try on these two quotes for size.

"Ladies, let me give you some advice. You can throw out all your f-ing chick-lit, self-help, why-doesn't-he-love-me books, because this is all you need to know: Men will treat you the way you let them. There is no such thing as "deserving" respect; you get what you demand from people... if you demand respect, he will either respect you or he will not associate with you. It really is that simple."
           —Tucker Max, author, *I Hope They Serve Beer in Hell*

"All I'm asking

For a little respect when I come home, hey now,

Hey, hey hey, yeah now....

R-E-S-P-E-C-T, find out what it means to me,

R-E-S-P-E-C-T, take care, TCB."—Aretha Franklin, in collaboration with Otis Redding

(***Note:*** TCB= Taking Care of Business)

Choose to Schmooze #8. Give Your-Self-Forgiveness
(See Chapter 39)

Of course it is difficult to put challenging, even traumatic, events out of your mind and not have them gnaw at you in your waking hours or in your sleep. You want to move on from that painful hurt, intense anger, deep sorrow, and shocking betrayal, but the truth is that some of these challenges replay in your mind.

Read Chapter 39. Try practicing *Helen's* and *Rae Jean's* exercises with your PODs!

Choose to Schmooze #9. Your Luna List
(See Chapter 43, Lesson 2)

Try making a *Luna List,* from the Latin *luna,* or *lucere,* meaning "to shine." Start your *Luna List* by naming three things you have always wanted to do. What activities will have you beaming from sea to shining sea?

(Note: This is *not* a Bucket List! Buckets bring up images of a mop and bucket and the last thing you have always wanted to do is mop the kitchen floor!)

Why not tap into your wildest fantasies? After all, dreaming is free!

My Luna List

#1. _____

#2. _____

#3. _____

Share with your PODs or put your *Luna Lists* in a bowl, draw at random, and act them out with charades.

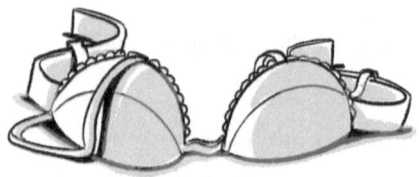

Choose to Schmooze #10. Burning Bras (or SPANX): Community & Global Luna Lists (See Chapter 44)

Discuss how your Pee POD could form a *Community & Global Luna List* to give back to the community and the world as a group. Get inspired to move into action —with those orthopedic sneakers—by these quotes.

"Can we understand how creating a new world will require, rather demand, our well-being? From small-town collections and national organizations to strategy and pop-ed sessions to shared meals and parties—it is our responsibility not as individuals but as communities to create structures in which self-care changes to community care... in which we are cared-for and able to care for others."
—Yashna Maya Padamsee

"I like to believe I am part of a global support group of 3.5 billion. Imagine—if you fall back on the 3.5 billion sisters, and the many good men who are with us, what could we possibly not achieve?"
—Nicole Kidman

CHAPTER 49. AFTER SOME TEARS: CHOOSE TO SCHMOOZE

Choose to Schmooze #11. Gender Discrimination Quease Disease
(Chapter 40, Lesson 2)

The Women's Truth Foundation (WTF) has identified a silent disease that causes silence in Human Females when confronted with Human Males' improper words and sexually-inappropriate actions.

GDQD: Gender Discrimination Quease Dis-ease. Noun. The queasiness, or dis-ease that a female feels in her stomach when a situation involves sexual inappropriateness, be it sexual discrimination, sexual politics, sexual intimations, or sexual acting out. This queasiness may not be consciously experienced until after the incident has passed.

Suggested anti-dote for the quease: *The Erma Edict*

"That won't work for me!" are five simple words that set the limit, no apologies, no excuses!

We AHFemales all have incidents in our lives when we were confronted by sexually intimidating circumstances with a man. Share your GDQD experience with your PODS. Do you wish you had responded differently at the time?

This can be a heavy topic. Why not lighten it up and empower yourself by doing a role play with your PODs. Think of a situation you've experienced in the past. Act it out, and empower yourself with a strong, "That won't work for me!" Share how that feels. Does changing your past behavior during the role play change how you feel now?

Chapter 50.
Getting Up Close & Personal: Flow and Tell

"You can't be brave if you've only had wonderful things happen to you."
—Mary Tyler Moore

Flow and Tell #1. The Goddess's Prayer

Try on this modern rendering of a sacred text... and if it's too controversial, write your own!

> **Our Goddess, Who creates artwork like heaven,**
>
> **Hallowed be our cheekbones,**
>
> **Thy queendom come in bed,**
>
> **Thy will be heard,**
>
> **From birth until we reach one hundred and seven.**
>
> **Give to each crone, our daily scone,**
>
> **And forgive us our womansplaining as we forgive those who mansplain to us.**
>
> **Lead us not into chocolate temptation, but deliver us from self-doubt,**
>
> **For thine is the queendom, the power, and the glory of femalehood,**
>
> **Forever and ever.**
>
> **Ah-women.**

CHAPTER 50. GETTING UP CLOSE & PERSONAL: FLOW AND TELL

Flow and Tell #2. Your Lust List (See Chapter 1, Lesson 5)

So what exactly is a *Lust List*? A *Lust List* is a list of personal turn-ons, ahem, very personal, very sexual turn-ons. What turns you on and gets you off? Chocolate? Flowers? Soft touches in the right places? Sweet words? Sexy movies or books? Your man cooking dinner?

Hand out four pieces of paper to each POD. Invite each POD to write the following on her first piece of paper

Lust List #1. I get very turned on when my AHMale...

and have her finish the sentence with her response—and no names, please!

Then each POD writes *Lust List #2, #3, and #4* and her responses (no names, again!) on her other pieces of paper.

Lust List # 2. I get very turned on when I....

Lust List #3. My hottest sexual experience was when....

Lust List #4. My favorite sex toys/activities/aphrodisiacs/books/songs/movies/thoughts are...

Put all the papers in a hat. Each POD chooses one piece of paper. Choose an activity:

Activity #1. Hot Poetry: Go around the circle reading aloud and see what wild group party poem emerges! And why not add some of these turn-ons to your personal *Lust List?*

Activity #2. Lusty Charades: Act out the *Lust List* turn-on for other PODs to guess.

Flow and Tell #3. Talk to Your Inner Helen and Your Inner Rae Jean

There is a *Helen* and a *Rae Jean* inside of all of us! How are you like *Helen* or *Rae Jean,* or a combo of both? And who would you most want at your POD Party: *Helen* or *Rae Jean?*

Helen-isms

"Humor eases the heart and allows love to flow in."

"His sense of his competence is as crucial to an Aging Human Male as her sense of her beauty is to an Aging Human Female—without question."

"Womanhandle...To expertly engage the cooperation of an Aging Human Male."

"It's not vanity to love yourself, it's sanity."

"To err is human, to self-forgive is divine."

"The key to being kind to yourself is truly believing in your heart that everyone at every moment is doing the very best that they can at that moment… If you believe everyone is trying their best, compassion and forgiveness arise… If you believe this for yourself, self-compassion and self-forgiveness arise."

"Self-love is a strength!"

Rae Jean-isms

"Be a badass with a good ass."

"Sex is crotch motion for an Aging Human Male."

"Mansplaining… A simple explanation from a simple man simply looking for trouble."

"I prefer my pretzels for eating, not as the shape I need to bend myself into to please my man."

"Other than Bruce Springsteen, who gets to be THE BOSS for life?"

"Wine glass half full, wine glass half empty… why not make it a *full on whine* experience."

"Your butt can't be kicked if you are proud of your butt."

CHAPTER 50. GETTING UP CLOSE & PERSONAL: FLOW AND TELL

Flow and Tell #4. Talk to Your Younger-You
(See Chapter 40, Lesson 5)

Think of yourself at 21. Try to recall a photo of you at that young age. Keep that photo of your Younger-You in your mind. Imagine you and your Younger-You have each ordered a latte at Cafe Cocoa and are sitting across the table from each other. Your Younger-You says, "You seem to have survived many challenges and enjoyed many adventures. C'mon, please share your wisdom with me?!"

Ease into the conversation. Take your time. What joys and sorrows, challenges and triumphs, hurts and revealings will you share? What regrets and great decisions will you re-live? What advice will you give your Younger-You? You and your Younger-You are two BFFs sharing coffee talk.

Jot down your thoughts and your feelings. Share aloud with your PODs.

Flow and Tell #5. Re-version Yourself (See Chapter 43, Lesson 1)

Name two women you admire and fill in the blanks.

Woman # 1: _____
Quality most admired: _____

Woman # 2: _____
Quality most admired: _____

The New Me: Is there a way to embrace these qualities in yourself? Try them on with the following statements. How does this feel. Share with your PODs.

*I am (quality #1)*_____ *and I am (quality #2)*_____.

Flow and Tell # 6. Your One Wild and Precious Life
(See Chapter 45)

Explore this important question from the poem, "The Summer Day," by Mary Oliver:

"Tell me, what is it you plan to do with your one wild and precious life?"

And why not get this sharing party started with some thoughts from **Helen** and **Rae Jean?**

Helen and Her One Wild and Precious Life

I love the life I have created in my retirement.

I hope to…

Keep my brain cells together.

Have twenty more happy, snappy years with my very special Aging Human Male and my sisters of the heart, my dear PODS.

Spend more time traveling to the exciting sights of my daughter, son, and daughter-in-love.

Have grandchildren.

Be strong amidst the changes and losses of who I love and what I love.

Care well for my body, my oldest friend, so it can stay strong enough to play racquetball, kayak, bike, hike, and orgasm.

Create passionately, forever, whether it is writing or beading or re-organizing the linen closet. A day without creating is a day without sunshine.

CHAPTER 50. GETTING UP CLOSE & PERSONAL: FLOW AND TELL

Write a coming-of-age book about the adventurous summer of 1967 when my best friend Jill and I traveled 10,000 miles coast-to-coast across the USA and into Canada in an old turquoise station wagon that started with a speedometer reading 100,000 miles.

Perfect a gluten-free pancake recipe.

Wake up every day with joy and excitement (despite the muscle aches).

Rae Jean and Her One Wild and Precious Life

I love my retired life and I want more!

I want to…

Remain cancer-free.

Switch my life to a slightly lower gear and have breakfast every morning with the sunrise as my breakfast buddy.

Go on an African Safari.

Be strong amidst the losses of people I love.

Buy a sporty red JEEP and ride it on the beach.

Teach my granddaughters to be strong, brave and loving.

Go line dancing *every* Saturday night with my high-kicking PODs.

Walk the Appalachian Trail on my 80th birthday, well, at least some of it, in bits and pieces.

Protest with my PODs at more women's marches for equality.

Go out kicking and screaming and loving.

Chapter 51.
Thank You Toasts

"I want to say thank you to all the people who walked into my life and made it outstanding, and all the people who walked out of my life and made it fantastic." —Anonymous

Every night at the end of his *Tonight* show, Jimmy Fallon offers thanks to all the special people and things he featured in his show. At the end of the Pee POD Poise Party, invite each POD to raise her glass in a special toast to say, "Thank You!" for a thought, a feeling, an apology, a pat on the back (for herself or another Boomer Chick), or a tip for dealing with her Boomer Buddy. Anything goes!

> *Claudia:* "Thank you, Jane, for sharing your frustration with your aging man about how he never appreciates your cooking with a kind word. Jane, I adored your brownies!"
>
> *Lynn:* "Thank you, everyone, for putting up with me crying about my fight with Hal. I was just so upset and angry. And thanks, Carla, for passing the tissues."
>
> *Alice:* "Thank you, thank you, thank you, to you gals for helping me feel like my life and my thoughts and my feelings are **NOT CRAZY**! It helps me appreciate myself and my guy!"
>
> *Evelyn:* "Thanks for listening to my kvetching and for being so freaking understanding about my cussing! And for being so real! I feel more at peace. And thanks to Janet for her great hosting, I can't wait to host the next Pee Party at my place!"

Chapter 52.
The Grand Finale

"It's easy to impress me. I don't need a fancy party to be happy. Just good friends, good food, and good laughs. I'm happy. I'm satisfied. I'm content."
— Maria Sharapova, tennis player

Close with a Group Toast.

"To us, may we be forever BADASS! And may we survive and thrive with our Aging Human Male Partners, with our Precious Old Dames, and with our own spectacular, shining Dame Diamond selves!"

And a Group Selfie.

Document the laughs and the pees in the pants?! Heck yes! And why not post the Group Selfie and email your story and your photo to Irene@sassyprimer.com.

P.S. The Party never stops!

Why not join more head-shaking and eye-rolling at the online Precious Old Dame's Poise Party at SassyPrimer.com?!

Use this space below for contact info for your Precious Old Dames.

Epilogue: The Reveal

"You are the exquisite product of thousands of years of your loving ancestors' best hopes and dreams." —Belleruth Naparstek, psychologist

Dear Precious Old Dame,

What's a **Sassy Primer** without a little something revealing?

I am the nice sweet Jewish girl, **Helen Weels**, who wasn't allowed to date, wear lipstick, or shave her legs until she was sixteen. (A very quiet rebel, when Helen was thirteen she would timidly steal her father's razor before leaving the house for her Friday night babysitting job, put it in her purse, and after the kids were asleep, she would shave her legs in the bathroom.)

And I am also the badass hot mama, **Rae Jean Beech**, who, in 1967, at age twenty-one, was strolling down the sidewalks of Haight-Ashbury, wearing a mini-skirt up to her pippick (Yiddish for belly-button), silver bracelets from wrist to elbow, and ironed-straight black hair to her waist, as she breathed in the maryjane smoke wafting through the streets of San Francisco.

Both the softer good-girl **Helen** (although her name reads like **Hell-on-Weels**) and the sassyass, tougher **Rae Jean** (whose name is, yes, like **Ragin' B____**), are me, **Irene Shere**. Using these two different personas was crucial to my honest writing of this book.

And after two and a half years of this honest writing, the book was finished and the cover was designed with **Helen** and **Rae Jean** as the only authors. My daughter took one look at the cover and said, "Mom, you spent years writing this book—you have to own it!" Well! Okay! I guess I needed a public declaration that I was the Aging Human Female behind **Helen** and **Rae Jean**! And I also realized that my friends would never find this book unless I was also listed as an author. So I plopped my name on to the cover of the book

EPILOGUE: THE REVEAL

and popped myself into the text of the book, while still leaving most of the sweetness and spice to my alter egos *Helen* and *Rae Jean*.

There, that confession is over. Phew! And I can assume—in fact, know—that you totally identify with both the sweet babycakes and the badass babe, even if one of these is hidden deeper inside of your bodacious self.

This is a reveal that is also a personal reveal-ation. Writing this book reflected to me the ways in which I needed to change in my own Aging Human Relationship with my partner **Bill** and with my own Aging Human Self. It was a see-saw revelation. First there was catharsis in the bitching and moaning about **Bill**, and then there was, as this **Primer** progressed, true self-learning.

A few months before I finished writing the first draft, my guy **Bill** and I had a terrible fight, one of those fights where you go on and on and on, and one of you leaves the room and then comes back to add a nasty comment, then leaves again, and then comes back to add another nasty comment… you get it. It was one of those fights where no one talks for days after, and you don't even want to be in the same room, let alone the same house, or the same planet, or the same universe with this guy! Days later, we made up, though things were a bit cold for a few days more. I had plenty of time to think during those post-fight days. **Bill** had said that I was critical and judgmental. I was sure that I was infinitely patient (if only he knew) and accepting (sooo accepting!). But then I thought about some of the suggestions and issues and advice that I had just written in **The Roadmap**. *I wasn't applying any of the ideas or advice in the book to myself or my partnership!*

I had broken every one of my **Primer's** fight club rules. I was acknowledging the differences between me and **Bill**, but I was not accepting them, and was certainly not appreciating and applauding them!

I wanted **Bill** *to be like me!*

Right?! Why isn't it that simple?! I didn't think **Bill** could be happy watching sports 24/7 on ESPN and not meeting friends for lunch. I didn't think **Bill** could be happy not wanting to travel and bop around cities. I thought long and hard about this. I decided that I needed to really let **Bill** live his life as he wanted (duh—**The Geezer Triangle** I had written about) and I would lead my life as I wished (duh—*The Dame Diamond* I had written about).

This revelation has seriously changed my relationship with **Bill**. I don't noodge him anymore... well, hardly ever. I am so much happier with him. I am letting **Bill** be **Bill**, and I feel that I have embraced our relationship with open arms. And **Bill** seems so much happier in response to my changes. **Bill** is **Bill**. I am me—*Helen* and *Rae Jean*, all in one package! I am me—the complex, colorful, frustrated and joyous tapestry that is my Aging Human Female self. Thank goodness!

After this fight, when I fully embraced what I had written in this book, I was overcome with tears. I was thunderstruck by this epiphany: *I had written this book for me! OMG! OMGODDESS!* With that realization, I felt complete. I felt that if no one else ever read this book, just having written this book for myself was enough.

As I continued to write this **Primer**, several more reveal-ations appeared.

I empowered myself as my writing went beyond the words.

This book truly did evolve from a complain-us (*Rae Jean's* intro) to a treat-us (*Helen's* intro). Initially, I would have an argument with **Bill** or a mutterance (a low-growled utterance) and I would sit down and spew out a cathartic chapter about "THAT AGING HUMAN MALE!" Initially this **Primer** was solely a diatribe about that tribe of Aging Human Males that my PODs and I suffered with and laughed about during many a lunch. In writing **The Field Guy-ed**, I initially found humor and catharsis in complaining about and teasing—and yes, I admit, at times, mocking—AHMales. But I also began feeling more compassion toward our brave men traversing aging for the first time.

While writing **The Roadmap**, I began voicing my true feelings and my opinions more easily with **Bill**. In our partnership I felt more compassion and less anger, so I spoke with a softer voice and more care. I felt a new wave of gentleness. I also kept silent more easily, not offering help or suggestions, realizing that my nurturing helped diminish **Bill**'s feelings of competence and undercut his strong need for independence. While writing **The Dame Digest** I was my own rah-rah coach to myself. I was my own best mother to myself. I was my own best POD to myself. I began to feel stronger. I felt more self-

EPILOGUE: THE REVEAL

compassion toward my Aging Human Female self. I began to revere, rather than revolt against, aging, embracing the freedom of truly being myself that aging offered me. I began to think of myself as a cute crone. I began to think of myself as a WOW, a Woman Of Wisdom!

As I wrote these chapters, I lived them. I learned so many lessons in this **Sassy Primer** the hard way, after stripping myself naked in front of the mirror of my laptop and then re-dressing myself on the advice of the relationship fashionista that appeared as my fingers flew over my keyboard.

The "amateur psychoanalyst me" believes that this **Primer** emerged from the "unconscious knowing" that would arise in my dreams and would send me to my laptop at three in the morning with a full-blown chapter in my head. The "spiritual me" believes that my ancestors—my mother **Rebecca**, my grandmothers *Molly* and **Pauline**, and my great-grandmothers **ANNA**, **Rifka**, **Scheindle**, and *Toba*—wanted to share their survival strategies and nurturing love with me as they guided my fingers to record their wisdom line by line. After all, has the Aging Human Male Species changed all that much over the millennia, the cavemen hunters, seeking game and a woman? And, then again, have we Aging Human Females changed all that much from the cavewomen PODs gathered around the campfire sharing personal stories, a babe in one arm while stirring the saber-toothed tiger stew?

I re-wrote myself in my Aging Human Partnership as my writing began to touch my heart.

I had been in therapy for 30 years and **Bill** had not, so I had always thought that I was The Wiser One in our relationship; I was also The Gifted Partner who was so in touch with her feelings. I had been so pumped up with myself that I wasn't listening carefully enough to **Bill**. I realized that when I repeated myself—my questions, my opinions, or my offers of help—**Bill** felt grilled and unheard. I was offering a lot of UA, "Unsolicited Advice."

I had tried to change **Bill** to be more like me and to be more in touch with his feelings. When I stopped trying to change **Bill**, I could see him more clearly. I saw that he loved sports, music, and debating politics, and that he didn't need as many people, activities, or emotional processing sessions as I did, if any at all. And that was okay.

As my ego diminished and I realized that I was not The Better Person or The More Evolved One, I began to hear **Bill** on a deeper level, and my self-righteousness transformed into respect. As I changed within our relationship, our relationship deepened. I moved from acknowledging our differences to accepting our differences to applauding our differences. Ouch! This was where the rubber met the road. It was not easy navigating **The Roadmap's** GPS for a smooth AHPartnership to get to a happy ending!

I outed my Inner Sass!

Amidst the hard work of early morning book writing, it was so much fun to come up with new twisty words, wavy concepts, and warped ideas! Much to my surprise, this Inner Sass and Badass Talk started leaking into my daily conversation. I played with words, tossing them into the air and juggling them in give-and-talk exchanges with my Precious Old Dames. As I wondered where that sass and wordsmithing came from, I remembered that, despite her depression, my mother **Rebecca** got a laugh out of entering word contests and recipe contests such as "Name the Cocker Spaniel and Win the Cocker Spaniel Pup" (her entry: Taffy) and "Come up with a Recipe using Lentil Beans, Name It, and Win a Year's Supply of Lentil Beans" (her creation: Veg-ay Pate). My mom didn't win the contests—sadly for us kids in the case of the pup, happily in the case of the lentil beans—but I won in inheriting her Inner Playfulness. I truly thank you, Mom!

I realized my Luna List #1 from 50 years ago. I wrote a very personal book from my life and my heart!

I wrote the first chapter, **The Little Blue... Isn't He a Pill?**, after I got home from a whiney, winey luncheon with my girlfriends and sat down at my computer to dish cathartically about "Those men!" Little did I know that this little "Little Blue Pill" would grow into this big published book.

My wish as a teenager, who read a book a day in the summers and always read with a dictionary by her side to learn new words, was that someday I would create a book from my imagination. In writing this book, I often felt joy and excitement as if I were sixteen again. This **Primer** has made my Aging Human Female self feel like a Teenage Human Female.

EPILOGUE: THE REVEAL

I was overwhelmed by all the love in my life.

(Cue humble thank-you bows and mega shout-outs with drums and tambourines and dancing in the background.)

I am forever thankful to my female oxygen, my Precious Old Dames, who have shared their hearts, and their anecdotes, with me. Special hugs of gratitude to my DC Dames Erma, Stef, Nicole, Gail, Terry, Erin, and Gloria; to my Florida Fab Five Madelaine, Linda, Barb, Carolyn, and Jeannine; to my African Queen Magogodi; and to my British Boomer Babe, Maggie.

And huge hugs to the super males—both new age and old age—in my life: Brett, Mark, Ade, and Ron.

Fist bumps to my racquetball guys at the Y, loving mentors teaching me, both on and off the court, about the Aging Human Male Species!

Writing this **Sassy Primer** was a joy ride accompanied by my two best PYDs (Precious Young Dames), my Wonder-Woman Book Editor Rachel Abileah and my Sparkle-Plenty Inspirational Best-Friend-Daughter Holly Taya Mâ Shere. Both Rachel and Holly Taya lovingly held my hand, cradled my heart, and waved cheerleader pom poms as we traveled The Book Journey together.

This book came to life when my cover artist Mary Ann Smith used her digital paintbrush to totally nail the front cover; when Andy "Doodles" Baker breathed life into my wacky words with retro laugh-out-loud cartoons and sexy sketches; and when designer and typographer Asya Blue transformed my simple Word document into a shining, fresh, lively **Primer!** Thank you, thank you, thank you!

And, of course, there are not enough thank yous for **Bill** (don't worry, **Bill**, more private thank yous to come, ahem, later!) **Bill** has my heart. **Bill** is my rock. **Bill** had me at, "Can I coach you in racquetball?"

My fondest hope is that as you have read this **Sassy Primer**, you have strengthened your wishbone, your funny bone, and your backbone. And hopefully you have deepened your appreciation and compassion for your beloved Aging Human Male, your beloved Aging Human Partnership, your beloved Precious Old Dames, and your beloved Aging Human Female Self.

Helen and *Rae Jean* and I want to thank you, dear Precious Old Dame, for riding shotgun with us on this fun and funky journey! We wish you the ride of your life as you and your Aging Human Male traverse the pitstops and potholes, and enjoy the romantic scenic views along Route 66+!

We raise our glasses in a toast in tribute to you—all you are and all you will become! Wahoo!

Amen, Ahhh-men, Ahhh-Women,

Irene

PS. I am certain you have lived so many chapters that you could add to this **Sassy Primer!** Please share your stories, anecdotes, trials, travails, triumphs, and tried-and-true advice at the ongoing online Pee POD Poise Party at SassyPrimer.com or contact me at Irene@sassyprimer.com.

A to Z for the Glossary-Eyed

"I am so clever that sometimes I don't understand a single word of what I am saying." —Oscar Wilde, author

A to Z for the Glossary-Eyed is The Women's Truth Foundation (WTF) collection of new, fun, scandalous aging-relationship words and concepts. It is chock full of all kinds of sexy junk. (e.g., ***Junk***. *Noun.* What comes in the male.)

A

Acute Neurological Geriatric Enraged Response (ANGER). *Noun.* A syndrome of feelings of madness and frustration that may be experienced by geezers and gezesses as they come to the final pit stop in the NASCAR of life, as their pit crew of doctors and family and friends help them re-tire their vehicle, fix any oil leakages, grease their spark plugs, wipe their windshield for better sight, adjust their horn so it can be heard, re-adjust their seat belts to muffin-top mode, and give them a new safety helmet. A daily dose of this **Primer** helps ease this ***ANGER*** syndrome, especially when used in combination with Pee Parties!

ADHD. *Noun.* <u>A</u>ctivated <u>D</u>rive to <u>H</u>unt it or <u>D</u>o it. Condition of the Aging Human Male described in the secret *Women's Psychiatric Diagnostic Satirical Man-ual,* specifically condition DSM #36-24-36.

Ageism. *Noun.* Prejudice, discrimination, and stereotypes based on a person's age, a prejudice that targets people's future selves.

Age-shaming. *Noun.* Shaming older people for becoming older!

Aging Human Female (AHFemale). *Noun.* 1. Any woman over the age of 18 who is with an Aging Human Male, as being with an Aging Human Male can age any Human Female, often astonishingly rapidly. 2. A Precious Old Dame (POD). 3. A geezess. 4. A cute crone. 5. A Boomer Babe. 6. A WOW, a <u>W</u>oman <u>O</u>f <u>W</u>isdom.

Aging Human Male (AHMale). *Noun.* 1. Sweetheart. 2. Curmudgeon, 3. Fuggetaboutit, see **The Field Guy-ed Intro** for The Dirty Dozen: Checklist for the Aging Human Male.

Alimony. *Noun.* Spousal support after a divorce. "I used to joke they were going to call it 'all the money,' but they changed it to 'alimony.'"—Robin Williams

AMIBLU. *Noun.* Assessment of Mental Illness Because of Large Undersexment, a psychological test instrument that measures low self-esteem and depression due to lack of sex.

Aging So Sucks (ASS) Rash. *Noun.* A skin outbreak that occurs in geezers and geezesses and is characterized by an acute itchiness for a better life. A daily dose of this **Primer** alleviates *ASS Rash.*

B

Badass. *Adjective.* Tough, feisty, strong.

Badderass. *Adjective.* More than badass.

Bakedcouchuspotato. *Noun.* The area of the AHMale brain that enables an Aging Human Male body to lie inert in the same position on a couch until the cows come home, which they never do if you don't own a farm.

Big Ovaries. *Noun.* 1. Power and guts. 2. Female equivalent to the male "big balls." "She did that! WOW! She has *big ovaries*!"

BJ. *Noun.* Protein shake.

BJ. *Verb.* To Bring Joy.

Bods. *Noun.* Bodies. One of the four essential facets of **The Dame Diamond**, involving an Aging Human Female's attitudes toward her body image, her body choices, her clothes, her health, and her sex life.

Bookend of Farts. *Noun.* Farts that occur from top to bottom, from brain farts to tushy farts, i.e. from the AHMale brain areas **Memorees Kapputtus** to **Wrectus Rectumus.**

Boomer. *Noun.* An Aging Human Male or an Aging Human Female whose heart still goes boom in the presence of someone or something they love (and whose mind still goes ka-boom after a good joke).

Buttonmylippius. *Noun.* Section of the Aging Human Female brain that deactivates her mouth, tongue, and voicebox. This area of the AHFemale brain can be strengthened with practice and the practice of patience.

C

Carton of Codgers. *Noun.* 1. A collection of *codgers*. 2. Male friendships.

Cementus Mentis. *Noun.* Area of the Aging Human Male brain in which decisions are written in stone, never to be questioned or revisited.

CHAT. *Noun.* The section of the brain known as the <u>C</u>onnected <u>H</u>umans <u>A</u>ll <u>T</u>alk area that regulates speech.

CHAT buds. *Noun.* The sensitive covering on an aging woman's tongue—adjacent to the taste buds—that is activated by her *CHAT* brain area and that stimulates her to talk during meals.

ChestPuffer. *Noun.* 1. A question designed to cause an Aging Human Male's chest to puff up, which automatically and instantaneously activates and massages the ***Everlasting God Omnipotence (EGO)*** section of the male brain, resulting in a smoothing of interactions, e.g., "How did you ever get so smart?" 2. A no-brainer.

C.L.A.P. *Noun.* <u>C</u>ompliment <u>L</u>eading to <u>A</u>pplauding your <u>P</u>artner.

C.L.O.P. *Noun.* <u>C</u>riticism <u>L</u>eading to <u>O</u>stracizing your <u>P</u>artner.

Codger. *Noun.* An elderly man, especially one who is old-fashioned or eccentric.

Cometab. *Noun.* 1. An area in the right hemisphere of an Aging Human Male's brain—an AHMale is always right— that unconsciously keeps a running count of how many times a week he has come with his Aging Human Female. 2. Not how you call your pussy.

Competence Area of the Brain. *Noun.* Area in the Aging Human Male brain that controls life skills and whose size may be perceived—either correctly or incorrectly—by an AHMale as decreasing with age; this decrease in life skills may manifest in areas such as the inability to make oneself a sandwich.

Competence Question. *Noun.* A Competence Question is any question that calls into account an Aging Human Male's competence by using the word "right" along with "?" in the same sentence, such as "Are we going in the right direction?"

Compliment Count. *Noun.* Count of an Aging Human Female's positive statements, which is easily discerned since it is the same as an Aging Human Male's Smile Count.

Constipation of the Brain. *Noun.* Stubbornness. See glossary "TLC" definitions for cures for this condition.

Crimson Clit. *Noun.* 1. Unfulfilled, non-orgasmic female sexual pleasure. 2. Female equivalent of male blue balls. "That make-out session left me with a *crimson clit*."

Criticism Count. *Noun.* Count of an Aging Human Female's negative statements, which is easily discerned by the number of times that smoke comes out of an Aging Human Male's ears.

Crone. *Noun.* 1. A cruel or ugly old woman (TRUTH, *Merriam-Webster Dictionary*). 2. A WOW, a <u>W</u>oman <u>O</u>f <u>W</u>isdom. 3. <u>C</u>ute <u>R</u>aunchy <u>O</u>ldster with <u>N</u>ever-ending <u>E</u>xpertise. 4. <u>C</u>reative <u>R</u>egal <u>O</u>ldie <u>N</u>oted for <u>E</u>xperience. (see **The POD Party Playbook**, Chapter 48, Chick Chat #2 for more *crone* definitions.)

##

Dame. *Noun.* A badass older woman, as in "[a] confident, desirable, and witty woman with mischievous sexuality." (TRUTH, Ash Pariseau, *Dames That Know*, www.damesthatknow.com)

Dame Diamond. *Noun.* The four needs (facets) of an Aging Human Female's ***Dame Diamond*** are ***Feelings ◊ Revealings ◊ Bods ◊ PODs***.

Divorce. *Noun.* Splitting up a partnership, separating, deciding that "good enough" is not good enough. "*Divorce* is… ripping your heart out through your wallet."—Robin Williams

Dooris Slammo Whammo. *Noun.* Portion of an Aging Human Male's or Aging Human Female's brain that is activated when someone who can't stand the heat gets out of the kitchen.

D/Witis. *Noun. (abbreviation for Dishwasheritis).* A virus that attacks the reptilian portion of an Aging Human Male brain and causes an AHMale to feel anxious and out of control. This virus initially appears as a need to control the loading of a dishwasher (D/W). It later spreads and man-ifests as a need for control in all interactions. Information about *D/Witis* is provided by the Crones for Disease Control (CDC).

E

Eatdaintily. *Noun.* The part of the Aging Human Female part of the brain that gets activated while eating. The *Eatdaintily* brain area then activates the ***"CHAT buds"*** on an AHFemale's tongue, stimulating additional need to speak during a meal.

Erma Edict. *Noun.* "That won't work for me." These five words compose a complete sentence, believe it or not! No excuses necessary! No apologies necessary! And no more womansplaining needed for ***The Erma Edict***.

Everlasting God Omnipotence (EGO). *Noun.* Area of the Aging Human Male brain that gets activated when the competence of an AHMale is threatened, either directly or indirectly, by an Aging Human Female.

F

Family Jewel Time. *Noun.* When an Aging Human Male's Family Jewels are happy so that an Aging Human Female can cash in on her own need for female jewels.

Fault Vault of Unfinished Forgiveness. *Noun.* Storehouse of angry, hurt feelings that are unresolved after a fight, a storehouse with a combination lock that has "NEVER" as its time release.

Fatlippius. *Noun.* A lip that is fat as a result of a mouth that should have been shut when it was opened.

Feelingafeelingafobia. *Noun.* A condition in human males, from utero through forever, that man-ifests as a fear of feeling a feeling. This condition resides in the area of the brain called the ***frefrontal fobes.***

Feelings. *Noun.* 1. Emotions, one essential part of ***The Dame Diamond*** facets of an Aging Human Female. 2. "Huh?" to an Aging Human Male.

Fewandfar Betweenus. *Noun.* Area of the Aging Human Male brain that keeps a tally of the kind deeds offered by an Aging Human Female.

Focuspocus. *Noun.* The magic of poking the focus to ignore the negative and focus on the positive, especially when looking in the mirror first thing in the morning. Example: She looked in the mirror and admired her smile so that she didn't notice that her last haircut left her with a permanent bedhead.

FOG (Female Orgasm Gone). *Noun.* Condition wherein Aging Human Females may experience a decrease in the frequency and intensity of their orgasms as they age.

Frefrontal fobes. *Noun.* The area of the Male brain where the condition ***feelingafeelingafobia*** resides. The ***frefrontal fobes*** enlarge throughout life as a male baby matures into an Aging Human Male.

Friend. *Noun.* 1. For an Aging Human Female, a person with whom someone shares feelings; chatter matters. (Source: WTF—Women's Truth Foundation). 2. For an Aging Human Male, a person with whom one shares grunts while engaging in a common activity, such as drinking, golfing or watching TV. (Source: WATUPS—What? Ask or Tell Ur Personal Story Foundation).

G

GainpowerthruNO. *Noun.* Area of the brain in an Aging Human Male that is activated in the slightest power struggle with an Aging Human Female.

GDQD. Gender Discrimination Quease Dis-ease. Noun. The queasiness, or dis-ease, that a female feels when a situation involves sexual inappropriateness, be it sexual discrimination, sexual politics, sexual intimations, or sexual acting out. This queasiness may not be consciously experienced until after the incident has passed. A remedy for this dis-ease is **The Erma Edict**.

Geeze. Noun. (Pronunciation: hard "g" as in "go away.") Gender neutral version of geezer or geezess.

Geezer. Noun. (Pronunciation, hard "g" as in "goat.") 1. *Traditionally:* an older man, specifically one who is cranky or eccentric. 2. *Affectionately:* a sweet Aging Human Male.

Geezer Triangle. Noun. The three basic needs of an Aging Human Male: **Sex ▲ SustenanceS ▲ Sports**. See **The Field Guy-ed** Chapter 1, Lesson 2.

Geezess. Noun. (Pronunciation: hard "g," as the first "g" in "gorgeous.") 1. *Traditionally:* an older woman, specifically one who is sometimes cranky or eccentric. (AHFemales demand equality, even on the cranky and eccentric side!) 2. *Affectionately:* a sweet Aging Human Female

Gender Discrimination Quease Dis-ease. GDQD. Noun. The queasiness, or dis-ease, that a female feels when a situation involves sexual inappropriateness, be it sexual discrimination, sexual politics, sexual intimations, or sexual acting out. This queasiness may not be consciously experienced until after the incident has passed. A remedy for this dis-ease is **The Erma Edict**.

Genitals Test. Noun. Test of gender bias for household chores: Does this chore require a clitoris/breasts or a penis? See also *Naked Genitals Test*.

Genitalus Maximus. Noun. Part of the male brain that develops and enlarges during adolescence.

Genitalus Uberallis. Noun. Part of the male brain that enlarges after adolescence; eventual size is governed by the size of the **EGO *(Everlasting God Omnipotence)*.**

Gluttonusbuttonus. *Noun.* The brain area of an Aging Human Male that is activated during a meal. When the ***Gluttonusbuttonus*** is activated, it shortcircuits the connection to the **Connected Humans All Talk (CHAT)** section of the male brain.

GMS. *Noun.* <u>G</u>eezer <u>M</u>oodiness <u>S</u>yndrome. Monthly Aging Human Male moodiness or crudiness or rudeness caused by all manner of hormones that ignore all manners.

Golfismymistress. *Noun.* The Aging Human Male part of the brain responsible for the belief that, as pro golfer Jimmy Demaret says, "Golf and sex are about the only things you can enjoy without being good at."

Gonads. *Noun.* 1. Body parts in the male and female <u>G</u>enerally <u>O</u>ver <u>N</u>oticed <u>A</u>nd <u>D</u>emanding <u>S</u>ex. 2. The hoo-ha in an Aging Human Female and the balls in an Aging Human Male.

GPS. *Noun.* GPS (from <u>G</u>ood <u>P</u>artnership <u>S</u>chemes or <u>G</u>ood <u>P</u>artnership <u>S</u>hit!) offered by AAA, The Aging Automobile Association, to help Aging Human Partners navigate the curves and pitfalls of traveling on Route 66+ during the road trip of their life.

Grow a vagina. *Phrase.* 1. Become tough. 2. Female equivalent to "grow some balls." As comedian Sheng Wang says, "Why do people say 'grow some balls?' Balls are weak and sensitive. If you want to be tough, *grow a vagina.* Those things can take a pounding."

Guy-ed. *Noun.* 1. A guy guide. 2. A guide with balls, for a gal with big ovaries!

H

Halfbakedcouchuspotato. *Noun.* A very small, mushy area of an Aging Human Male brain that results in verbalizations of "Huh?" every other sentence while lying supine on a couch or in a Lazy Boy recliner (aka Lazy Aging Human Male recliner).

Healings. *Noun.* Passions of an Aging Human Female that result in nurturing and creativity, an essential facet of ***The Dame Diamond.***

Heethemaster and Hegottajohnson. *Nouns.* Sex researchers in The Women's Truth Foundation (WTF).

Homeostayinplacis. *Noun.* A disease in which the Aging Human Male remains in a petrified body position for 24 hours or more, mesmerized by any TV or electronic screen or device that shows endless sports or big boobs or video games or card games.

Hoo-ha. *Noun.* Vayjayjay, vag, lady garden, girly parts, nether regions, hot box, cherry, vagina.

H.E.R.S. *Noun.* <u>H</u>ormonal <u>E</u>ruptions <u>R</u>unning the <u>S</u>how is a female developmental stage that begins in puberty and continues forever.

H.I.S. *Noun.* <u>H</u>ard <u>I</u>nto <u>S</u>oft defines the developmental stages of a male as he ages; oftentimes, his penis goes *Hard into Soft* and, hopefully, his heart will go *Hard into Soft*.

I

Ignorus Ignoramus. *Noun.* Part of the Aging Human Female brain that is activated to help her ignore that ignoramus.

I=KING (I=KnowImNaturallyGreat). *Noun.* Area of the Aging Human Male brain that is activated by sunspots and which cause an aging man to believe that he is the center of the solar system and the King of Knowledge. When this AHMale brain area is stimulated, mansplaining is triggered.

I'm Sorry. *Sentence.* 1. An apology. Sorry, but this phrase suffers from overuse. Sorry, but this phrase should be used minimally in a sentence by an Aging Human Female, and only in circumstances in which she is actually responsible. 2. Irene wishes "I'm sorry" wasn't overused. See **Irene's "I Wish"** (Chapter 40, Lesson 1) for an anti-dote.

Incompetence Detestus (ID). *Noun.* Section of the Aging Human Male brain that gets activated when the answer to a question is not known, thus causing the *ID* brain area to light up like a Christmas tree (or a Hannukah Menorah or a Kwanzaa Kinara).

Incompetence Mentis. *Noun.* Section of the Aging Human Male brain that triggers meshuggeneh behavior.

Irene's "I wish." *Phrase.* Resets regret about circumstances beyond an Aging Human Female's control. Encourages not apologizing for the past, but wishing for a different past. Replaces an apology, "I'm sorry," with a positive desired outcome, "I wish." "I wish I could have been at your birthday party to help you celebrate, but I was wrestling with a bad cold." See **Irene's "I Wish"** (Chapter 40, Lesson 1).

J

JULIETS. *Noun.* Just Us Ladies Into Enormous Tasty Salads.

Junk. *Noun.* The stuff that comes in the male.

K

Kakaland. *Noun.* That part of the Aging Human Partnership Universe of Conflict where you do-do not want to be.

Kvetch. *Verb. (Derivation: Yiddish.)* Moan, nag, grumble, squawk, grouch, fuss, gripe, crab, bellyache, yammer.

L

Legal Tender. *Noun.* Money that folds or jangles in your pocket; more technically, dollar bills and coins, not checks or bank notes or electronic transfers. **Note:** all tender-ness of the emotional kind is legal and welcome!

LGBTQIA. *Adjectives.* 1. Lesbian-Gay-Bisexual-Trans-Queer-Intersex-Asexual. 2. A list of sexuality and gender terms for a progressive Boomer Babe's "List for Learning More About."

Libido. *Noun.* The Hots.

Libid-go. *Noun.* Three alarm fire.

Libid-lo. *Noun.* Not even a lukewarm spark.

Libid-O. Noun. O, yeah, the ultimate libido.

Luna List. Noun. *(Derivation: Latin "luna" or "lucere" meaning "to shine.")* An itemized list of things to-do and ways to-be for an Aging Human Female as she shines and outs her outrageous self.

Lust List. Noun. A list that turns "Not" into "Hot to Trot." A *Lust List* is better than aspirin for a headache.

M

Man-age-ment. Noun. The study of the Human Male as he ages, and as he ages the Human Female in his life.

Manly Trap Door. Noun. The area of the Aging Human Male brain that controls the *Cementis Mentis*. Once the *Manly Trap Door* activates a decision in the *Cementis Mentis,* the *Door* cannot re-activate that decision.

Manopause. Noun. Change of life for an Aging Human Male. "The hot flashbacks, the Moody Blues, the muffin bottom, the extra wrinkles on his penis, the brain sag—he is definitely showing the wear and tear of *manopause.*"

Mansplaining. Noun. A simple explanation from a simple man simply looking for trouble. Contrast with *womansplaining.*

Manthropology. Noun. The anthropological study of Human Male behavior and culture.

Meis Innocentus. Noun. Area of the Aging Human Female brain where her behavior is identified as innocent and kind and totally undeserving of the Aging Human Male verbiage that is being thrown her way.

Memorees Kaputtus. Noun. The Brain Fart sections of an Aging Human Male brain.

Mengineering. Noun. The study of relationship principles in order to design a model wherein an Aging Human Male—despite being occasionally well-oiled and equipped with some obsolete parts—can function optimally in building an Aging Human Partnership.

Meshuggeneh. *Adjective. (Derivation: Yiddish.)* Crazy, nuts, insane, stupid.

MMPI. *Noun.* <u>M</u>acho <u>M</u>ale <u>P</u>enis <u>I</u>ndex, a psychological test instrument assessing optimism and pessimism and how it relates to Aging Human Male frequency of sexual satisfaction.

N

Naggus Maximus. *Noun.* The area of an Aging Human Female's brain that activates nagging.

Naked Genitals Subtest. *Noun.* Test of gender bias for household chores: "Does this chore endanger a clitoris/breasts or a penis if the chore person were naked?" See also ***Genitals Test.***

Need-to-Control Area of the Brain. *Noun.* The brain area in an Aging Human Male that may increase in size with age and may manifest as increased complaining, crankiness, and bossiness.

No. *Noun. Verb. Adjective. Adverb. Gerund. Non-dangling participle. Declarative sentence. Imperative sentence.* 1. No (as in, "No means no!"). 2. "No." is a complete sentence.

Nookie. *Noun. (Derivation: the Arabic "niki" or the Dutch "neuken" meaning "to copulate with.")* Getting it on, having sex, making whoopie, dancing in the sheets.

Nookie number. *Noun.* The score kept in the ***Cometab*** section of an Aging Human Male brain that keeps track of how many times whoopie occurs in any given week. The ***nookie number*** resets to 0 every week and the previous week's ***nookie number*** is permanently erased from ***Cometab*** memory, as every Aging Human Female knows.

O

O. *Noun.* The BIG **O**. As in **ORGASM**! As in Libid-**O**! Not as in **OH NO**!

Old. *Adjective.* 1. Aging. 2. Longtime, as "longtime" friends. Sometimes the friendly bond is only minutes old; connections happen fast when time is precious!

Ovary. *Adjective.* 1. Strong, powerful and risky. 2. Female equivalent to the male "ballsy." "She demanded a raise from her boss. That was so *ovary* of her."

Own Your Crone Party. *Noun.* A celebration of the rite of passage of an Aging Human Female as she owns her crone as a WOW—a Woman Of Wisdom. She is feted and feasted by her Precious Old Dames in an honoring of her strength, courage, and the light that shines within her, as well as the light she shines upon the world.

P

PATIENCE. *Noun.* A registered trademark of The WTF (Women's Truth Foundation), referenced by every Aging Human Female sharing life with an Aging Human Male.

Patienceisgolden. *Noun.* The large section of the Aging Human Female brain that is as necessary for her survival as air, water, chocolate, and compliments.

POD. *Noun.* 1. A POD is a gathering of Precious Old Dames. "Old" is used affectionately, as in "Old" friends. "Dames" is used sweetly, as for an older cutie. 2. Any group of Aging Human Females. 3. A gathering of AHFemale Besties. 4. An essential facet of *The Dame Diamond*.

Pee POD. *Noun.* A Pee POD is any gathering of Precious Old Dames who laugh so hard they pee their pants.

Pee POD Poise Party. *Noun.* A **Pee POD Poise Party** is a group of two or more Precious Old Dames, who gather like peas in a pod and who laugh so hard they pee their pants, while keeping their poise. **Pee POD Poise Parties** strengthen Aging Human Female funny bones, backbones, and wishbones.

Pippick. *Noun. (Derivation: Yiddish.)* Belly-button.

PMMS. *Noun.* Prized Mega-Maturity Status for an Aging Human Female after womenopause, a status that an AHFemale carries with honor and with a moody swing of her hips. He: "Do you have PMMS?" She: "Yes, thank you!"

Precious. *Adjective.* Has great value and is well-loved, such as precious gemstones like sparkling diamonds and Old Dames.

POP Jeans. *Noun.* The bad answer to "MOM Jeans"—no buts about it, his butt will never look good in those jeans again —and, yes, it is the jeans AND IT IS HIS BUTT!

Primer. *Noun.* A book that presents the most basic elements of any subject. And what could be more basic than your average Aging Human Male? ***Note on pronunciation:*** 1. *Primer* can be pronounced with a "short i," which then sounds like "primmer" and this **Primer** is definitely not prim or even primmer or 2. *Primer* can be pronounced with a "long i," which then sounds like pr-eye-mer, as in primer like preparing to paint, and this **Primer** definitely prepares you to paint a _____ (fill-in-the-blankety-blank) picture of your Aging Human Male.

Pulsar. *Noun.* 1. A pulsed emission of a highly magnetized star. 2. Female sexual arousal, the female equivalent of a boner. "I took one look at him and I felt a *pulsar* in my vagina."

Putz. *Noun. (Derivation: Yiddish. Derogatory.)* Penis, but not in a good way.

Q

Questions. *Noun.* 1. Oxygen for aging women. Questioning her Aging Human Male is like breathing to an Aging Human Female. 2. Anathema for aging men. Being questioned as an Aging Human Male can activate the **Incompetent Detestus (ID)** portion of the AMale brain and concomitant verbal releases, such as "F(reeze) U(rself)."

Quinceañera. *Noun.* The "fiesta de quince años," a religious and social celebration of a Latina girl's fifteenth birthday. (What is this doing here in this glossary? Check out Chapter 33, Lesson 5.)

R

Rebecca Rule. *Noun.* "Listen to everything your man says. Then do what you want." Named after **Irene's** mother **Rebecca.**

Retiring. *Verb.* Putting new tires on an old car.

Retirement. *Noun.* The state of having nothing to do and all day to do it.

ROMEOs. *Noun.* Retired Old Men Eating Out.

Rubius Reddus Slipperus. *Noun.* Portion of the Aging Human Male brain that becomes activated when an AHMale is asked a question to which he doesn't know the answer. Activation of this brain area expresses an unconscious desire to escape the situation and return home to Kansas.

S

Sassyass. *Noun.* 1. A feisty, mouthy, "in your face, in your face" Aging Human Female who says it all—and says it all with a twinkle in her eye. 2. A Boomer Chick who tells it like she sees it—post cataract surgery!

Sex. *Noun.* 1. Whatever turns you on and gets you off. 2. What two-thirds of this **Primer** is about. 3. What one-third of **The Geezer Triangle** is about. 4. What the *Bods* facet of the *Dame Diamond* is about.

Sexual Incompatibility Erectus. *Noun.* A condition of incompatibility that e-wrecks the sex life of the Aging Human Male and Aging Human Female.

Sexus Maximus: Sexual Campus Type 1. *Noun.* 1. Libid—OH! 2. An Aging Human Male whose brain has evolved into *Sexual Campus Type 1* has a raging sexual fire burning 24/7, with smoldering rarely occurring, and then only when dampened by rain (or alcohol).

Sexus Maximus: Sexual Campus Type 2. *Noun.* 1. Libid-lo. 2. An Aging Human Male whose brain has evolved into *Sexual Campus Type 2* no longer has a raging sexual fire burning and there is no way to light this fire, not with a match or a tinderbox, come rain or come shine (or come alcohol)—actually, come nothing. Nothing comes.

Sexus Maybeus. *Noun.* Area of the female brain where decisions about sex—yes, no, maybe so—are determined.

Shmear. *Noun.* (Derivation: Yiddish.) A smear or spread of something delicious, as in a shmear of cream cheese on a bagel with lox.

SimpleNeedsSimpleDeeds Supposition. Noun. This supposition posits that if a person has simple needs, simply little needs doing. A geezer has simple needs (**The Geezer Triangle** of **Sex▲Sustenance▲Sports**). Thus, if a need exists outside that triangular tunnel vision, then the deed requires, in an Aging Human Male's mind and body, a Herculean effort.

SimplePimple Principle. Noun. Ignoring geeze acne when looking in the mirror. "If I don't look at it, zit's not there."

Size. Noun. Only matters in T-shirts.

Snippyus Withmylippius. Noun. Part of the Aging Human Male brain that short circuits verbal constructs and activates the mouth before a gentle tone and a kind thought has been wisely formulated. This part of the AHMale brain is activated by a perceived threat to an AHMale's competence.

SNL. Noun. Saturday Night Live—the TV show, not your date night!

Sustenance. Noun. 1. Food and drink. 2. When used within the context of **The Geezer Triangle** of**Sex▲Sustenance▲Sports**, "food" refers to any food with "Nachos," "Chili" or "BBQ" in the name. 3. When used in the context of **The Geezer Triangle**, "drink" refers to any drink that has sat in an old wooden container to ripen with age to help the aged ripen.

T

T & A Personality Diagnostic Assessment. Noun. A test to determine whether a person is prone to tango-ing or tangling in conflict situations.

Tabbis Humongous. Noun. Area of the Aging Human Female brain which keeps an ongoing count of the generous deeds of an AHFemale for her AHMale.

TickTockOrgasmaclock. Noun. An area in the left hemisphere of the Aging Human Female brain that consists of an automatic brain counter, a second-by-second timer of how long it takes from first kiss to the "end," the "end" being AHMale satisfaction. "Her *TickTockOrgasmaclock* had only just begun to tick when, poof, it was over in a wild explosion almost as soon as it began."

TLC. *Noun.* 1. Truly Lacy Clothes when used as the antidote for AHMale ***Constipation of the Brain.*** 2. Tender Loving Care when offered for empathy and illness. 3. Truly Lost Compassion when the offer for Tender Loving Care is rejected.

(TRUTH). *Noun.* The Real Deal. True Research Using Tested Humans. "(TRUTH)" indicates that the information cited was NOT concocted at a Pee POD Poise Party after four drinks by Aging Human Females who were at the height of their game.

Tushy. *Noun. (Derivation: Yiddish).* Nothing but a butt.

U

Underwear. *Noun. (Derivation: Olde English medieval term for "panties." Obsolete.)* Thongs, g-strings. A word currently used only by those who think a Brazilian is a person who comes from Brazil.

Unsolicited Advice (UA). *Noun.* Unsolicited Advice. Mansplaining. Unrequested, unwanted simple advice from a simple man simply looking for trouble.

V

Visitme Doctoris. *Noun.* The area of an Aging Human Male or Aging Human Female brain related to the willingness of a person to visit a doctor for medical issues; the larger the ***Visitme Doctoris***, the more likely the person is to consult a medical professional when health needs call. The ***Visitme Doctoris*** in 98% of AHFemales is markedly larger than the ***Visitme Doctoris*** in a typical AHMale.

W

Wazoo. *Noun.* 1. The place you don't want things to go, as in "up the *wazoo.*" 2. Vayjayjay.

Wet-and-set. *Adjective.* Sexually aroused female equivalent to a male boner. "He looked dreamily into her eyes and she knew she was *wet-and-set.*"

WhataPutz. *Noun.* Area of the Aging Human Male brain that is activated by the ***Gainpowerthru NO*** and is identified on a brain MRI with millions of "???"s.

WhatsaGirltodo. *Noun.* Area of the Aging Human Female brain that is activated to deal with an Aging Human Male's brain farts and/or tushy farts.

Whereiswhiteball. *Noun.* The optical area of the Aging Human Male brain that searches on the golf course for a round white sphere to curse at. This area is activated by the ***Golfismymistress*** section of the male brain.

WISER. *Noun.* A <u>W</u>oman of <u>I</u>ntelligence <u>S</u>pirit <u>E</u>xperience and <u>R</u>esilience! With strength and heart and the help of her Precious Old Dames, an Aging Human Female becomes <u>WISER</u>.

Woman: *Noun.* A female equal to a man. "Step up! Be a *woman!*"

Womanhandle. *Verb.* 1. To move or manage by female human force or will. 2. To expertly engage the cooperation of an Aging Human Male, often without his knowing what is happening.

Womenopause. *Noun. (Derivation: from the French word for "moon cessation," although during and after womenopause, no self-respecting Aging Human Female loses her ability to moon a deserving AHMale.)* Commonly called "menopause."

Womansplaining. *Noun.* A simple explanation from a simply marvelous woman simply telling the truth. Contrast with *mansplaining.*

Wonderwomb. *Noun.* Womb. "A female fetus is born with all the eggs she will ever have in her lifetime. So when your Grandmother was carrying your Mother in her womb, you were a tiny egg in your Mother's ovaries. The three of you have been connected for a very long time. Women are amazing!" (TRUTH, The MindsJournal.com) Wonderwombs are truly a wonder!

WOW. *Noun.* 1. A <u>W</u>oman <u>O</u>f <u>W</u>isdom. 2. An Aging Human Female.

Wrectus Rectumus. *Noun.* The Tushy Fart section of an Aging Human Male brain.

WTF. *Expletive.* What the f___? Fudge, anyone?

WTF. Women's Truth Foundation. *Noun.* The Women's Truth Foundation, a research organization based in La-La Land that studies partnership interactions in which the Aging Human Male is driving under the influence (of testosterone) and the Aging Human Female is the designated driver. WTF's slogan: "WTF Says It All!"

X

X-Rated. *Adjective.* X-citing fun for those so inclined… or standing up or on the kitchen table or on the washing machine.

Y

YES! List. *Noun.* A delicious litany of future adventures.

Yes-ing. *Verb.* Embracing the adventures of life.

Yes Night. *Noun.* A night where all questions have to be answered, "Yes!"

Yoni. *Noun.* *(Derivation: Sanskrit.)* New age, hip feminist word for womb/uterus. As in, "We females all own-y a *yoni*."

YY. *Noun.* 1. Age demarcation that stands for "Years Young." 2. Time to get your "ya-ya's" on!

Z

Zaftig. *Adjective.* *(Derivation: Yiddish.)* Having a full, rounded figure, plump, juicy.

Zzzzzs. *Noun.* CPAP on high. Ahh… sweet dreams.